Charles Haddon Spurgeon

Messages to the multitude

Being ten representative sermons

Charles Haddon Spurgeon

Messages to the multitude
Being ten representative sermons

ISBN/EAN: 9783337104733

Printed in Europe, USA, Canada, Australia, Japan

Cover: Foto ©Lupo / pixelio.de

More available books at **www.hansebooks.com**

Yours very heartily,

C. H. Spurgeon

BEING

TEN REPRESENTATIVE SERMONS SELECTED AT
MENTONE, AND TWO UNPUBLISHED
ADDRESSES DELIVERED ON
MEMORABLE OCCASIONS

BY

CHARLES HADDON SPURGEON

" Take my lips, and let them be
Filled with messages from Thee "

LONDON

SAMPSON LOW, MARSTON & COMPANY
LIMITED
St. Dunstan's House
FETTER LANE, FLEET STREET, E.C.
1892

LONDON :
PRINTED BY WILLIAM CLOWES AND SONS, LIMITED,
STAMFORD STREET AND CHARING CROSS.

PUBLISHERS' NOTE.

Just twelve months ago, Mr. Spurgeon kindly consented to contribute a group of sermons to the present series, but almost immediately afterwards he was seized with critical illness, and it seemed in the early autumn as if he never would be able to carry out his purpose. At the request of the publishers, his brother and colleague, the Rev. J. A. Spurgeon, undertook to make the selection, but towards the end of the year Mr. Spurgeon recovered sufficiently, amid the sunshine of Mentone, to feel a revived interest in the task. He accordingly took the matter once more into his own hands, and in December last selected the majority of these sermons as typical of his pulpit teaching during the entire period of his ministry at the Metropolitan Tabernacle. He showed keen interest in the preparation of the volume for the press, and was busily engaged in the revision of the printed slips, when the sudden return of his illness in an aggravated form compelled him to lay down finally his busy pen. In a letter to the publishers, dated January 12, 1892, he said, " Call the volume ' Messages to the Multitude,' " and he added, " I will write three or four pages of preface." That letter was hardly despatched, when his illness assumed an alarming character, and it is needless to add that the words of greeting which the great preacher had intended to address through these pages to his absent friends remain unwritten. The two concluding addresses were both delivered on special occasions, and neither of them have hitherto been published; they were selected from Mr. Spurgeon's papers preserved in the library at Westwood. The publishers desire to thank the Rev. J. A. Spurgeon for writing a preface to the book, and they are not less indebted to the Rev. J. W. Harrald—Mr. Spurgeon's private secretary and companion at Mentone—for the painstaking and loving care with which he has seen the volume through the press.

PREFACE.

This volume has passed—as to the chief part of it—under the author's own revision. He took much interest in it during the closing weeks of his life, and it is amongst the last of his literary productions. Other hands have put some final touches, but it may be accepted as substantially his own, alike as to authorship and as to the choice of the sermons to represent him amongst the preachers of his age. It is a sad task to compose an introduction to a book which the departed one should himself have penned, but perhaps a brother can fitly say what must have been under those circumstances left unsaid.

The preacher will ever be remembered as the teacher of the people. One who spoke forcefully the thoughts of the great heart of Christendom on the eternal verities of the gospel. As unchangeable in his system of theology as the shape of a circle, and as fixed in principles as the multiplication table; and for the same reasons, that he was resting on fundamental truths which have no variation. Some have deemed this a weakness, and called it a limited range of thought; but in this holy trafficking of truth we are glad he has not had divers weights and measures in his bag. The standard has ever been the shekel of the sanctuary, and therefore fixedly the same. Through the nearly forty years represented in this selection from his ministerial preaching, there are no old terms applied with new and contradictory meaning. The progress—and such there is—has always been in and not out of the truth as it is in Jesus, and this ever along the lines of thought sanctified by the experience and witness of the Church's leaders ever since apostolic times.

With this unity of creed, the reader will discover a deepening and mellowing of thought and utterance, such as might well be expected from the ripening powers of a great worker and a greater sufferer. The style of the speaker has been advisedly modified in the preparation for the press, to meet the eye rather than the ear of the student of truth. It were a great advantage for some public speakers to be compelled to peruse their own productions after delivery. Here the preacher was continually reperusing his own treatises with the desire to produce the same impression under altered circumstances. This has affected them somewhat as orations, and has occasionally reduced an oratorical effect, and tamed down the thrilling utterance to a calmer mood more suited to the quiet thought of the closet. But what has been lost to emotion has been richly repaid in unction and spiritual power. This fact must, therefore, be remembered in any comparison with other public speakers of his age. With an unaltered theme, the great preacher has found ample scope for the display of his undoubted talents, both of mind and utterance.

The style of the author is as clear as the day, because illumed all through with accurate acquaintance with his subject and his own views upon it. In his depths there is no darkness, and in his heights he has not entered the clouds, and yet in both height and depth of thought he has few equals. The range of illustration, metaphor, and information exhibited in the sermons, of which these are a small specimen, is immense; and every art, trade, science, and realm has been laid under tribute to enrich the discourses and enforce the truths. This is the result of no mere accidental possession of natural powers. On the contrary, the accurate scholar of tenacious memory and facile mind has studied carefully, noted down copiously, and by persistent efforts has given the perfected product of much conscientious toil for the benefit of those listening to him. In the earlier years of his preaching, the preparation extended even to the wording of the sermon in almost its entirety, gradually lessening in detail as years ripened the speaker's pulpit powers, but always including a careful and written division of matter, with due arrangement of illustration, argument, and appeal. The freshness of the sermons has thus been maintained by dint of hard work, which is perhaps the main characteristic of what is called genius in every department of human life.

But two other reasons are manifestly to be noted. The preacher was a great Bible student, and honoured his text by expounding it, illustrating it, enforcing it in perfect loyalty to the mind of the Spirit as therein revealed. This textual style ensured a fresh sermon with each portion of the sacred record taken from time to time for review and exposition. But last of all, and chief of all other reasons of his perennial variety—he was a live man, full of the Holy Ghost and power, and spake as the Spirit gave him utterance. On that he relied, and to it he never failed to give all the praise. The same influence which of old gave the revelation of the truth to the first utterers of it, was with him to aid in the exposition of the themes thus first of all penned by an inspiration Divine. The Spirit of all truth was in him, and under a power distinctly given from above he brought forth these many manner of fruits in due season, and thus these leaves in ceaseless verdure have been for the healing of the nations. In this no claim is made beyond that which all truly God-sent and God-helped men will share, but on this we lay the greatest stress of all, as we indicate the reasons for a power which has made this preacher's sermons, both as spoken and perused, a spiritual phenomenon of the age.

May the same Almighty Lord, whom His now departed servant sought to honour, enforce the publication of these truths in their present form as richly as when they were first proclaimed, and make this new issue of them one more memento of the preacher's faithfulness, and of the Master's power to solace, sanctify, and save!

JAMES A. SPURGEON.

METROPOLITAN TABERNACLE,
NEWINGTON BUTTS, S.E.,
April 4, 1892.

CONTENTS.

———

CONTENTS.

"LET US PRAY."

B—8

"LET US PRAY."[1]

" But it is good for me to draw near to God."—Ps. lxxiii. 28.

THERE are many ways by which the true believer can "draw near to God." The gates of the King's palace are many; and through the love of Jesus, and the grace of His Spirit, it is our delight, by any of these gates of pearl, to enter, and approach our heavenly Father. Foremost among these is communion, that converse which man holds with God; that state of nearness to God, in which our mutual secrets are revealed—*our* hearts being open unto Him, *His* heart being manifested to us. Here it is we see the invisible, and hear the unutterable. The outward symbol of fellowship is the sacred Supper of the Lord, at which, by means of simple emblems, we are divinely enabled to feed, after a spiritual sort, upon the flesh and blood of the Redeemer. This is a golden gate of fellowship, a royal road which our feet delight to tread. Blessed are the feet that tread this sunny pathway. But we may as truly draw near to God if with sighs and tears we tread the pathway of penitence, when our desolate spirit longs for His sacred presence,

[1] It was the desire of the publishers that the sermons should illustrate different periods of my long ministry. Hence this early one has in it allusions to events in the year 1859. It was preached in the Music Hall, Royal Surrey Gardens, November 6, 1859.

and cries, "Whom have I in heaven but Thee? and there is none upon earth that I desire beside Thee !" Equally does a firm trust " draw near to God," for it clings to Him. So often as we read the promise written in Holy Scripture, and are enabled to receive it and rest upon it as the very word of a covenant God, we do really " draw near " to Him.

Nevertheless, *prayer is the best used means of drawing near to God.* You will excuse me, then, if, in considering my text this morning, I confine myself entirely to the subject of prayer. It is in prayer, mainly, that we draw near to God ; and certainly by each gracious man it can be said emphatically of prayer, " It is good for me to draw near to God." Prayer is good for every man who knoweth how to practise that heavenly art, for in it he is privileged " to draw near to God."

To assist your memories, that the sermon may abide with you in after-days, I shall divide my discourse in a somewhat singular manner. First, I shall look upon my text as being a *touchstone,* by which we may try our prayers, ay, and try ourselves too; then I shall take the text as *a whetstone* to sharpen our desires, to make us more earnest, and more diligent in supplication, because " it is good to draw near to God ; " and then I shall have the solemn task, in the last place, of using it as *a tombstone,* with a direful epitaph upon it for those who do not know what it is to draw near to God ; since " a prayerless soul is a Christless soul."

I. First, you may regard my text as A TOUCHSTONE by which you may test your prayers, and try yourselves.

That is not prayer of which it cannot be said that there was in it a drawing near unto God. Come hither, then, with your supplications. I see one coming forward who says, "I am in the daily habit of using a form of prayer both at morning and at evening. I could not be happy if I went abroad before I had first repeated my morning prayer, nor could I rest at night without again going over the holy sentences appointed for use at eventide. Sir, my form is the very best that could possibly be written; it was compiled by a famous bishop and confessor, who was glorified in martyrdom, and ascended to his God in a chariot of flame." My friend, I am glad, if you use a form of prayer, that you use the best. If we have forms at all, let them be of the most excellent kind. So far so good. But let me ask you a question. I am not about to condemn you for any form you may have used; but tell me now, and tell me honestly from your inmost soul, have you drawn near to God while you have been repeating those words? for if not—oh, solemn thought!—all the prayers you have ever uttered have been an idle mockery. You have *said* prayers, but you have never prayed in your life. Imagine not that any enchantment resides in any particular set of words. You might as well repeat the alphabet backwards, or the "Abracadabra" of a wizard, as go over the best form in the world, unless there is something more than form in the act. *Have you drawn near to God?* That is the essential point. Suppose that one of us should desire to present a petition to the House of Commons. We wisely ask in what manner the petition should be worded, and we employ the prescribed phrases. Now, suppose that in the morning we rise and read this form, or repeat it to ourselves; and duly conclude with, "And your petitioners will ever pray," and the like. Imagine that we do the same at night, and the next day, and the next, for many months. What have we done? One day, meeting a member of the House, we accost him, and astonish him by saying, "Sir, I wonder I have never had an answer from the House of Commons; I have been petitioning these last six months, and the form that I used was the most accurate that could be procured." "But," says he, "how was your petition presented?" "*Presented!* I had not thought of that; I have repeated the form of petition with much care. Is not that enough?" "No," he would say. "You may repeat it many a long day before any good comes from it; it is not the repeating it, but the presenting of the petition, and having it pleaded by some able friend, that will get you the boon you desire." And so it may be, my friend, that you have been repeating collects and prayers; and have ignorantly imagined that you have prayed, and yet have never prayed because you have not had to do with God in the whole business. Your prayer has never been presented to God. You have not laid it before Jesus, the Great High-priest, and have not asked Him to take it for you into the sacred place where God abideth, and there to present the petition with His own merits before His Father's throne. I will not bid you cease from your form; but I do beseech you, by the living God, either cease from it or else beg the Holy Spirit to enable you to draw near to God in it. I entreat you not to be vexed with me, so as to take what I may say for a piece of bitter censoriousness; I speak now as God's own messenger in this matter. Your prayer has not been heard, and it neither can nor will be answered unless there be in it a true and real desire " to draw near to God."

"Ah," saith another, "I am pleased to hear these remarks, for I am in the habit of offering extempore prayer every morning and evening, and at other times; and I am pleased to hear you discourage the use of forms of prayer." Mark, I did not speak against forms of prayer; that is not my subject upon this occasion. One class of sinners is always pleased to hear another class of sinners found fault with. You say you offer an extempore supplication. I must bring your prayer to the same touchstone as the former. What is there in the form that you extemporize, that it should be so much better than that which was composed by a man of God of a former age? Possibly your extempore form is not worth a farthing, and if it could be written out in black and white, it might be a disgrace to prayer-makers. That also is no concern of mine just now. I bring you at once to the test—*have you in your prayer drawn near to God?* When you have been on your knees in the morning, have you thought that you were talking to the King of heaven and earth? Have you breathed your desires, not to wandering winds, but to the ear of the Eternal? Have you desired to come to Him, and tell to Him your wants, and have you sought at His hand the answer to your requests? Remember, you have not prayed successfully or acceptably unless you have in prayer endeavoured to draw near to God. Suppose now (to take a case) that I should desire some favour of a friend. I shut myself up alone, and I commence delivering an oration, pleading earnestly for the boon I need. I repeat this at night, and so on month after month, extemporizing appeals to my friend's bounty and goodness. At last I meet my friend, and I tell him that I have been asking a favour of him, and that he has never answered my prayer. "Nay," saith he, "I have never seen you; you have never spoken to me." "Ah, but you should have heard what I said; if you had but heard it, surely it would have moved your heart!"

"Ah," saith he, "but then you did not address it to me! You wrote a letter, you tell me, in moving strains; but did you post the letter? Did you make sure that it was delivered at my door?" "No, no," you say; "I kept the letter after I had written it. I never sent it to you." Now, mark, the case is parallel with your offering extempore prayer without drawing near to God in it. You plead; but if you are not pleading *with God*, to what effect is your pleading? You talk; but if you are not talking to a manifestly present God, to what effect is all your talking? If you do not seek to come near to Him, what have you done? You have offered sacrifice, mayhap; but it has been upon your own high places, and the sacrifice has been an abomination. You have not brought it up to God's *one* altar; you have not approached the mercy-seat, where is His own visible presence. You have not drawn near to God, and consequently your prayers, though they be multiplied by tens of thousands, are utterly valueless to your soul's benefit. Drawing near to God is an indispensable requisite in accepted prayer.

But now, lest I should be misunderstood as to this drawing near to God, let me attempt to describe it in its degrees; for all men cannot draw near to God with the same nearness of access. When first the life of grace begins in the soul, you will draw near to God, but it will be *with great fear and trembling.* The soul conscious of guilt, and humbled thereby, is overawed with the solemnity of its position; it is bowed to the earth by a sense of the grandeur of God in whose presence it stands. I remember the first time I sincerely prayed; but the words I used I remember not. Surely there were few enough words in that petition. I had often repeated a form; I had been

in the habit of continually repeating it. At last I came
really to pray; and then I saw myself standing before God,
in the immediate presence of the heart-searching Jehovah,
and I said within myself, "I have heard of Thee by the
hearing of the ear: but now mine eye seeth Thee. Wherefore I abhor myself, and repent in dust and ashes." I felt
like Esther when she stood before the king, faint and
overcome with dread. I was full of penitence of heart,
because of His majesty and my sinfulness. I think the only
sounds I could utter were rather breathings than words.
The only complete sentence was, "God be merciful to
me a sinner!" The overwhelming splendour of His
majesty, the greatness of His power, the severity of His
justice, the immaculate character of His holiness, and all
His dreadful grandeur,—these things overpowered my soul,
and I fell down in utter prostration of spirit. But there
was in that a true and real drawing to God.

If you, who gather in your churches and chapels, did but
realize that you are in God's presence, surely we might
expect to see scenes more marvellous than any of the con-
vulsions of the Irish revival. If you knew that God was
there, that you were speaking to Him, that in His ear you
were offering that oft-repeated confession, "We have done
the things that we ought not to have done, we have left
undone the things that we ought to have done," there
would be among you a deep humility and a solemn abase-
ment of spirit, which would prostrate you on your faces.
May God grant to us all, as often as we offer prayer of
any sort, that we may truly and really draw near to Him,
even if it be only in this sense!

In after-life, as the Christian grows in grace, he
draws near to God *with joyful trust.* Although he will

never forget the solemnity of his position, and will never
lose that holy awe which must overshadow a gracious
man when he is in the presence of a God who can create
or can destroy, yet that fear has all its terror taken out of
it; it becomes a holy reverence, and no more a slavish,
abject dread. Then the man of God, walking amid the
splendours of Deity, and veiling his face, like the glorious
cherubim, with those twin wings, the blood and righteousness of Jesus Christ, will, reverent and bowed in spirit,
approach the throne. Seeing there the God of love, of
goodness, and of mercy, he will realize rather the covenant
character of God than His absolute Deity. He will see in
God rather His goodness than His greatness, and more of
His mercy than of His majesty. Then will the soul, bowing
again as reverently as before, enjoy a sacred liberty of
intercession; for while humbled in the presence of the
Infinite, it will yet be sustained by the happy consciousness
of being in the presence of mercy and of love in infinite
degree. This is a state to which men reach after they have
had their sins forgiven, after they have passed from death
unto life : then they come to rejoice in God, and draw near
to Him with confidence.

There is yet a third and higher stage, which I fear too
few among us ever arrive at; when the child of God, awed
by the splendour, and delighting in the goodness of God,
sees something which is more enchanting to him than
either of these, namely, the fact of his relationship to God;
and draws near *with filial boldness*. He sees on the throne,
not simply goodness, but his Father's goodness; not merely
love, but love which has from all eternity been set upon
him ; love which has made *him* its darling, which has written
his name upon its breast; love which for his sake did even

deign to die. Then the child of God comes near to the throne of his Father; he taketh hold of his Father's knees, and though conscious of the greatness of the God, yet is he still more alive to the love of the Father, and he cries, "Our Father, hear our prayer and grant our request, for Jesu's sake." In this position it sometimes happens that the child of God may pray in such a way that others cannot understand him at all. If you had heard Martin Luther pray, some of you would have been shocked; and perhaps it would be presumption should you try to imitate him, because Martin Luther was God's own son, and you, alas! may be destitute of sonship. He had a liberty to talk to God as another man might not. If you are not the son of God, if you have neither regeneration nor adoption, the utmost you can do is to come into the King's court as a humble beggar seeking an alms. But happy is the man who has received his full adoption, and knows himself to be born of the Spirit. It were rudeness for any one to do or to say that to a king which a king's son may freely do and say. There are words of high and hallowed familiarity, and of close and sacred communing between God and His own adopted child, that I could not repeat in a stranger's ear. There are words allowable between God and the purified soul, that are something like what Paul heard in Paradise; things not lawful for a man to utter in public, though in private he knows their sweetness. Ah! my dear hearers, some of you, I doubt not, know more about this than I do; but this I know, it is the happiest moment in our lives when we can go up to our Father and our God in Christ Jesus, and can know and feel of a surety that His infinite love is set on *us*, and that our love is all engrossed by Him. There is an embrace of faith which is as heaven below. No chariots of Amminadib can describe the heavenly rapture. Even Solomon's Song itself, glowing though its figures be, can scarcely reach the mystery—the length, the breadth, the height of the approach to God known by the communing heart, and the condescending revelation of God to the enraptured mind. It is not essential to the success of your prayers that you should come up to this last point. Possibly you never may attain to this eminence of grace. Nor do I even think that it is absolutely necessary that your prayer should come to the second degree to be prevailing prayer. Your drawing near to God should be growingly close; and it will be so if you grow in grace. But, mark well, that you must draw near to God in some one of these three grades—either in a lowly sense of His majesty, or in a delightful consciousness of His goodness, or in a ravishing sense of your own relationship to Him—or else your prayer is as worthless as the chaff which is blown from the threshing-floor. It is as though you whispered to the wind, or uttered a cry to the desert air, where no ear can hear, and no hand can help.

Bring your prayers, then, to this *touchstone*, and may God help you to examine them, and to be honest with yourselves, for your own soul's sake!

II. This must suffice upon the touchstone; we now come to the second head of the discourse, which was THE WHETSTONE, to whet your desires, to make you more anxious to be much in prayer, and to be more earnest in it. "It is good for me to draw near to God."

Now, first and foremost, let us remark that the goodness of prayer does not lie in any merit that there is in prayer itself. There is no merit whatever in prayer; and wherever the idea of the merit of prayer could come from, one is at a loss to know, except that it must have come from that Popery which is a native weed in every human heart. The Pharisee of old had this notion, and he seems to have bequeathed it to the Church of Rome. The notion that we deserve anything because we pray for it, is absurd and wicked. If a beggar should be always on your door-step, or should be always meeting you in the street, or stopping you on your journeys, and asking you to give him help, I suppose the last thing you would understand would be the merit of his prayers. You would say, "I can understand their impudence; I can believe their earnestness; I can comprehend their importunity; but as for *merit*, what merit can there be in a beggar's cry?" Remember, your prayers at the best are nothing, apart from the grace of God, but a beggar's cry. Apart from what grace has done for you, you still stand as beggars at the gate of mercy, asking for the dole of God's charity, for the love of Jesus. He gives freely; yet He gives, not because of your prayers, but because of Christ's blood and Christ's merit. Your prayers are the empty vessels into which He puts the alms of His mercy; but the merit by which the mercy comes is in the veins of Christ, and nowhere else. Remember that there can be no merit in a beggar's cry, nor in our prayers.

But now let us note that it nevertheless is good, practically good, for us to pray and draw near to God; and the first thing which should whet our desires in prayer is this: *Prayer explains mysteries.* I utter that first because t is in the psalm. Poor Asaph had been greatly troubled. He had been trying to untie that Gordian knot concerning the righteousness of a providence which permits the wicked to flourish and the godly to be tried; and because he could not untie that knot, he tried to cut it; but he cut his own

fingers in the act, and became greatly troubled. He could
not understand how it was that God could be just and yet
give riches to the wicked while His own people were in
poverty. At last Asaph understood it all, for he went into
the house of his God, and there he understood their end.
Therefore he says, looking back upon his discovery of a clue
to this great labyrinth, " It is good for me to draw near to
God." Beloved hearers, if you would more clearly understand the Word of God in its knotty points, if you would
more fully comprehend the mystery of the gospel of Christ,
remember that Christ's scholars must study upon their knees.
Depend upon it, the best commentator upon the Word
of God is its Author, the Holy Ghost; and if you would
know 'the meaning of Scripture, you must go to Him in
prayer. Often, when a verse has staggered me, I have
knelt down, and tried to read it over in that position, and
some one word in the text has leaped up, and has become
the key to the whole passage. To pray yourself into the
spirit of the text, and then to employ that Scripture in the
way of prayer: that is the way to learn the sacred Word
and its theology. What you learn upon your knees you
will never unlearn. That which men teach you, men can
unteach you, if I may be allowed the term. If I am merely
convinced by my friend's reasoning, a better reasoner may
force me in the opposite direction. If I merely hold my
doctrinal opinions because they seem to me to be correct,
I may be led to think differently another day. But if God's
own Holy Spirit has taught me in answer to prayer, I have
not learned amiss, and I have so learned that I shall
never forget.

Behold, believer, art thou this day in a labyrinth? Whenever thou comest to a turning-point, where there is a road

to the right and another to the left, if thou wouldst know
which way to go, fall on thy knees, and then rise and pursue
thy journey. When thou comest to the next turning-place,
fall on thy knees again, and so learn the right road. The
one clue to the labyrinths of providence, of doctrinal
opinion, and of sacred thought, will be found in the
hallowed exercise of prayer, whereby we draw near to God,
and so find guidance. Continue much in prayer, and
neither Satan nor the world shall deceive you. Behold
before you the sacred casket of truth. But where is the
key? It hangs upon the silver nail of prayer. Go and
reach it down, unlock the casket, and be rich.

A second whetstone for your prayers shall be this:
Prayer brings deliverances. In an old author I met with
the following allegory. As I found it, so I tell it to you.
Once upon a time, the King of Jerusalem left his city in the
custody of an eminent captain, whose name was Zeal. He
gave unto Zeal many choice warriors, to assist him in the
protection of the city. Zeal was a right-hearted man, one
who never wearied in the day of battle, but would fight
all day and all night, even though his sword did cleave to
his hand as the blood ran down his arm. But it happened
about this time that the King of Arabia, getting unto himself exceeding great hosts and armies, surrounded the city,
and prevented any introduction of food for the soldiers, or
of ammunition to continue the war. Driven to the last extremity, Captain Zeal called a council of war, and asked the
members what course he should take. Many things were
proposed, but they all failed to effect the purpose, and they
came to the sad conclusion that nothing was before them
but the surrender of the city, although upon the hardest
terms. Zeal took the resolution of the council of war; but

when he read it, he could not bear it.   His soul abhorred it.
"Better," said he, "to be cut in pieces than surrender.
Better for us to be destroyed while we are faithful, than
to give up the keys of this royal city."   In his great distress
he met a friend of his, called Prayer, and Prayer said to
him, "Oh, captain, I can deliver this city."   Now, Prayer
was not a soldier—at least, he did not look much like a
warrior, for he wore the garments of a priest.   In fact, he
was the king's chaplain, and was the priest of the holy city
of Jerusalem.   But, nevertheless, this Prayer was a valiant
man, and wore armour beneath his robes.   "Oh, captain,"
said he, "give me three companions, and I will deliver this
city—their names must be Sincerity, Importunity, and
Faith."   Now these four brave men went out of the city
at the dead of night.   When the prospects of Jerusalem
were the very blackest, they cut their way right through the
hosts that surrounded the city.   With many wounds and
much struggling they made their escape, and travelled all
that night as quickly as they could across the plain, to
reach the camp of the King of Jerusalem.   When they
flagged a little, Importunity would hasten them on; and
when at any time they grew faint, Faith would give them
a drink from his bottle, and they would recover.   They
came at last to the palace of the great king.   The door was
shut, but Importunity knocked long, and at last it was
opened.   Faith stepped in.   Sincerity threw himself on
his face before the throne of the great king; and then
Prayer began to speak.   He told the king of the great
straits in which the beloved city was now placed, the
dangers that surrounded it, and the almost certainty that
all the brave warriors would be cut in pieces by the morrow.
Importunity rehearsed again and again the wants of the city.

Faith pleaded hard the royal promise and covenant. At last the king said to Captain Prayer, "Take with thee soldiers, and go back; lo, I am with thee to deliver this city." At the morning light, just when the day broke—for they had returned more swiftly than could have been expected, for though the journey seemed long in going there, it was very short in coming back, in fact they seemed to have gained time on the road—they arrived before the bulwarks, fell upon the hosts of the King of Arabia, took him prisoner, slew his army, and divided the spoil, and then entered the gates of the city of Jerusalem in triumph. Zeal put a crown of gold upon the head of Prayer, and decreed that henceforth, whenever Zeal went forth to battle, Prayer should be the standard-bearer, and should lead the van. The allegory is full of truth; let him that heareth understand. If we would have deliverance in the hour of need, "Let us pray." Prayer shall soon bring seasonable and merciful deliverances from the throne of our faithful God. This is the second sharpening of your desires upon the whetstone; let us proceed to the third.

It is written of faith, in that mighty chapter, the eleventh of the Hebrews, that faith "stopped the mouths of lions", and wrought other wonders; but one singular thing that faith did, which is as great a miracle as any, was this: faith "obtained promises." The like can be truly said of prayer. *Prayer obtains promises;* therefore "it is good for me to draw near to God." We read a story in the history of England, whether true or not we cannot tell, that Queen Elizabeth gave to the Earl of Essex a ring, as a token of her favour. "When thou art in disgrace," she said, "send this ring to me. When I see it, I will forgive thee, and restore thee again to favour." You know the story of that

ill-fated noble, how he sent the ring by a faithless messenger,
and it was never delivered; and therefore he perished at
the block. Learn the lesson: our God has given to each
one of His people the sacred ring of promise; saying, "As
often as thou art in need, show it to Me, and I will deliver
thee." Take heed then, believer, that thou employest a
faithful messenger. And what messenger canst thou employ
so excellent as true, real, earnest prayer? But take heed it
be real prayer; for if thy messenger miscarry, and the
promise be not brought to God's remembrance, thou
mayest never obtain the blessing. Draw near to God with
living, loving prayer; present the promise, and thou shalt
obtain the fulfilment. Brave things might we say of prayer;
our old divines are full of encomiums concerning it. The
early fathers spake of it as if they were writing sonnets.
Chrysostom preached of it as if he saw it incarnate in some
heavenly form. The choicest metaphors were gathered
together by the saints to describe with rapture the power, nay,
the omnipotence, of prayer. Would to God that we loved
prayer as our fathers did of old! It is said of James the
Less, that he was so much in prayer that his knees had
become hard like those of a camel. It may have been
only a legend, but legends are often based on truth.
Certain it is that Hugh Latimer, that blessed saint and
martyr of our God, was accustomed to pray so earnestly in
his old age, when he was imprisoned, that he would often
pray until he had no strength left to rise, and the prison
attendants had need to lift him from his knees. Where
see we men like these? O angel of the covenant, where
canst thou find them? When the Son of man cometh,
shall He find prayer on the earth? Our prayers are not
worthy of the name of supplications. Oh, that we had

learned that sacred art of drawing near to God, and pleading His promise! Cowper has put several thoughts together in one verse of his hymn. Prayer clears the sky;—

> "Prayer makes the darkened cloud withdraw."

Prayer climbs to heaven;—

> "Prayer climbs the ladder Jacob saw."

Prayer makes the powers of darkness quail;—

> "And Satan trembles when he sees
> The weakest saint upon his knees."

I have thus given you three reasons why we should be diligent in prayer. Let me add yet another, for we must not leave this part of the whetstone until we have thoroughly entered into the reasons why "it is good for us to draw near unto God." Let me remark, that *prayer has a mighty power to sustain the soul in every season of its distress and sorrow.* Whenever your soul becomes weak, use the heavenly strengthening plaster of prayer. It was while He prayed that an angel appeared unto our Lord, and strengthened Him. That angel has appeared to many of us, and we have not forgotten the strength which we received when on our knees. In the ancient mythology they tell of one who, as often as he was thrown down, recovered strength because he touched his mother earth. It is so with the believer. As often as he is thrown down, and falls upon his knees, he recovers himself, for he touches the great source of his strength. If thou hast a heavy burden pressing thy back, be much in prayer, for thou shalt carry it well if thou canst pray. Once on a time, a pilgrim had upon his shoulder a terrible burden, that crushed him to the earth, so that he could not stand upright, but crept along on his hands and knees. There appeared to him a fair and comely damsel, holding in her hand a wand, and she touched the burden. It was there, in all its outward shape and fashion, but without weight. That which had crushed him to the earth had now become so light that he could leap beneath it. Beloved, do you understand this? Have you not gone to God with mountains of trouble on your shoulders, unable to carry them? Have you not seen them remaining in the same shape, but lightened, so as to be no more a load to your heart? They became blessings instead of curses. What you thought was an iron cross, suddenly turned out to be a wooden one, and you carried it with joy, following your Master.

I will give but one other reason, lest I should weary you, and that certainly is not my desire. Beloved, there is one reason why those of us who are engaged in the Lord's work should be diligent in prayer, and it is—*prayer will ensure success.* Two labourers in God's harvest met each other once upon a time, and they sat down to compare notes. One was a man of sorrowful spirit, and the other joyous, for God had given him the desire of his heart. The sad brother said, "Friend, I cannot understand how it is that everything you do is sure to prosper. You scatter seed with both your hands very diligently, and it springs up plenteously, and so rapidly too, that the reaper treads upon the heels of the sower. I have sown," said he, "as you have done, and I trust I have been diligent. The soil has been the same, for we have laboured side by side in the same town. The seed has been of the same quality, for I have taken mine where you have taken yours—from the common granary of Holy Scripture. But, alas! *my* seed never springs up. I sow it, and it is as if I sowed upon the waves. I never see a harvest. Here and there I have discovered, with great and diligent search, a sickly blade of wheat; but small is the reward of my labours." They talked long together, for the brother who was successful was one of a tender heart, and therefore he sought to comfort his mourning brother. They compared notes; they looked through all the rules of husbandry; but they could not solve the mystery, why one was successful and the other laboured in vain. At last one said to the other, "I must retire." "Wherefore?" said the other. "Why, this is the time," said he, "when I must go alone to steep my seed." "Steep your seed?" said the other. "Yes, my brother, I always steep my seed before I sow it. I steep it till it begins to swell, and germinate, and I can almost see a green blade springing from it; and then you know it speedily grows after it is sown." "Ah," said the other, "but I understand not what you mean! How do you steep your seed, and in what mysterious mixture?" "Brother," said he, "it is a composition made of one part of the tears of agony for the souls of men, and the other part of drops of the cordial of confidence in God as the Hearer of prayer: this mixture, if you drop your seed in it, hath a transcendent efficacy to quicken the growth of every grain, so that none of it is lost." The other rose, and went on his way, and forgot not what he had learned, for he too began to steep his seed. He spent less time in his study, and more in his closet: he was less abroad, and more at home; less with man, and more with God. He went to the field, and scattered his seed; and he, too, saw a harvest, and the Lord was glorified in them twain. Brethren, I do feel this with regard to myself; and, therefore, when I speak of others, I speak not uncharitably, that the reason of the non-success

of many ministries will be found in restraining prayer.
If I were addressing students in the college, I should
say to them, Set prayer first in your labours; let your
subject be well prepared; think out well your discourse;
but best of all, pray over it.   Study on your knees.
Speaking to the present assembly, containing Sabbath-school
teachers, and others who in their way are labouring for
Christ, let me beseech you, whatever you do, go not about
your work except you have first saturated your soul and
your seed with the spirit of prayer.   We are in these days
demanding more labourers—it is a right prayer : our
Saviour bade us pray the Lord of the harvest to thrust out
more labourers.   We are seeking that the Word preached
should be of the best sort—it is a right demand.   But
let us not forget to ask of God that men may be led to
preach, agonizing for souls while they speak.   I like to
preach with a burden on my heart—the burden of other
men's sins, the burden of other men's hard-heartedness,
the burden of their unbelief, the burden of their desperate
estate, which must ere long end in perdition unless they
repent.   There is no preaching, I am persuaded, like that;
for then we preach as though—

> " We ne'er might preach again,
>   As dying men to dying men."

May each of you labour as those who live near to God,
whose very breath is prayer, and whose dependence is
upon heavenly help ! Commit your work to God, and you
will find it good to draw near to Him.

I will tell you here an incident of the revival. It is one
I know to be correct ; it is told by a good brother who
would not add a word thereunto, I am sure. It happened,
not long ago, that, in a school which is sustained by the

Corporation of the City of London, in the north of Ireland, one of the older boys had been converted to God; and one day, in the midst of school, a smaller lad was greatly oppressed by a sense of sin, and so overwhelmed did he become that the master plainly perceived that he could not work, and therefore he said to him, "You had better go home, and plead with God in prayer in private." He said, however, to the bigger boy, who was all rejoicing in hope, "Go with him; take him home, and pray with him." They started together. On the road they saw an empty house; the two boys went in, and there began to pray; the plaintive cry of the younger one after a little time changed into a note of joy, when, suddenly springing up, he said, "I have found rest in Jesus; I have never felt as I do now. My sins, which are many, are all forgiven." The proposal was to go home; but the younger lad forbade this. No, he must go back, and tell the master of the school that he had found Christ. So, hurrying back, he rushed in, and said, "Oh! sir, I have found the Lord Jesus Christ." All the boys in the school, who had seen him sitting sad and dull upon the form, remarked the joy that flashed from his eye when he cried, "I have found Christ." The effect was electric. The boys suddenly and mysteriously disappeared; the master knew not where they were gone; but, looking over into the play-ground, he saw by the wall a number of boys, in prayer asking for mercy, one by one. He said to the elder youth, "Cannot you go and tell these boys the way of salvation? Run and tell them what they must do to be saved." He did so, and the prayer that was being offered was suddenly changed into a loud piercing shriek; the boys understood what this cry meant, and, impelled by the great Spirit, they all fell on their knees, and began to plead for mercy through the blood of Christ. But this was not all. There was a girls' schoolroom in the same building overhead, and the girls too became affected by the same Spirit; and began to cry aloud for the forgiveness of their sins. Here was an interruption for school! Was ever such a thing known before in a schoolroom? Classes were all put aside, and books forgotten, while poor sinners were kneeling at the foot of the cross, seeking for pardon. The cry was heard throughout the various offices attached to this large school, and it was heard also across the street, and passers-by were attracted. Men of God, ministers and clergymen of the neighbourhood, were brought in; the whole day was spent in prayer, and they continued until almost midnight. They separated with songs of joy, for it was believed that the girls and boys, and men and women, who had crowded the two schoolrooms, had all found the Saviour.

Our good brother, Dr. Arthur, says that, while travelling in Ireland, he met with a youth, and he said to him, "Do you love the Saviour?" And he answered, "I trust I do." "How did you come to love Him?" "Oh," said he, "I was converted in the big schoolroom that night! My mother heard that there was a revival going on there, and she sent me to fetch my little brother away; she did not want him, she said, to get convinced. I went to fetch away my brother, but he was on his knees, crying, 'Lord, have mercy upon me, a sinner!' I stopped, and I prayed too, and the Lord saved us both." Now, to what are we to attribute this? I know many of the brethren there—Presbyterian ministers and others—and I do not think there is any superiority in their ministry over that which is common in London. They themselves would subscribe to the truth of what I assert. The difference is this: there has been prayer for

Ireland. Living, hearty prayer has been offered continually, perhaps, by some who do not live in Ireland, but
have laid that island to heart. God alone knows where that
revival really began. Some woman on her bed may have
been exercised in her soul for that district, and may have
been wrestling with God in prayer; and then the blessing
has descended. If God shall help you and me to bear upon
our hearts the neighbourhood in which we live, the family
over which we preside, the congregation we have to address,
the class we have to teach, the labourers we employ, or
any of these; surely then by mighty prayer we shall bring
down a great blessing upon them from on high. Prayer is
never lost; preaching *may* be, but prayer *never* is. Praying
breath can ne'er be spent in vain. The Lord send to all
the Churches of Great Britain, first of all, the power of
prayer, and then conversions by tens of thousands, through
the outpoured energy of the Holy One of Israel!

III. I have little time for the third point, further than to
remark that, while I have been preaching, I do hope that
many have heard for themselves; and have begun to pray.
If so, there will be the less need to dwell upon the sorrowful
business of setting up A TOMBSTONE. Alas for those who
do not pray, for in truth they do not *live* in the best sense
of life!

Ah, my hearers, religion is more solemn work than some
men think it to be! I am often shocked with the brutality
of what are called the lower classes of society, and with
their coarse blasphemies; but there is one thing more
shocking still, and that is, the frivolous way in which the
mass of our higher classes spend their time. How little
worth the doing is even attempted by numbers of the
wealthy! A round of calls is frequently a mere pretence

for wasting time. What are most amusements but an attempt to kill the time that hangs laboriously on idle hands? What are many of your employments but an industrious idleness, wasting precious hours, which, God knows, will be few enough when you come to look back upon them from a dying bed? Oh! if you did but know your high destiny, many of you would no longer waste your time in the paltry things that occupy your hands, and enslave your souls. God Almighty forgive those wasted hours which, if you be Christians, ought to be employed for the good of others! God forgive those moments of frivolity which ought to have been occupied in prayer! If such a congregation as this could but be solemnly alive to the interests of this land, and the poverty of it, to its miseries, to its wickedness, what results might come of it! If but such a host as I have here could solemnly begin to pray "Thy kingdom come," how much would be attempted and achieved! This would be the best form of Missionary Society. So many hearts full of tenderness and affection, all beating high with anxious desire to see sinners brought to Christ! Though we cannot approve of the doctrines of the Romish Church, we sometimes stand abashed at its zeal. Would God that we had sisters of mercy who were merciful indeed; not dressed in fanciful garb, but yet going from house to house, to comfort the sick, and help the needy! Would that you all were Brothers of the Heart of Jesus, or Sisters of the Compassionate One, whose mother's heart was pierced with agony, when He died, that we might be saved. This I speak with an earnest anxiety that the words may be prophetic of a better age.

Certain of you have never prayed in your lives, toying like glittering insects, wasting your little day. You know

not that death is near you. If you have never sought and
have never found the Saviour, how terrible is your danger!
However bright those eyes, if they have never seen the
wounds of Christ, if they have never looked to Jesus, they
shall not simply be sealed in death, but they must eternally
behold sights of fearful woe. May God grant you grace to
pray; may He lead each one of you home to your house, to
fall on your knees, and for the first time to cry, "Lord, have
mercy upon me!" Remember, you have sins to confess,
and if you think you have not, you are in a sad state of
heart; it proves that you are dead in trespasses and sins—
yes, *dead* in them. Go home, and ask the Lord to give you
a new heart and a right spirit; and may He who will inspire
the prayer graciously hear it at once! May you, and I,
and all of us, when this life has passed away, and time is
exchanged for eternity, stand before the throne of God
at last, "accepted in the Beloved"! I have to preach continually to a congregation in which I know there are many
drunkards, swearers, and the like—with these men I know
how to deal, and God has given me success; but I sometimes tremble for you amiable, excellent, upright daughters,
who make glad your father's house, and I fear for you
wives who train up your children tenderly. Remember, if
you have not the root of the matter in you, outward religion
will not avail. "Except a man be born again, he cannot
see the kingdom of God." You must draw near to God in
simple, penitent faith, or you will not find eternal good.
As I must be honest with the poor, so must I be with the
rich; and I must tell you that you must be converted, and
become as little children, or you cannot enter the kingdom
of heaven. As we must lay the axe to the root of the tree
with the drunkard and the swearer, so must we with you.

You are as much lost as they are, and shall as surely perish
as they do, unless you are born again.   There is but one
road to heaven for you all alike.   As a minister of the
gospel, I know no rich men and no poor men; I know
no working classes and no gentlemen; I know simply God's
sinful creatures, bidden to come to Christ and find mercy
through His atonement.   He will not reject you; put the
black thought away.   He is able to save; doubt Him not.
Come to Him; come and welcome.   God help you to
draw near to Him at once, through Jesus Christ our Lord.
Amen.

THE TALKING BOOK

THE TALKING BOOK.

Preached at the Metropolitan Tabernacle, October 22, 1871.

" When thou awakest, it shall talk with thee."—PROV. vi. 22.

IT is a very happy circumstance when the commandment
of our father and the law of our mother are also the commandment of God and the law of the Lord. Happy are
they who have a double force to draw them to the right—
the bonds of nature, and the cords of grace. They sin
with a vengeance who sin both against a father on earth
and the great Father in heaven ; and they exhibit a virulence
and a violence of sin who do despite to the tender obliga-
tions of childhood, as well as to the demands of conscience
and of God. Solomon, in the passage before us, evidently
speaks of those who find in their parents' law and in God's
law the same thing ; and he admonishes such to bind the
law of God about their heart, and to tie it about their
neck ; by which he intends inward affection and open
avowal. The law of God should be so dear to us, that it
should be bound about the most vital organ of our being,
braided about our heart. That which a man carries in his
hand he may forget and lose, that which he wears upon his
person may be torn from him ; but that which is bound
about his heart will remain there as long as life remains.
We are to love the Word of God with all our heart, and

mind, and soul, and strength; with the full force of our
nature we are to embrace it; all our warmest affections are
to be bound up with it. When the wise man tells us, also,
to wear it about our necks, he means that we are never to
be ashamed of it. No blush is to mantle our cheek when
we are mentioned as God-fearing men: we are never to
speak with 'bated breath in any company concerning the
things of God. Manfully must we take up our cross; cheerfully must we avow ourselves to belong to those who have
respect unto the Divine testimonies. Let us count true
religion to be our highest ornament; and, as magistrates
put upon them their gold chains, and think themselves
adorned thereby, so let us tie about our neck the commands
and the gospel of the Lord our God.

In order that we may be persuaded so to do, Solomon
gives us three telling reasons. He says that God's law—by
which I understand the whole run of Scripture, and especially the gospel of Jesus Christ—will be a guide to us:
"When thou goest, it shall lead thee." It will be a
guardian to us: "When thou sleepest,"—when thou art
defenceless and off thy guard,—"it shall keep thee." And
it shall also be a dear companion to us: "When thou
awakest, it shall talk with thee." Any one of these three
arguments might surely suffice to make us seek a nearer
acquaintance with the sacred Word. We all need a *guide*,
for "it is not in man that walketh to direct his steps."
Left to our own wisdom, we soon excel in folly. There are
dilemmas in all lives where a guide is more precious than a
wedge of gold. The Word of God, as an infallible director
for human life, should be sought unto by us, and it will lead
us in the highway of safety. Equally powerful is the second
reason: the Word of God will become the *guardian* of our

days. "Whoso hearkeneth unto it shall dwell safely, and be quiet from fear of evil." Unguarded moments there may be; times, inevitable to our imperfection, there will be, when, unless some other power protect us, we shall fall into the hands of the foe. Blessed is he who has God's Law so written on his heart, and wears it so about his neck as armour of proof, that at all times he is invulnerable, "kept by the power of God through faith unto salvation."

But I prefer, this morning, to keep to the third reason for loving God's Word. It is this, that it becomes *our sweet companion:* "When thou awakest, it shall talk with thee." The inspired Law of God, which David in the hundred and nineteenth psalm calls God's testimonies, precepts, statutes, and the like, is the friend of the righteous. Its essence and marrow is the gospel of Jesus, the Law-fulfiller, and this also is the special solace of believers. Of the whole sacred volume it may be said, "When thou awakest, it shall talk with thee." The Book of books *talks* with those who lovingly obey its precepts. The statement is homely; and we rejoice that it is one whose truth we are all of us able to prove. The Word of God has talked with us, even with us. I gather four or five thoughts from this expression, and upon these I will speak.

I. We perceive here that THE WORD IS LIVING. How else could it be said, "It shall talk with thee"? A dead book cannot talk, nor can a dumb book speak. It is clearly a living Book, then, and a speaking Book: "The Word of God, which liveth and abideth for ever." How many of us have found this to be most certainly true! A large pro-portion of human books are long ago dead, and even shrivelled like Egyptian mummies; the mere course of years has rendered them worthless, their teaching is disproved, and they have no life for us. Entomb them in your public libraries if you will; but henceforth they will stir no man's pulse, and warm no man's heart. But this thrice-blessed Book of God, though it has been extant among men these many hundreds of years, is immortal in its life, unwithering in its strength. The .dew of its youth is still upon it; its speech still drops as the rain fresh from heaven; its truths are overflowing founts of ever-fresh consolation. Never book spake like this Book; its voice, being the voice of God, is powerful and full of majesty.

Whence comes it that the Word of God is living? Is it not, first, because *it is pure truth?* Error is death, truth is life. No matter how well established an error may be by philosophy, or by force of arms, or the current of human thought, the day cometh that shall burn as an oven, and all untruth shall be as stubble before the fire. The tooth of time devours all lies. Falsehoods are soon cut down, and they wither as the green herb. Truth never dies; it dates its origin from the immortals. Kindled at the source of light, its flame cannot be quenched; if by persecution it be for a time covered, it shall blaze forth anew to take reprisals upon its adversaries. Many a once-venerated system of error now rots in the dead past, among the tombs of the forgotten; but the truth as it is in Jesus knows no sepulchre, and fears no funeral; it lives on, and must live while the Eternal fills His throne.

The Word of God is living, because *it is the utterance of an immutable, self-existing God.* God doth not speak to-day what He meant not yesterday, neither will He to-morrow blot out what He records to-day. When we read a promise spoken three thousand years ago, it is as fresh as though it fell from the eternal lips to-day. There are, indeed, no dates to the Divine promises; they are not of private interpretation, nor to be monopolized by any generation. We say again, the eternal Word drops from the Almighty's lips as fresh to-day as when He uttered it to Moses, or to Elias, or spake it by the tongue of Isaiah or Jeremiah. The Word is always sure, steadfast, and full of power. It is never out of date. Scripture bubbles up evermore with good matters; it is an eternal Geyser, or—shall I say?—a spiritual Niagara of grace, for ever falling, flashing, and flowing on; it is never stagnant, brackish, or defiled, but always clear, crystal, fresh, and refreshing; because it is evermore the living water.

The Word lives, again, because *it enshrines the living heart of Christ.* The heart of Christ is the most living of all existences: it was once pierced with a spear, but it lives on, and yearns towards sinners, and is as tender and compassionate as in the days of our Lord's sojourn on earth. Jesus, the Sinner's Friend, walks in the avenues of Scripture as once He traversed the plains and hills of Palestine; you can see Him still, if you have opened eyes, in the ancient prophecies; you can behold Him more clearly in the four Gospels; He opens and lays bare His inmost soul to you in the Epistles, and makes you hear the footsteps of His approaching Advent in the symbols of the Apocalypse. The living Christ is in the Book; you behold His face almost in every page; and, consequently, it is a Book that can talk. The Christ of the mount of benedictions speaks in it still; the God who said, " Let there be light," gives forth from its pages the same divine fiat; while the incorruptible truth, which saturated every line and syllable of it when first it was penned, abides therein in full force, and preserves it from the finger of decay.

"The grass withereth, and the flower thereof falleth away : but the Word of the Lord endureth for ever."

Over and above all this, *the Holy Spirit has a peculiar connection with the Word of God.* We know that He works in the ministries of all His servants whom He hath ordained to preach ; but, for the most part, we have remarked that the work of the Spirit of God in men's hearts is rather in connection with the texts we quote than with our explanations of them. "Depend upon it," says a deeply-spiritual writer, "it is God's Word, not man's comment on it, which saves souls." God does save souls by our comment, but still it is true that the majority of conversions have been wrought by the agency of a text of Scripture. It is the Word of God that is living and powerful, and sharper than any two-edged sword. There must be life in it, for by it men are born again. As for believers, the Holy Spirit often sets the Word on a blaze while they are studying it. The letters were at one time before us as mere letters ; but the Holy Ghost suddenly came upon them, and they spake with tongues. The chapter is lowly as the bush at Horeb, but the Spirit descends upon it, and lo ! it glows with celestial splendour ! God appears in the words, so that we feel like Moses when he put off his shoes from off his feet, because the place whereon he stood was holy ground. It is true, the mass of readers understand not this, and look upon the Bible as a common book ; but if they understand it not, at least let them allow the truthfulness of our assertion, when we declare that, hundreds of times, we have as surely felt the presence of God in the pages of Scripture as ever Elijah did when he heard the Lord speaking in a still small voice. The Bible has often appeared to us as the dwelling of God, and the posts of its doors have moved at the voice of

Him that cried, whose train also has filled the temple. We have been constrained adoringly to cry, with the seraphim, "Holy, holy, holy, is the Lord God of hosts." The Jews place as a frontispiece to their great Bible the text, "Surely God is in this place. It is none other than the house of God, and the very gate of heaven." And they say well. It is, indeed, a spiritual temple, a most holy house, garnished with precious stones for beauty, and overlaid within and without with pure gold for truth, having for its chief glory the presence of the Lord, so gloriously revealed, that oftentimes the priests of the Lord cannot stand to minister, by reason of the glory of the Lord which fills the house. God the Holy Spirit vivifies the letter with His presence, and then it is to us a living Word indeed.

And now, dear brethren, if these things be so—and our experience certifies them—let us take care how we trifle with the Book which is so instinct with life. Might not many of you remember your faults this day were we to ask you whether you are habitual students of Holy Writ? Readers of it I believe you are; but are you searchers? The blessing is not for those who merely read, but for those who delight in the law of the Lord, and meditate therein both day and night. Are you sitting at the feet of Jesus, with His Word as your school-book? If not, remember, though you may be saved, you lack very much of the blessing which otherwise you might enjoy. Have you been back-sliding? Refresh your soul by meditating in the divine statutes, and you will say with David, "Thy Word hath quickened me." Are you faint and weary? Go and talk with this living Book; it will give you back your energy, and you shall mount again as with the wings of eagles. But are you unconverted altogether? Then I cannot direct you to Bible-reading as being the way of salvation, nor speak of it as though it had any merit in it; but I would, nevertheless, urge upon you unconverted people great reverence for Scripture, an intimate acquaintance with its contents, and a frequent perusal of its pages, for it has occurred, ten thousand times over, that when men have been studying the Word of life, the Word has brought life to them. "The entrance of Thy Word giveth light." Like Elisha with the dead child, the Word has stretched itself upon them, and their dead souls have been made to live. One of the likeliest places in which to find Christ is in the garden of the Scriptures, for there He delights to walk. As of old the blind men were wont to sit by the wayside begging, so that, if Jesus passed by, they might cry to Him, so would I have you sit down by the wayside of the Holy Scriptures. Hear the promises, listen to their gracious words—they are the footsteps of the Saviour; and, as you hear them, may you be led to cry, "Thou Son of David, have mercy upon me!" Attend most those ministries which preach God's Word most. Do not select those that are fullest of fine speaking, and that dazzle you with ex-pressions which are rather ornamental than edifying; but get to a ministry that is full of God's own Word, and, above all, study God's Word itself. Read it with a desire to know its meaning, and I am persuaded that, thereby, many of you who are now far from God will be brought near to Him, and led to a saving faith in Jesus; for "the Word of the Lord is perfect, converting the soul." "Faith cometh by hearing, and hearing by the Word of God."

II. As the text says, "When thou awakest, it shall talk with thee," then it is clear THE WORD IS PERSONAL. "It shall talk with *thee*." It is not written, "It shall speak to the air, and thou shalt hear its voice," but, "It shall talk *with thee.*" You know exactly what the expression means. I am not exactly talking with any one of you this morning; there are too many of you, and I am but one; but, when you are on the road home, each one will talk with his fellow: then is it truly *talk* when man speaks to man. Now, the Word of God has the condescending habit of talking to men, speaking personally to them; and, herein, I desire to commend the Word of God to your love. Oh, that you might esteem it very highly for this reason!

"It shall talk *with thee*," that is to say, *God's Word talks about men, and about modern men;* it speaks of ourselves, and of these latter days, as precisely as if it had only appeared this last week. Some go to the Word of God with the idea that they shall find historical information about the ancient ages; and so they will, but that is not the object of the Word. Others look for facts upon geology, and great attempts have been made either to bring geology round to Scripture, or Scripture to geology. We may always rest assured that truth never contradicts itself; but, as nobody as yet can fully expound geology—for its facts have not yet been compressed into a satisfactory theory—we will wait till the philosophers settle their own private matters, being confident that when they find out the truth, it will be quite consistent with what God has revealed. At any rate, we may leave the sciences to the scientific. The main teachings of Holy Scripture are about men, about the Paradise of unfallen manhood, the fall, the degeneracy of the race, and the means of its redemption. The Book speaks of victims and sacrifices, priests and washings, and so points us to the divine plan by which man can be elevated from the fall, and be reconciled to God. Read Scripture through, and

you shall find that its great subject is that which concerns
the race as to its most important interests; and concerns
the race, not as Jews or as Gentiles, but as made of one
blood; not as barbarians, or Scythians, or Greek, or bond,
or free, but as men who are called to the feast of grace;
and he does not read the Word of God aright who does
not hear it talking to him about things which intimately
concern both himself and his fellows.

It is a book that talks, and that talks personally to us.
It deals with things not in the moon, nor in the planet
Jupiter, nor alone in the distant ages long gone by, nor
chiefly of the periods yet to come; but it deals with *us*, with
the business of to-day—how sin may be to-day forgiven,
and our souls brought at once into union with Christ.

Moreover, this Book is so personal, that *it speaks to men
in all states and conditions before God.* How it talks to
sinners—talks, I say, for it puts it thus: " Come now, and
let us reason together : though your sins be as scarlet, they
shall be as white as snow ; though they be red like crimson,
they shall be as wool." It has many very tender expostula-
tions for sinners. It bows itself to their condition and
position. If they will not stoop to mercy, it shows, as it
were, eternal mercy stooping to them. It talks of feasts of fat
things, of fat things full of marrow ; and the Book, as it talks,
reasons with men's hunger, and bids them eat and be satisfied.
It speaks of garments woven in the loom of infinite wisdom
and love ; and so it talks to man's nakedness, and entreats
him to be arrayed in the divine righteousness. There is no
person, in any condition, who may dare say that there is
nothing in the Word of God to suit his case. If thou hast
been a persecutor, Saul's history talks to thee ; if thou hast
greatly offended, David's repentance instructs thee ; if thou

hast been a harlot or a thief, there are special instances
recorded to meet thy case. In all conditions into which
the sinner can be cast, there is a word that is spoken on
purpose for him.

And, certainly, *when we become the children of God, the
Book talks with us wondrously.* In the family of heaven it is
"The child's own Book." We no sooner know our Father than
this dear writing comes to us as a love-letter from the far-off
country, signed with our own Father's hand, and perfumed
with His tender love. If we grow in grace, or if we back-
slide, in either case Scripture still talks with us. Whatever
our position before the eternal God, the Book seems to be
written on purpose to meet that position. Beloved friends,
you will find that it talks to you as you are : it addresses
you not only as you should be, or as others have been,
but as you personally find yourself just now.

Have you never noticed how personal the Book is as to
all your states of mind, in reference to sadness or to joy?
There was a time with some of us when we were very
gloomy and sore depressed, and then the Book of Job
mourned to the same dolorous tune. I have turned over
the Lamentations of Jeremiah, and thought that I could have
written what Jeremiah wrote. The Book mourns unto us
when we lament. On the other hand, when the soul gets
up to the exceeding high mountains, to the top of Amana
and Lebanon, when we behold visions of glory, and see our
Beloved face to face, lo! the Word is at our side, and in the
delightful language of the Psalms, or in the yet sweeter
expressions of the Song of Solomon, it tells us all that is in
our heart. It talks to us as a living friend who has been
in the deeps, and has been on the heights, has known the
overwhelmings of affliction, and has rejoiced in the triumphs

of delight. The Word of God is to me my own book. I have no doubt, brother, it is the same to you. There could not be a Bible that suited *me* better; it seems written on purpose for me. Dear sister, have not you often felt, as you have put your finger on a promise, "Ah, that is my promise; if there were no other soul, whose tearful eyes would bedew that page, and say, 'It is mine,' yet I, a poor afflicted one, can do so"? Oh, yes; the book is divinely personal; for it goes into minute details of personal experience, let our state be what it may.

And how very faithful it always is! You never find the Word of God keeping back that which is profitable to you. Like Nathan, it cries, "Thou art the man." It never allows our sins to go unrebuked, nor our backslidings to escape notice till they grow into overt sin. It gives us timely notice; it cries to us as soon as we begin to go aside. "Awake thou that sleepest," "Watch and pray," "Keep thine heart with all diligence," and a thousand other words of warning does it address personally to each one of us.

I would suggest, before I leave this point, a little self-examination, as a healthy exercise for each of us. Does the Word of God speak to my soul after this fashion? Then it is gross folly to lose by generalizations that precious thing which can only be realized by a personal grasp. How sayest thou, dear hearer? Dost thou read the Book for thyself, and does the Book speak *to thee?* Has it ever condemned thee? Hast thou trembled before the Word of God? Has it ever pointed thee to Christ, and hast thou looked to Jesus the incarnate Saviour? Does the Book now seal, as with the witness of the Spirit, the witness of thine own spirit that thou art born of God? Art thou in the habit of going to the Book to know thine own condition, to see thine own face as in a glass? Is it thy family medicine? Is it thy test and tell-tale to let thee know thy spiritual condition? Oh, do not treat the Book otherwise than thus, for if thou dealest well with it, and takest it to be thy personal friend, happy art thou, since God will dwell with the man who is humble and contrite, and who trembles at His Word. But if thou treatest it as anybody's book rather than thine own, then beware, lest thou be numbered with the wicked who despise God's statutes.

III. From the text we learn that HOLY SCRIPTURE IS VERY FAMILIAR. "When thou awakest, it shall *talk with thee.*" To talk signifies fellowship, communion, familiarity. It does not say, "It shall preach to thee." Many persons have a high esteem for the Book; but they look upon it as though it were some strangely-elevated teacher speaking to them from a lofty tribunal, while they stand far below. I will not in the least condemn such reverence, but it were far better if they would understand the familiarity of God's Word; it does not so much preach to us as *talk* to us. It is not, "When thou awakest, it shall lecture thee," or, "it shall scold thee." No, no, "it shall *talk* with thee." We sit at its feet, or rather at the feet of Jesus, in the Word, and it comes down to us; it is familiar with us, as a man talketh to his friend. And here let me remind you of the delightful familiarity of Scripture in this respect, that *it speaks the language of men.* If God had written us a book in His own language, we could not have comprehended it, or what little we understood would have so alarmed us, that we should have besought that those words should not be spoken to us any more; but the Lord, in His Word, often uses language which, though it be infallibly true in its

meaning, is not after the knowledge of God, but according
to the manner of man.   I mean this, that the Word uses
similes and analogies of which we may say that they speak
humanly, and not according to the absolute truth as God
Himself sees it.   As men conversing with babes use their
broken speech, so doth the condescending Word.   The
Book is not written in the celestial tongue, but in the *patois*
of this lowland country, condescending to men of low estate.
It feeds us on bread broken down to our capacity, "food
convenient for us."   It speaks of God's arm, His hand, His
finger, His wings, and even of His feathers.   Now, all this
is familiar picturing, to meet our childish capacities; for
the Infinite One is not to be conceived of as though such
similitudes were literal facts.   It is an amazing instance of
divine love, that He uses homely parables so that we may
be helped to grasp sublime truths.   Let us thank the Lord
of the Word for this.

   How tenderly Scripture comes down to our simplicity!
Suppose the sacred Volume had all been like the Book of
the Prophet Ezekiel, small would have been its service to
the generality of mankind.   Imagine that the entire Volume
had been as mysterious as the Book of Revelation : it
might have been our duty to study it; but if its benefit
depended upon our understanding it, we should have failed
to attain it.   But how simple are the Gospels!   How plain
these words, "He that believeth and is baptized shall be
saved"!   How deliciously clear those parables about the lost
piece of money, the stray sheep, and the prodigal son!
Wherever the Word touches upon vital points, it is as bright
as a sunbeam.   Mysteries there are, and profound doctrines
deeps where leviathan can swim ; but where it has to do
immediately with what concerns us for eternity, it is so

plain that the babe in grace may safely wade in its refreshing streams. In the gospel narrative the wayfaring man,
though a fool, need not err. It is familiar talk; it is God's
great mind brought down to our littleness, that it may lift
us up to His greatness.

How familiar the Book is, too,—I speak now as to my
own feelings—*as to all that concerns us!* It talks about my
flesh, and my corruptions, and my sins, as only one that
knew me could speak. It talks of my trials in the wisest
way. Some I dare not tell, it knows all about. It talks
about my difficulties. Some would sneer at them, and laugh;
but this Book sympathizes with them. It knows my tremb-
lings, my fears, my doubts, and all the storm that rages
within the little world of my nature. This Book has been
through all my experience; somehow or other it maps out all
my way, and talks with me as if it were a fellow-pilgrim. It
does not speak to me unpractically, and scold me, and look
down upon me from an awful height of stern perfection, as
if it were an angel, and could not sympathize with fallen
men; but, like the Lord whom it reveals, the Book seems as
if it were touched with a feeling of my infirmities, and had
been tempted in all points as I am. Have you not often
wondered at the human utterances of the divine Word?
It thunders like God, and yet it weeps like man. Nothing
is too little for the Word of God to notice, or too bitter,
or even too sinful for that Book to overlook. It touches
humanity at all points. Everywhere it is a personal, familiar
acquaintance, and seems to say to itself, " Shall I hide this
thing from Abraham my friend?"

And *how often the Book has answered inquiries!* I have
been amazed, in times of difficulty, to see how plain the
oracle is. You have asked friends, and they could not

advise you; but you have gone to your Bible, and it has told you. You have questioned, and you have puzzled, and you have tried to elucidate the problem, and lo! in the chapter read at morning prayer, or in a passage of Scripture that lay open before you, the direction has been given. Have we not seen a text, as it were, plume its wings, and fly from the Book like a seraph, and touch our lips with a live altar-coal? It lay like a slumbering angel amidst the beds of spices of the sacred Word; but it received a divine mission, and brought consolation and instruction to your heart.

The Word of God, then, talks with us in the sense of being familiar with us. Do we understand this? Who, then, that finds God's Word so dear and kind a friend, would forget or neglect it? If any of you have despised it, what shall I say to you? If it were a dreary book, written within and without with curses and lamentations, whose every letter flashed with declarations of vengeance, I might see some reason why you should neglect it; but, O precious, priceless companion, dear friend of all my sorrows, making my bed in my sickness, the light of my darkness, and the joy of my soul, how can I forget thee, how can I forsake thee? I have heard of one who said that the dust on some men's Bibles lay there so thick and long that you might write "*Damnation*" on it. I am afraid that such is the case with some of you. Mr. Rogers, of Dedham, on one occasion, after preaching about the preciousness of the Bible, took it away from the front of the pulpit, and, putting it down behind him, pictured God as saying, "You do not read the Book; you do not care about it; I will take it back. You shall not be wearied with it any more." And then he portrayed the grief of wise men's hearts when they found the blessed revelation withdrawn from men; and how they would besiege the throne of grace, day and night, to ask it back. I am sure he spoke the truth. Though we too much neglect it, yet ought we to prize it beyond all price; for if it were taken from us, we should have lost our kindest comforter in the hour of need. God grant us to love the Scriptures more!

IV. Fourthly, and with brevity, our text evidently shows that THE WORD IS RESPONSIVE. "When thou awakest, it shall talk *with* thee," not "*to* thee." Now, talk *with* a man is not all on one side. To talk with a man needs answering talk from him. You have both of you something to say when you talk together. It is a conversation to which each one contributes his part. Now, Scripture is a marvellously conversational book; it talks, and makes men talk. It is ever ready to respond to us. Suppose you go to the Scriptures in a certain state of spiritual life: you must have noticed, I think, that the Word answers to that state. If you are dark and gloomy, it will appear as though it had put itself in mourning, so that it might lament with you. When you are on the dunghill, there sits Scripture, with dust and ashes on its head, weeping side by side with you, and not upbraiding like Job's miserable comforters. But suppose you come to the Book with gleaming eyes of joy, you will hear it laugh; it will sing and play to you as with psaltery and harp; it will bring forth the high-sounding cymbals. Enter its goodly land in a happy state, and you shall go forth with joy, and be led forth with peace; its mountains and its hills shall break forth before you into singing, and all the trees of the field shall clap their hands. As in water the face is reflected, so in the living stream of revealed truth a man sees his own image.

If you come to Holy Scripture with growth in grace, and with aspirations for yet higher attainments, the Book grows with you, and grows upon you. It is also ever beyond you, cheerily cries, "Higher yet! Excelsior!" Many books in my library are now behind and beneath me; I read them, years ago, with considerable pleasure; I have read them since, with disappointment; I shall never read them again, for they are of no service to me. They were good in their way once, and so were the clothes I wore when I was ten years old; but I have outgrown them. I know more than these books know, and know wherein they are faulty. Nobody ever outgrows Scripture; the Book widens and deepens with our years. It is true, it cannot really grow, for it is perfect; but it does so to our apprehension. The deeper you dig into Scripture, the more you find that it is a great mine of truth. The beginner learns four or five points of orthodoxy, and says, "I understand the gospel, I have grasped all the truth." Wait a bit, and when his soul grows and knows more of Christ, he will confess, "Thy commandment is exceeding broad; I have only begun to understand it."

There is one thing about God's Word which shows its responsiveness to us, and that is, when you reveal your heart to it, *it reveals its heart to you.* If, as you read the Word, you say, "O blessed truth, thou art indeed realized in my experience; come thou still further into my heart; I give up my prejudices, I assign myself, like the wax, to be stamped with thy seal;"—when you do that, and open your heart to Scripture, Scripture will open its heart to you; for it has secrets which it does not tell to the casual reader, it has precious things of the everlasting hills which can only be discovered by miners who know how to dig and open the secret places, and penetrate great veins of everlasting riches. Give thyself up to the Bible, and the Bible will give itself up to thee. Be candid with it, and honest with thy soul, and the Scripture will take down its golden key, and open one door after another, and show to thy astonished gaze ingots of silver which thou couldst not weigh, and heaps of gold which thou couldst not measure. Happy is that man who, in talking with the Bible, tells it all his heart, and learns the secret of the Lord which is with them that fear Him.

And how, too, if you love the Bible, and talk out your love to it, *the Bible will love you!* Its wisdom says, " I love them that love me." Embrace the Word of God, and the Word of God embraces you at once. When you prize its every letter, then it smiles upon you graciously, greets you with many welcomes, and treats you as an honoured guest. I am always sorry to be on bad terms with the Bible, for then I must be on bad terms with God. Whenever my creed does not square with God's Word, I think it is time to mould my creed into another form. As for God's words, they must not be touched with hammer or axe. Oh, the chiselling and cutting and hammering in certain commentaries to make God's Bible orthodox and systematic ! How much better to leave it alone ! The Word is right, and we are wrong, wherein we agree not with it. The teachings of God's Word are infallible, and must be reverenced as such. Now, when you love it so well that you would not alter a single line of it, and prize it so much that you would even die for the defence of one of its truths, then it is dear to you, and you will be dear to it. It will henceforth unfold itself to you as it does not to the world.

Dear brethren and sisters, I must leave this point, but it shall be with this remark—Do you talk to God? Does God talk to you? Does your heart go up to heaven, and does His Word come fresh from heaven to your soul? If not, you do not know the experience of the living child of God, and I earnestly pray that you may. May you this day be brought to see Christ Jesus in the Word, to see a crucified Saviour there, and to put your trust in Him, and then, from this day forward, the Word will echo to your heart, it will respond to your emotions!

V. Lastly, SCRIPTURE IS INFLUENTIAL. That I gather from the fact that Solomon says, " When thou awakest, it shall talk with thee," and follows it up with the remark that it keeps man from the strange woman, and from other sins which he goes on to mention. When the Word of God talks with us, it influences us. All talk influences more or less. I believe there is more done in this world for good or bad by talking than there is by preaching; indeed, the preacher preaches best when he talks. No oratory in the world surpasses natural talk; it is the model of eloquence, and all your rhetorician's action and verbiage are so much artificial rubbish. The most efficient way of preaching is simply talking; the man permitting his heart to run over at his lips into other men's hearts. Now, this sacred Book, as it talks with us, influences us, and it does so in many ways.

It soothes our sorrows, and encourages us. Many a warrior has been ready to steal away from God's battle; but the Word has laid its hand on him, and said, " Stand on thy feet; be not discouraged; be of good cheer; I will help thee; yea, I will strengthen thee; yea, I will uphold thee with the right hand of My righteousness." Brave saints we have heard of; but we little know how often they would have been arrant cowards, only the good Word came to them, and strengthened them, and they went back to the fight stronger than lions and swifter than eagles.

While the Book thus soothes and cheers, *it has a wonderfully quickening power.* Have you never felt it put fresh life-blood into you? You have upbraided your own slackness, and said, " How can I bear to live at such a dying rate as this in which I have too long continued? I must press forward at a faster rate." The Word has put wings to your heels, and spurs to your sides. Read that part of the Word which tells of the agonies of your Master, and you will feel—

> " Now for the love I bear His name,
> What was my gain I count my loss ;
> My former pride I call my shame,
> And nail my glory to His cross."

Read of the glories of heaven which this Book reveals, and you will feel that you must run the race with quickened speed, because a crown so bright is glittering in your view. Nothing can so lift a man above the gross considerations of carnal gain, or human applause, as to have his soul saturated with the Spirit of truth, with which Holy Scripture is filled. It elevates as well as cheers.

Then, too, *how often it warns and restrains!* I had gone to the right or to the left if the law of the Lord had not said, "Let thine eyes look right on, and let thine eyelids look straight before thee." This is the storm-signal which bids us keep in port since tempests await incautious mariners.

This Book's consecrated talk *sanctifies and moulds the mind into the image of Christ.* You cannot expect to grow in grace if you do not read the Scriptures. If you are not

familiar with the Word, you cannot expect to become like
Him that spake it. Our experience is, as it were, the
potter's wheel on which we revolve; and the hand of God
is in the Scriptures to mould us after the fashion and image
which He intends to bring us to. Be much with the
holy Word of God, and you will be holy. Be much with
the silly novels of the day, and the foolish trifles of the
hour, and you will degenerate into vapid wasters of your
time; but be much with the solid teaching of God's Word,
and you will become solid and substantial men and women.
Drink in the Word, and feed upon it, and you shall be conformed to that whereon you feed, and the world shall stand
astonished at you.

Lastly, let the Scripture talk with you, and *it will
confirm and settle you.* We hear every now and then of
apostates from the gospel. They must have been little
taught in the truth as it is in Jesus. A great outcry is
made, every now and then, about our all being perverted to
Rome. A good man lately assured me, with a great deal
of alarm, that all England would be subdued by Popery.
I told him I did not know what kind of God he worshipped,
but my God was much greater than the devil, and did not
intend to let Satan have his way in this land of the martyrs
and of the Bible. I am not half as much afraid of the
pope at Rome as of the Ritualists and Rationalists at home.
But mark you, there was some truth in my friend's fear.
There will be a going over to one form of error or another,
unless there be in the Christian Church a more honest,
industrious, and general reading of Holy Scripture. What
if I were to say that many even among Church members
do not search the Scriptures: should I be slandering them?
You hear on the Sabbath day a chapter read, and you

perhaps read a passage at family prayer; but you do not search the Bible privately and regularly. Is it not so? Too many take their religion out of the monthly magazine, or accept it from the minister's lips. Oh, for the Berean spirit back again, to "search the Scriptures" to see if these things be so! I would like to see a huge pile of all the books, good and bad, that were ever written by men—yes, prayer-books, sermons, hymn-books, and all—consumed in one flame, if the reading of those books should be keeping you away from reading the Bible. A ton weight of human literature is not worth an ounce of Scripture. One single drop of the essential tincture of the Word of God is better than a sea full of our commentings and sermonizings. We must live upon the pure, infallible Word of God if we are to become strong against error, and tenacious of truth. Brethren, may you be established in the faith, rooted, grounded, built up in it! But I know you cannot be except you search the Scriptures continually.

The time is coming when we shall all fall asleep in death. Oh, how blessed it will be to find, when we awake, that the Word of God will talk with us then, and will renew its ancient friendship! Then the promise which we loved before shall be fulfilled; the charming intimations of a blessed future shall be all realized; and the face of Christ, whom we saw as through a glass darkly, shall be all un-covered, and He shall shine upon us as the sun in its strength. God grant us to love the Word, and feed thereon, that we may live to the glory of God all our days! Amen.

FAITH: WHAT IS IT? HOW CAN IT BE OBTAINED?

FAITH: WHAT IS IT? HOW CAN IT BE OBTAINED?

Preached at the Metropolitan Tabernacle, July 17, 1881.

" By grace are ye saved through faith."—Eph. ii. 8.

I MEAN to dwell mainly upon that expression, "through faith." I call attention, however, first of all, to the fountain-head of our salvation, which is the grace of God. " By grace are ye saved." Because God is gracious, therefore sinful men are forgiven, converted, purified, and saved. It is not because of anything in them, or that ever can be in them, that they are saved; but because of the boundless love, goodness, pity, compassion, mercy, and grace of God. Tarry a moment, then, at the well-head. Behold the pure river of water of life as it proceeds out of the throne of God and of the Lamb. What an abyss is the grace of God ! Who can fathom it? Like all the rest of the divine attributes, it is infinite. God is full of love, for "God is love." God is full of goodness, and the very name "God" is but short for "good." Unbounded goodness and love enter into the very essence of the Godhead. It is because " His mercy endureth for ever," that men are not destroyed; because " His compassions fail not," that sinners are brought to Himself, and forgiven. Right well remember this, for else you may fall into error by fixing your minds so much upon the faith which is the channel of salvation as to forget the grace which is the fountain and source even of faith itself. Faith is the work of God's grace in us. No man can say that Jesus is the Christ but by the Holy Ghost. "No man cometh unto Me," saith Christ, "except the Father which hath sent Me draw him." So that faith, which is coming to Christ, is the result of divine drawing. Grace is the first and last moving cause of salvation; and faith, important as it is, is only an essential part of the machinery which grace employs. We are saved "through faith," but it is "by grace." Sound forth those words as with the archangel's trumpet: "By grace are ye saved."

Faith occupies the position of a channel or conduit-pipe. Grace is the fountain and the stream; faith is the aqueduct along which the flood of mercy flows down to refresh the thirsty sons of men. It is a great pity when the aqueduct is broken. It is a sad sight to see, around Rome, the many noble aqueducts which no longer convey water into the city, because the arches are broken, and the marvellous structures are in ruins. The aqueduct must be kept entire to convey the current; and, even so, faith must be true and sound, leading right up to God, and coming right down to ourselves, that it may become a serviceable channel of mercy to our souls. Still, I again remind you that faith is only the channel or aqueduct, and not the fountain-head; and we must not look so much to it as to exalt it above the divine source of all blessing which lies in the grace of God. Never make a Christ out of your faith, nor think of it as if it were the independent source of your salvation. Our life is found in "looking unto Jesus," not in looking to our own faith. By faith, all things become possible to us ; yet the power is not in the faith, but in the God upon whom faith relies. Grace is the locomotive, and faith is the link by which the carriage of the soul is attached to the great motive power. The righteousness of faith is not the moral excellence of faith, but the righteousness of Jesus Christ which faith grasps and appropriates. The peace within the soul is not derived from the contemplation of our own faith ; but it comes to us from Him who is our peace, the hem of whose garment faith touches, and virtue comes out of Him into the soul.

However, it is a very important thing that we look well to faith as the channel of grace, and therefore at this time we will consider, as God, the Holy Ghost, shall enable us, First, Faith, *what is it?* Next, Faith, *why is it selected as the channel of blessing?* Then, Faith, *how can it be obtained and increased?*

I. FAITH, WHAT IS IT? What is this faith concerning which it is said, " By grace are ye saved *through faith*" ? There are many descriptions of faith ; but almost all the definitions I have met with have made me understand it less than I did before I saw them. The negro preacher said, when he read the chapter from the pulpit, that he would proceed to *confound* it ; and it is very likely that he did do so, though he meant to expound it. So, brethren, we may explain faith till nobody understands it. I hope I shall not be guilty of that fault. Faith is the simplest of all mental acts ; and perhaps, because of its simplicity, it is the more difficult to explain.

What is faith? *It is made up of three things—knowledge, belief, and trust.*

Knowledge comes first in order. Some Romanist divines

hold that a man can believe what he does not know.
Perhaps a Romanist can; but I cannot. "How shall they
believe in Him of whom they have not heard?" I want to
be informed of a fact before I can possibly believe it. I
believe this, I believe that; but I cannot say that I believe
a great many things of which I have never heard. "Faith
cometh by hearing:" we must first hear, in order that we
may know what is to be believed. "They that know Thy
name will put their trust in Thee." A measure of knowledge is essential to faith; hence the importance of getting
knowledge. "Incline your ear, and come unto Me; hear,
and your soul shall live,"—such was the word of the ancient
prophet, and it is the word of the gospel still. Search the
Scriptures, and learn what the Holy Spirit teacheth concerning Christ and His salvation. Seek to know "that God is,
and that He is the Rewarder of them that diligently seek
Him." May He give you "the spirit of knowledge and of
the fear of the Lord"! Know the gospel: know what the
good news is, how it talks of free forgiveness and of change
of heart, of adoption into the family of God, and of countless other blessings. Know God, know His gospel, and
know especially Jesus Christ the Son of God, the Saviour of
men, united to us by His human nature, and united to God,
seeing He is divine, and thus able to act as Mediator between God and man, able to lay His hand upon both, and
to be the connecting link between the sinner and the Judge
of all the earth. Endeavour to know more and more of
Christ. After Paul had been converted more than twenty
years, he told the Philippians that he desired to know
Christ; and depend upon it, the more we know of Jesus,
the more we shall wish to know of Him, that so our faith in
Him may increase. Endeavour especially to know the doc-

trine of the sacrifice of Christ, for that is the centre of the target at which faith aims; that is the point upon which saving faith mainly fixes itself, that "God was in Christ, reconciling the world unto Himself, not imputing their trespasses unto them." Know that He was made a curse for us, as it is written, "Cursed is every one that hangeth on a tree." Drink deep into the doctrine of the substitutionary work of Christ, for therein lies the sweetest possible comfort to the guilty sons of men, since the Lord " made Him to be sin for us, who knew no sin, that we might be made the righteousness of God in Him." Faith, then, begins with knowledge; hence the value of being taught in divine truth; for to know Christ is life eternal.

Then the mind goes on to *believe* that these things are true. The soul believes that God is, and that He hears the cries of sincere hearts; that the gospel is from God; that justification by faith is the grand truth that God hath revealed in these last days by His Spirit more clearly than before. Then the heart believes that Jesus is verily and in truth our God and Saviour, the Redeemer of men, the Prophet, Priest, and King unto His people. Dear hearers, I pray that you may at once come to this. Get firmly to believe that "the blood of Jesus Christ, God's dear Son, cleanseth us from all sin;" that His sacrifice is complete and fully accepted by God on man's behalf, so that he that believeth on Jesus is not condemned.

So far you have made a considerable advance towards faith; but one more ingredient is absolutely necessary to complete saving faith, and that ingredient is *trust*. Commit yourself to the merciful God; rest your hope on the gracious gospel; trust your soul on the dying and living Saviour; wash away your sins in the atoning blood; accept His per-

fect righteousness, and all is well. Trust is the life-blood
of faith ; there is no saving faith without it. The Puritans
were accustomed to explain trust by the word "recum-
bency." You know what it means. You see me leaning
upon this rail, leaning with all my weight upon it; even
thus lean upon Christ. It would be a better illustration
still if I were to stretch myself at full length, and rest my
whole person upon a rock, lying flat upon it. Fall flat
upon Christ. Cast yourself upon Him, rest in Him, commit yourself to Him. That done, you have exercised
saving faith. Faith is not a blind thing; for faith begins
with knowledge. It is not a speculative thing ; for faith
believes facts of which it is sure. It is not an unpractical,
dreamy thing ; for faith trusts, and stakes its destiny upon
the truth of revelation. Faith *ventures* its all upon the
truth of God ; it is not a pleasant word to use, but the poet
employed it, and it suggests my meaning—

> "Venture on Him, venture wholly ;
>   Let no other trust intrude."

That is one way of describing what faith is : I wonder
whether I have " confounded " it already.

Let me try again. *Faith is believing that Christ is what
He is said to be, that He will do what He has promised to do,
and expecting this of Him.* The Scriptures speak of Jesus
Christ as being God, God in human flesh ; as being perfect
in His character; as being made a sin-offering on our
behalf ; as bearing sin in His own body on the tree. The
Scriptures speak of Him as having finished transgression,
made an end of sin, and brought in everlasting righteousness. The Scriptures further tell us that He " rose again,"
that He " ever liveth to make intercession for us," that He

has gone up into the glory, and has taken possession of heaven on the behalf of His people, and that He will shortly come again "to judge the world in righteousness, and His people with equity." We are most firmly to believe that it is even so; for this is the testimony of God the Father when He said, "This is My beloved Son: hear ye Him." This also is testified by God the Holy Spirit; for the Spirit has borne witness to Christ, both by the Word and by divers miracles, and by His working in the hearts of men. We are to believe this testimony to be true.

Faith also believes that Christ will do what He has promised; that if He has promised to cast out none that come to Him, it is certain that He will not cast us out if we come to Him. Faith believes that if Jesus said, "The water that I shall give him shall be in him a well of water springing up into everlasting life," it must be true; and if we get this living water from Christ, it will abide in us, and will well up within us in streams of holy life. Whatever Christ has promised to do He will do, and we must believe this so as to look for pardon, justification, preservation, and eternal glory from His hands, according as He has promised.

Then comes the next necessary step. Jesus is what He is said to be, Jesus will do what He says He will do; therefore we must each one *trust Him*, saying, "He will be to me what He says He is, and He will do to me what He has promised to do; I leave myself in the hands of Him who is appointed to save, that He may save me. I rest upon His promise that He will do even as He has said." This is a saving faith, and he that hath it hath everlasting life. Whatever his dangers and difficulties, whatever his

darkness and depression, whatever his infirmities and sins,
he that believeth thus on Christ Jesus is not condemned,
and shall never come into condemnation. May that
explanation be of some service ! I trust it may be used by
the Spirit of God.

But now I thought, as it was a very hot and heavy
morning, that I had better give you a number of illustrations, lest anybody should be inclined to go to sleep.
The illustrations will be such as have been commonly
used; but perhaps I may be able to add one or two of
my own.

Faith exists in various degrees, according to the amount
of knowledge, or other varying circumstances. Sometimes faith is little more than a simple *clinging to Christ:* a
sense of dependence, and a willingness so to depend.
When you are at the seaside, as we might all of us wish to
be just now, you will see the limpet sticking to the rock ;
you walk with a soft tread up to the rock with your walking-
stick, and strike the limpet with a rapid blow, and off he
comes. Try the next limpet in that way. You have
given him warning; he heard the blow with which you
struck his neighbour, and he clings with all his might. You
will never get him off; not you ! Strike, and strike again,
but you may as soon break the rock. Our little friend, the
limpet, does not know much ; but he clings. He cannot tell
us concerning the geological formation of the rock ; but he
clings to it. He has found something to cling to, that is his
little bit of knowledge, and he uses it by clinging to the
utmost of his capacity ; it is the limpet's life to cling.
Thousands of God's people have no more faith than this ;

they know enough to cling to Jesus with all their heart and soul; and this suffices to save them. Jesus Christ is to them a Saviour strong and mighty, and like a rock immovable and immutable; they cleave to Him for dear life, and this clinging saves them.

God gives to His people the propensity to cling. Look at the sweet pea which grows in your garden. Perhaps it has fallen down upon the gravel walk. Lift it up against a shrub or trelliswork, or put a stick near it, and it catches hold directly, because there are little hooks ready prepared with which it grasps anything which comes in its way: it was meant to grow upwards, and so it is provided with tendrils. Every child of God has his tendrils about him—thoughts and desires and hopes with which he hooks on to Christ and the promise. Though this is a very simple sort of faith, it is a very complete and effectual form of it; and, in fact, it is the heart of all faith, and that to which we are often driven when we are in deep trouble, or when our mind is somewhat bemuddled by our being sickly or depressed in spirit. We can cling when we can do nothing else, and that is the very soul of faith. O poor heart, if thou dost not yet know as much about the gospel as we could wish thee to know, cling to what thou dost know! If as yet thou art only like a lamb that wades a little into the river of life, and not like leviathan who stirs the mighty deep to the bottom, yet drink; for it is drinking, and not diving, that will save thee. Cling, then! Cling to Jesus; for that is faith.

Another form of faith is this, in which a man depends upon another from a knowledge of his superiority, and therefore *follows his lead*. I do not think the limpet knows much about the rock, but in this next phase of faith there

F—8

is more knowledge. A blind man trusts himself with his guide because he knows that his friend can see; and trusting, he walks where his guide conducts him. If the poor man was born blind, he does not know what sight is; but he knows that there is such a thing as sight, and that it is possessed by his friend, and therefore he freely puts his hand into the hand of the seeing one, and follows his leadership. This is as good an image of faith as well can be : we know that Jesus has about Him merit and power and blessing which we do not possess, and therefore we gladly trust ourselves to Him, and He never betrays our confidence.

Every boy that goes to school has to exert faith while *learning of a master.* He teaches him geography, and instructs him as to continents and oceans, countries, cities, and empires. The boy does not himself know that these things are true, except that he believes in his teacher, and in the books put into his hands. That is what you will have to do with Christ if you are to be saved—you must just know because He tells you, and believe because He assures you it is even so ; and you must trust yourself with Him because He promises you salvation. Almost all that you and I know has come to us by faith. A scientific discovery has been made, and we are sure of it. On what ground do we believe it ? On the authority of certain well-known men of learning, whose repute is established. We have never made or seen their experiments, but we believe their witness. Just so you are to do with regard to Christ : because He teaches you certain truths, you are to be His disciple, and believe His words, and trust yourself with Him. He is infinitely superior to you, and presents Himself to your confidence as your

Master and Lord. If you will receive Him and His words, you shall be saved.

Another and a higher form of faith is that *faith which grows out of love.* Why does a boy trust his father? You and I may know more about his father than he does, and we do not rely upon him quite so implicitly; but the reason why the child trusts his father is because he loves him. Blessed and happy are they who have a sweet faith in Jesus, intertwined with deep affection for Him. They are charmed with His character, and delighted with His mission, they are carried away by the lovingkindness that He has manifested, and now they cannot help trusting Him because they so much admire, revere, and love Him. It is hard to make you doubt a person whom you love. If you are at last driven to it, then comes the awful passion of jealousy, which is strong as death, and cruel as the grave; but till such a crushing of the heart shall come, love is all trustfulness and confidence.

The way of loving trust in the Saviour may thus be illustrated. A lady is the wife of the most eminent physician of the day. She is seized with a dangerous illness, and is smitten down by its power; yet she is wonderfully calm and quiet, for her husband has made this disease his special study, and has healed thousands similarly afflicted. She is not in the least troubled, for she feels perfectly safe in the hands of one so dear to her, in whom skill and love are blended in their highest forms. Her faith is reasonable and natural, her husband from every point of view deserves it of her. This is the kind of faith which the happiest of believers exercise towards Christ. There is no physician like Him, none can save as He can; we love Him, and He loves us, and therefore we put ourselves into His hands, accept whatever He prescribes, and do whatever He bids.

We feel that nothing can be wrongly ordered while He is the Director of our affairs, for He loves us too well to let us perish, or suffer a single needless pang.

Faith also *realizes the presence of the living God and Saviour*, and thus it breeds in the soul a beautiful calm and quiet like that which was seen in a little child in the time of tempest. Her mother was alarmed, but the sweet girl was pleased; she clapped her hands with delight. Standing at the window when the flashes came most vividly, she cried in childish accents, "Look, mamma! How beautiful! How beautiful!" Her mother said, "My dear, come away, the lightning is terrible;" but she begged to be allowed to look out and see the lovely light which God was making all over the sky, for she was sure God would not do His little child any harm. "But hearken to the terrible thunder," said her mother. "Did you not say, mamma, that God was speaking in the thunder?" "Yes," said her trembling parent. "Oh," said the darling, "how nice it is to hear Him! He talks very loud, but I think it is because He wants the deaf people to hear Him. Is it not so, mamma?" Thus she went talking on; as merry as a bird was she, for God was real to her, and she trusted Him. To her the lightning was God's beautiful light, and the thunder was God's wonderful voice, and she was happy. I dare say her mother knew a good deal about the laws of nature and the energy of electricity; but little was the comfort which her knowledge brought her. The child's knowledge was less showy, but it was far more certain and precious. We are so conceited nowadays that we are too proud to be comforted by self-evident truth, and prefer to make ourselves wretched with questionable theories. Hood sang a deep spiritual truth when he merrily said—

> "I remember, I remember,
>   The fir trees dark and high;
> I used to think their slender tops
>   Were close against the sky.
> It was a childish ignorance,
>   But now 'tis little joy
> To know I'm farther off from heav'n
>   Than when I was a boy."

For my own part, I would rather be a child again than grow perversely wise. Faith is to be a child towards Christ, believing in Him as a real and present Person, at this very moment near us, and ready to bless us. This may seem to be a childish fancy; but it is such childishness as we must all come to if we would be happy in the Lord. "Except ye be converted, and become as little children, ye shall not enter into the kingdom of heaven." Faith takes Christ at His word, as a child believes his father, and trusts him in all simplicity with past, present, and future. God give us such faith!

A firm form of faith arises out of assured knowledge. This comes of growth in grace, and is the faith which believes Christ because it knows Him, and trusts Him because it has proved Him to be infallibly faithful. This faith asks not for signs and tokens, but bravely believes. Look at the faith of the master-mariner—I have often wondered at it. He looses his cable, and steams away from the shore. For days, weeks, or even months he never sees sail or shore, yet on he goes day and night without fear, till one morning he finds himself just opposite to the desired haven towards which he has been steering. How has he found his way over the trackless deep? He has trusted in his compass, his nautical almanack, his glass, and the heavenly bodies; and, obeying their guidance, without sighting shore, he has steered so accurately that he has not to change a

point to get into port. It is a wonderful thing, that sailing
without sight. Spiritually, it is a blessed thing to leave the
shores of sight, and say, "Good-bye to inward feelings,
cheering providences, signs, tokens, and so forth : I believe
in God, and I steer for heaven straight away." "Blessed
are they that have not seen, and yet have believed : " to
them shall be ministered an abundant entrance into
heaven at the last, and a safe voyage on the way.

This is the faith which makes it easy *to commit our
soul and all its eternal interests into the Saviour's keeping.*
One man goes to the bank, and puts his money into it with
unthinking confidence ; but another has looked into the
bank's accounts, and has been behind the scenes, and
made sure of its having a large reserve of well-invested
capital; he puts in his money with the utmost assurance.
He knows and is established in his faith, and so he cheerfully commits his all to the bank. Even so, we who know
Christ are glad to place our whole being in His hands,
knowing that He is able to keep us even unto the end.

God give us more and more of an assured confidence
in Jesus, until it comes to be an unwavering faith, so that
we never doubt, but unquestioningly believe ! Look at the
ploughman ; he labours with his plough in the wintry
months, when there is not a bough on the tree, nor a bird
that sings to cheer him, and after he has ploughed, he takes
the precious corn from the granary, of which perhaps he
hath little enough, and he buries it in the furrows, assured
that it will come up again. Because he has seen a harvest
fifty times already, he looks for another, and in faith he
scatters the precious grain. To all appearance, the most
absurd thing that ever was done by mortal man is to throw
away good corn, burying it in the ground. If you had

never seen or heard of its results, it would seem the way
of waste, and not the work of husbandry; yet the farmer
has no doubt, he longs to be allowed to cast away his seed:
in faith he even covets fair weather that he may bury his
corn; and if you tell him that he is doing an absurd thing,
he smiles at your ignorance, and tells you that thus harvests
come. This is a fair picture of the faith which grows of
experience; it helps us to act in a manner contrary to
appearances; it leads us to commit our all to the keeping of
Christ, burying our hopes and our very lives with Him in
joyful confidence that, if we be dead with Him, we shall also
live with Him. Jesus Christ, who rose from the dead, will
raise us up, through His death, unto newness of life, and give
us a harvest of joy and peace.

Give up everything into the hand of Christ, and you
shall have it back with an abundant increase. May we get
strong faith, so that, as we have no doubt of the rising and
setting of the sun, we may never doubt the Saviour's
working for us in every hour of need! We have already
trusted in our Lord and have never been confounded,
therefore let us go on to rely upon Him more and more
implicitly; for never shall our faith in Him surpass the
bounds of His deservings. Have faith in God, and then
hear Jesus say, "Ye believe in God, believe also in Me."

II. Thus far have I done my best to explain what faith
is; we shall now enquire, WHY IS FAITH SELECTED AS THE
CHANNEL OF SALVATION? "By grace are ye saved *through
faith.*" It becomes us to be modest in answering such a
question, for God's ways are not always to be understood;
but, as far as we can tell, faith has been selected as the
channel of grace because *there is a natural adaptation in
faith to be used as the receiver.* Suppose that I am about

to give a poor man an alms : I put it into his hand—why ?
Well, it would hardly be fitting to put it into his ear, or to
lay it upon his foot ; the hand seems made on purpose to
receive. So faith in the mental frame is created on purpose
to be a receiver; it is the hand of the man, and there is
a fitness in bestowing grace by its means. Do let me put
this very plainly. Faith which receives Christ is as simple
an act as when your child receives an apple from you,
because you hold it out, and promise to give him the apple
if he comes for it. The belief and the receiving relate only
to an apple ; but they make up precisely the same act as
the faith which deals with eternal salvation ; and what the
child's hand is to the apple, that your faith is to the perfect
salvation of Christ. The child's hand does not make the
apple, nor alter the apple, it only takes it ; and faith is
chosen by God to be the receiver of salvation, because it
does not pretend to make salvation, nor to help in it, but
it receives it.

Faith, again, is doubtless selected because *it gives all
the glory to God.* It is of faith that it might be by grace,
and it is of grace that there may be no boasting; for God
cannot endure pride. Paul saith, " Not of works, lest any
man should boast." The hand which receives charity
does not say, "I am to be thanked for accepting the gift ;"
that would be absurd. When the hand conveys bread to
the mouth, it does not say to the body, " Thank me, for
I feed you." It is a very simple thing that the hand does,
though a very necessary thing ; but it never arrogates glory
to itself for what it does. So God has selected faith to
receive the unspeakable gift of His grace, because it cannot
take to itself any credit, but must adore the gracious God
who is the Giver of all good.

Next, God selects faith as the channel of salvation because *it is a sure method, linking man with God.* When man confides in God, there is a point of union between them, and that union guarantees blessing. Faith saves us because it makes us cling to God, and so brings us into connection with Him. Years ago, above certain great falls, a boat was upset, and two men were being carried down the current, when persons on the shore managed to float a rope out to them, which rope was seized by them both. One of them held fast to it, and was safely drawn to the bank; but the other, seeing a great log come floating by, unwisely let go the rope, and clung to the log, for it was the bigger thing of the two, and apparently better to cling to. Alas! the log, with the man on it, went right over the vast abyss, because there was no union between the log and the shore. The size of the log was no benefit to him who grasped it; it needed a connection with the shore to pro-duce safety. So, when a man trusts to his works, or to sacraments, or to anything of that sort, he will not be saved, because there is no junction between him and Christ; but faith, though it may seem to be like a slender cord, is in the hand of the great God on the shore side; infinite power pulls in the connecting line, and thus draws the man from destruction. Oh, the blessedness of faith, because it unites us to God!

Faith is chosen, again, because *it touches the springs of action.* I wonder whether I shall be wrong if I say that we never do anything except through faith of some sort. If I walk across this platform, it is because I believe my legs will carry me. A man eats because he believes in the necessity of food. Columbus discovered America because he believed that there was another continent beyond the ocean : many another grand deed has also been born of faith, for faith works wonders. Commoner things are done on the same principle ; faith in its natural form is an all-prevailing force. God gives salvation to our faith, because He has thus touched the secret spring of all our emotions and actions. He has, so to speak, taken possession of the battery, and now He can send the sacred current to every part of our nature. When we believe in Christ, and the heart has come into the possession of God, then are we saved from sin, and are moved towards repentance, holiness, zeal, prayer, consecration, and every other gracious thing.

Faith, again, *has the power of working by love ;* it touches the secret spring of the affections, and draws the heart towards God. Faith is an act of the understanding ; but it also proceeds from the heart. "With the heart man believeth unto righteousness ; " and hence God gives salvation to faith because it resides next door to the affections, and is near akin to love ; and love, you know, is that which purifies the soul. Love to God is obedience, love to God is holiness : to love God and to love man is to be conformed to the image of Christ, and this is salvation.

Moreover, *faith creates peace and joy ;* he that hath it rests, and is tranquil, glad, and joyous ; and this is a preparation for heaven. God gives all the heavenly gifts to faith, because faith worketh in us the very life and spirit which are to be eternally manifested in the upper and better world. I have hastened over these points that I might not weary you on a day when, however willing the spirit may be, the flesh is weak. May the Holy Spirit bless what has been spoken !

III. We close with the third point : How CAN WE OBTAIN AND INCREASE FAITH ? A very earnest question this to many. We hear them say that they wish to believe, but cannot. A great deal of nonsense is talked upon this subject. Let us be practical in our dealing with it, and not raise absurd questions as an excuse for continuing in unbelief. Instead of asking, "What am I to do in order to believe?" let us believe at once, and have done with trifling. The shortest way to understand faith is to believe at once what we know to be true. If the Holy Spirit has made you honest and candid, you will believe as soon as the truth is set before you. You are bidden to trust in Jesus; and as you know that He is perfectly reliable, your wisdom is to trust him immediately. Anyhow, the gospel command is clear: "Believe in the Lord Jesus Christ, and thou shalt be saved."

But still, *if you have a difficulty, take it before God in prayer.* Tell the great Father exactly what it is that puzzles you, and beg Him by His Holy Spirit to solve the question. If I cannot believe a statement in a book, I am glad to enquire of the author what he meant, and if he is a true man, his explanation will satisfy me: much more will the divine explanation satisfy the heart of the true seeker. The Lord is willing to make Himself known; go to Him, and see if it be not so.

Furthermore, if faith seems difficult, it is possible that God the Holy Spirit will enable you to believe if you *hear very frequently and earnestly that which you are commanded to believe.* We believe many things because we have heard them so often. Do you not find it so in common life, that if you hear a thing fifty times a day, at last you come to believe it? Some men have come to believe that which is false by this process: I should not wonder but what God often blesses this method in working faith concerning that

which is true, for it is written, " Faith cometh by hearing."
If I earnestly and attentively hear the gospel, it may be that,
one of these days, I shall find myself believing that which I
hear, through the blessed operation of the Spirit upon my
mind.

If that, however, should seem poor advice, I would add,
next, *consider the testimony of others.* The Samaritans
believed because of what the woman told them concerning
Jesus. Many of our beliefs arise out of the testimony of
others. I believe that there is such a country as Japan : I
never saw it, and yet I believe that there is such a place
because others have been there. I believe I shall die : I
have never died, but a great many have done so whom I
once knew, and I have a conviction that I shall die also ;
the testimony of many convinces me of this fact. Listen,
then, to those who tell you how they were saved, how they
were pardoned, how they have been changed in character :
if you will but listen, you will find that somebody just like
yourself has been saved. If you have been a thief, you will
find that a thief rejoiced to wash away his sin in the fountain of Christ's blood. You that have been unchaste in
life, will find that others who have fallen that way have
been cleansed and changed. If you are in despair, you
have only to get among God's people, and enquire a little,
and some who have been equally in despair with yourself
will tell you how He saved them. As you listen to one
after another of those who have tried the Word of God, and
proved it, the Divine Spirit will lead you to believe. Have
you not heard of the African, who was told by the missionary
that water sometimes became so hard that a man could
walk on it ? He declared that he believed a great many
things the missionary had told him ; but he never would

believe that. When he visited England, it came to pass
that, one frosty day, he saw the river frozen; but he would
not venture on it. He knew that it was a river, and he was
certain that he would be drowned if he ventured upon it. He
could not be induced to walk on the ice till his friend went
upon it; then he was persuaded, and trusted himself where
others had ventured. So, mayhap, while you see others
believe, and notice their joy and peace, you will yourself
be gently led to trust Christ. It is one of God's ways of
helping us to faith, through His good Spirit.

A better plan still is this,—*note the authority upon which
you are commanded to believe*, and this will greatly help you.
The authority is not mine, or you might well reject it. It
is not even the pope's, or you might even reject that. But
you are commanded to believe upon the authority of God
Himself. *He* bids you believe in Jesus Christ, and you
must not refuse to obey your Maker. The foreman of
certain works in the north had often heard the gospel, but
he was troubled with the fear that he might not come to
Christ. His good master one day sent a card round to the
works—" Come to my house immediately after work." The
foreman appeared at his master's door, and the master came
out, and said somewhat roughly, " What do you want, John,
troubling me at this time? Work is done, what right have
you here?" " Sir," said he, " I had a card from you saying
that I was to come after work." " Do you mean to say
that, merely because you had a card from me, you are to
come up to my house, and call me out after business
hours?" "Well, sir," replied the foreman, " I do not
understand you; but it seems to me that, as you sent for me,
I had a right to come." " Come in, John," said his master;
" I have another message that I want to read to you," and

he sat down, and read these words, "Come unto Me, all ye that labour and are heavy laden, and I will give you rest." "Do you think, after such a message from Jesus, that you can be wrong in going to Him?" The poor man saw it all at once, and believed, because he saw that he had good warrant and authority for believing. So have you, poor soul; you have good authority for coming to Christ, for the Lord Himself bids you trust Him.

If that does not settle you, *think over what it is that you have to believe,*—that the Lord Jesus Christ suffered in the room and place and stead of men, and is able to save all who trust Him. Why, this is the most blessed fact that ever men were told to believe: the most suitable, the most comforting, the most divine truth that ever was set before men! I advise you to think much upon it, and search out the grace and love which it contains. Study the writings of the four Evangelists, study Paul's Epistles, and then see if the message is not such a credible one that you are forced to believe it.

If that is not enough, then *think upon the person of Jesus Christ;* think of who He is, and what He did, and where He is now, and what He is now; think often and deeply about the Son of God, and the Holy Spirit will create faith in your soul. When He, even such an One as He, bids you trust Him, surely then your heart will be persuaded; for how can you doubt *Him?*

If none of these things avail, then there is something wrong about you altogether, and my last word is, *submit yourself to God!* May the Spirit of God take away your enmity, and make you yield! You are a rebel, a proud rebel, and that is why you do not believe your God. Give up your rebellion; throw down your weapons; yield at discretion ; surrender to your King.   I believe that never did a soul throw up its hands in self-despair, and cry, "Lord, I yield," but what faith became easy to it before long.   It is because you still have a quarrel with God, and intend to have your own will and your own way, that therefore you cannot believe.   "How can ye believe," said Christ, "which receive honour one of another, and seek not the honour that cometh from God only?"   Proud self creates unbelief.   Submit, O man!   Yield to your God, and then shall you sweetly believe in your Saviour.   God bless you, for Christ's sake, and by His Holy Spirit bring you at this very moment to believe in the Lord Jesus!   Amen.

THE DYING THIEF IN A NEW LIGHT.

G--8

THE DYING THIEF IN A NEW LIGHT.

Preached at the Metropolitan Tabernacle, August 23, 1885.

"But the other answering rebuked him, saying, Dost not thou fear God, seeing thou art in the same condemnation? And we indeed justly; for we receive the due reward of our deeds: but this Man hath done nothing amiss. And he said unto Jesus, Lord, remember me when Thou comest into Thy kingdom."—LUKE xxiii. 40-42.

A GREAT many persons, whenever they hear of the conversion of the dying thief, remember that he was saved in the very article of death, and they dwell upon that fact, and that alone. He has always been quoted as a case of salvation at the eleventh hour; and so, indeed, he is. In his case it is proven that, as long as a man can repent, he can obtain forgiveness. The cross of Christ avails even for a man hanging on a gibbet, and drawing near to his last hour. He who is "mighty to save" was mighty, even during His own death, to pluck others from the grasp of the destroyer, though they were in the act of expiring.

But that is not everything which the story teaches us; and it is always a pity to look exclusively upon one point, and thus to miss everything else—perhaps miss that which is more important. So often has this been the case, that it

has produced a sort of revulsion of feeling in certain minds,
so that they have been driven in a wrong direction by their
wish to protest against what they think to be a common
error. I read, the other day, that this story of the dying
thief ought not to be taken as an encouragement to death-
bed repentance. Brethren, if the author meant—and I do
think he did mean—that this ought never to be so used
as to lead people to postpone repentance to a dying bed,
he spoke correctly. No Christian man could or would use
it so injuriously: he must be hopelessly bad who would
draw from God's long-suffering an argument for continuing
in sin. I trust, however, that the narrative is not often so
used, even by the worst of men; and I feel sure that it will
not be so used by any one of you. It cannot be properly
turned to such a purpose: it might be used as an encouragement to thieving just as much as to the delay of repentance.
I might say, "I may be a thief because this thief was saved,"
just as rationally as I might say, "I may put off repentance
because this thief was saved when he was about to die."
The fact is, there is nothing so good but men can pervert
it into evil, if they have evil hearts: the justice of God is
made a motive for despair, and His mercy an argument for
sin. Wicked men will drown themselves in the rivers of
truth as readily as in the pools of error. He that has a
mind to destroy himself can choke his soul with the Bread
of Life, or dash himself in pieces against the Rock of Ages.
There is no doctrine of the grace of God so gracious that
graceless men may not turn it into licentiousness.

I venture, however, to say that, if I stood by the bedside
of a dying man to-night, and I found him anxious about his
soul, but fearful that Christ could not save him because
repentance had been put off so late, I should certainly quote

the dying thief to him, and I should do it with a good conscience, and without hesitation. I should tell him that, though he was as near to dying as the thief upon the cross was, yet, if he repented of his sin, and turned his face to Christ believingly, he would find eternal life. I should do this with all my heart, rejoicing that I had such a story to tell to one at the gates of eternity. I do not think that I should be censured by the Holy Spirit for thus using a narrative which He has Himself recorded,—recorded with the foresight that it would be so used. I should feel, at any rate, in my own heart, a sweet conviction that I had treated the subject as I ought to have treated it, and as it was intended to be used for men *in extremis* when their hearts are turning towards the living God. Oh, yes, poor soul, whatever your age, or whatever the period of life to which you have come, you may now find eternal life by the exercise of faith in the Lord Jesus Christ ! Altering Cowper's hymn a very little, we may truly say—

> " The dying thief rejoiced to see
> That fountain in his day ;
> And there may you, though vile as he,
> Wash all your sins away."

Many good people think that they ought to guard the gospel ; but it is never so safe as when it stands out in its own naked majesty. It wants no covering from us. When we protect it with provisos, and guard it with exceptions, and qualify it with observations, it is like David in Saul's armour : it is hampered and hindered, and you may even hear it cry, " I cannot go with these." Preach the gospel just as it is, and it will prove itself to be " the power of God unto salvation to every one that believeth." Qualify it, and the salt has lost its savour. I will venture to put

the matter to you thus.   I have heard it said that few are
ever converted in old age; and this is thought to be a
statement which will prove exceedingly arousing and im-
pressive to the young.   It certainly wears that appearance;
but, on the other hand, it is very discouraging to the aged.
I demur to the frequent repetition of such statements, for
I do not find their counterpart in the teaching of Christ
and His apostles.   Assuredly, our Lord spoke of some who
entered the vineyard at the eleventh hour of the day; and
His miracles included, not only healing for those who were
dying, but even resurrection for the dead.   Nothing can be
concluded from the words of the Lord Jesus against the
salvation of men at any hour or any age.   I tell you that, in
the business of your acceptance with God, through faith in
Christ Jesus, it does not matter what age you have now
reached.   The command, for the present moment, to every
one of you is, "To-day if ye will hear His voice, harden
not your hearts;" and whether you are in the earliest stage
of life, or are within a few hours of eternity, if now you fly
for refuge to the hope set before you in the gospel, you
shall be saved.   The gospel that I preach excludes none
on the ground of either age or character.   Whoever you
may be, " Believe on the Lord Jesus Christ, and thou shalt
be saved," is the message we have to deliver to you.   If we
address to you the longer form of the gospel, " He that
believeth and is baptized shall be saved," this is true of
every living man, be his age whatever it may.   I am not
afraid that this story of the dying and repenting thief, who
went straight from the cross to the crown, will be used by
you amiss; but if you are wicked enough to misuse it, I
cannot help it.   Such conduct will only fulfil that solemn
Scripture which saith that preachers of the gospel are the

"savour of death unto death" to some, while they are the
"savour of life unto life" to others.

But I do not think, dear friends, that the only speciality
about the thief is the lateness of his repentance.   So far from
that being the only point of interest, it is not even the chief
point.   To some minds, at any rate, other points will be
even more remarkable.   I want to show you, very briefly,
first, that there was a speciality in his case as to *the means of
his conversion ;* secondly, a speciality in *his faith ;* thirdly, a
speciality in *the result of his faith while he was here below ;*
and, fourthly, a speciality in *the promise won by his faith—*
the promise fulfilled to him in Paradise.

I. First, then, I think you ought to notice very carefully
THE SINGULARITY AND SPECIALITY OF THE MEANS BY WHICH
THE THIEF WAS CONVERTED.

How do you think it was?   Well, we do not know.   We
cannot tell.   It seems to me that the man was an unconverted, impenitent thief when they nailed him to the cross,
because Matthew says, that when the chief priests, scribes,
and elders mocked the suffering Saviour, saying, "He
trusted in God; let Him deliver Him now, if He will have
Him : for He said, I am the Son of God. *The thieves also,*
which were crucified with Him, *cast the same in His teeth.*"
I know that this may have been a general statement, and
that it is reconcilable with its having been done by one
thief only, according to the methods commonly used by
critics ; but I am not enamoured of critics even when they
are friendly.   I have such respect for revelation that I
never in my own mind permit the idea of discrepancies and
mistakes; and when the Evangelist says " they ", I believe
he means thieves, and that both these malefactors did at first
rail at the Christ with whom they were crucified.   It would

appear that, by some means or other, this thief must have been converted while he was on the cross. Assuredly, nobody preached a sermon to him, no evangelistic address was delivered at the foot of his cross, and no meeting, of which we have any record, was held for special prayer on his account. He does not even seem to have had an instruction, or an invitation, or an expostulation addressed to him; and yet he became a sincere and accepted believer in the Lord Jesus Christ.

Dwell upon this fact, if you please, and note its practical bearing upon the cases of many around us. There are many among my hearers who have been instructed from their childhood, who have been admonished, and warned, and entreated, and invited, and yet they have not come to Christ; while this man, without any of these advantages, nevertheless believed in the Lord Jesus Christ, and found eternal life. O you who have lived under the sound of the gospel from your childhood, the dying thief does not comfort you, but he accuses you! Why do you abide so long in unbelief? Will you never believe the testimony of divine love?

What do you think must have converted this poor thief? It strikes me that it may have been—it must have been—*the sight of our great Lord and Saviour.* There was, to begin with, our Saviour's wonderful behaviour on the way to the cross. Perhaps the robber had mixed in all sorts of society; but he had never seen a man like this Man. Never had a cross been carried by a Cross-Bearer of His form and fashion. The robber might well marvel who this meek and majestic Personage could be. He heard the women weep, and he may have wondered within himself whether anybody would ever weep for him. He thought that this must be

some very singular Person that the people should crowd
around Him with tears in their eyes. When he heard
that mysterious Sufferer say so solemnly, "Daughters of
Jerusalem, weep not for Me, but weep for yourselves,
and for your children," he must have been struck with
wonder. When he came to think, in his death-pangs, of
the singular look of pity which Jesus cast on the women,
and of the self-forgetfulness which gleamed from His eyes,
he must have been smitten with a strange relenting : it was
as if an angel had crossed his path, and opened his eyes to
a new world, and to a new form of manhood, the like of
which he had never seen before. He and his companion
were coarse, rough fellows : but their fellow-Sufferer was a
delicately-fashioned Being, of a superior order to them ;
yes, and of a superior order to any other of the sons of
men. Who could He be? What must He be? Though
the thief could see that Jesus suffered and fainted as He
went along, he marked that there was no word of complain-
ing, no note of execration, in return for the revilings cast
upon Him. His eyes looked love even on those who
glared upon Him with hate. Surely that march along the
Via Dolorosa was the first part of the sermon which God
preached to that bad man's heart. It was preached to
many others who did not regard its teaching ; but upon
this man, by God's special grace, it had a softening effect
when he came to think over it, and consider it. Was it
not a likely and convincing means of grace ?

When he saw the Saviour surrounded by the Roman
soldiery—saw the executioners bring forth the hammers and
the nails, and lay him down upon His back, and drive the
nails into His hands and feet—this crucified criminal was
startled and astonished as he heard Him say, "Father, for-

give them ; for they know not what they do." He himself,
probably, had met his executioners with a curse ; but he
heard this Man breathe a prayer to the great Father ; and, as
a Jew, as he probably was, he understood what was meant
by such a prayer.   But it did astound him to hear Jesus
pray for His murderers.   That was a petition the like of which
he had never heard, nor even dreamed of.   From whose
lips could it come but from the lips of a divine Being ?
Such a loving, forgiving, God-like prayer, proved Him to be
the Messias.   Who else had ever prayed so ?   Certainly not
David and the kings of Israel, who, on the contrary, in all
honesty and heartiness, imprecated the wrath of God upon
their enemies.   Elias himself would not have prayed in that
fashion ; rather would he have called fire from heaven on the
centurion and his company.   It was a new, strange sound
to the malefactor.   I do not suppose that he appreciated
it to the full ; but I can well believe that it deeply
impressed him, and made him feel that his fellow-Sufferer
was a Being about whom there was an exceeding mystery
of goodness.

And when the central cross was lifted up, that thief,
hanging on his own cross, looked around, and I suppose he
could see Pilate's inscription written in Hebrew, Greek, and
Latin,—" Jesus of Nazareth, the King of the Jews."   If so,
that writing was his little Bible, his New Testament, and he
interpreted it by what he knew of the Old Testament.
Putting this and that together—that strange Person, incarnate loveliness, all patience and all majesty, that strange
prayer, and now this singular inscription, surely he who
knew the Old Testament, as I have no doubt he did,
would say to himself, " Is this HE ?   Is this truly the King
of the Jews ?   This is He who wrought miracles, and raised

the dead, and said that He was the Son of God; is it all true, and is He really our Messiah?" Then he would remember the words of the prophet Isaiah, " He is despised and rejected of men : a Man of sorrows, and acquainted with grief." "Surely He hath borne our griefs, and carried our sorrows." "The chastisement of our peace was upon Him." "Why," he would say to himself, "I never understood that passage in the prophet Esaias before, but it must point to Him! Can this be He who cried in the Psalms, 'They pierced My hands and My feet'?" As he looked at Him again, he felt in his soul, "It must be He? Could there be another so God-like, so divine?" He felt conviction creeping over his spirit. Then he looked again, and he marked how all men down below rejected, and despised, and hissed at Him, and hooted Him ; and all this would make the case the more clear. "All they that see Me laugh Me to scorn : they shoot out the lip, they shake the head, saying, He trusted on the Lord that He would deliver Him : let Him deliver Him, seeing He delighted in Him."

Peradventure, *the dying thief learned the gospel from the lips of Christ's enemies.* They said, "He saved others." "Ah!" thought he, "did He save others? Why should he not save *me?*" What a grand bit of gospel that was for the dying thief—" He saved others"! I think I could swim to heaven on that plank—"He saved others;" because, if He saved others, He can of a surety save me. Thus, the very things that Christ's enemies disdainfully threw at Him would be gospel to this poor dying man. When I have been obliged to read any of the wretched prints that are sent us out of scorn, in which our Lord is held up to ridicule, I have thought, "Why, perhaps those who read these loathsome blasphemies may, nevertheless, learn the gospel from them!" You may pick a diamond from a dunghill, and find its brilliance undiminished; and you may hear the gospel from a blasphemous mouth, and it shall be none the less the gospel of salvation. Peradventure, this man learned the gospel from those who jested at our dying Lord; and so the servants of Satan were unconsciously made to be the servants of the Saviour.

But, after all, surely that which won him most must have been to *look at Jesus again*, as He was hanging upon the cruel tree. Possibly nothing about the physical person of Christ would be attractive to him, for His visage was more marred than that of any man, and His form more than the sons of men; but yet there must have been in that blessed face a singular charm. Was it not the very image of perfection? As I conceive the face of Christ, it was very different from anything that any painter has yet been able to place upon his canvas. It was all goodness, and kindness, and unselfishness; and yet it was a royal face. It was a face of superlative justice and unrivalled tenderness. Righteousness and uprightness sat upon His brow; but infinite pity and good-will to men had also there taken up their abode. It was a face that would have struck you at once as one by itself, never to be forgotten, never to be fully understood. It was all sorrow, yet all love; all meekness, yet all resolution; all wisdom, yet all simplicity; the face of a child, or an angel, and yet peculiarly the face of a man. Majesty and misery, suffering and sacredness, were therein strangely combined; He was evidently the Lamb of God, and the Son of man. As the robber looked, he believed. Is it not singular that the sight of the Saviour won him? The sight of the Lord in agony, and shame, and death!

Scarcely a word; certainly no sermon; no attending worship on the Sabbath; no reading of gracious books; no appeal from mother, or teacher, or friend; but the sight of Jesus won him. I put it down as a very singular thing, a thing for you and for me to recollect, and dwell upon, with quite as much vividness as we do upon the lateness of this robber's conversion.

Oh, that God of His mercy might convert everybody in this Tabernacle! Oh, that I might have a share in it by the preaching of the Word! Yet I will be equally happy if you get to heaven anyhow; ay, if the Lord should take you there without any outward ministry, leading you to Jesus by some simple method such as He adopted with this thief. If you do but get there, He shall have the glory of it, and His poor servant will be overjoyed. Oh, that you would now look to Jesus, and live! Before your eyes He is set forth, evidently crucified among you. Look to Him, and be saved, even this very hour.

II. But now I want you to think with me a little upon THE SPECIALITY OF THIS MAN'S FAITH, for I think it was a very singular faith that this thief exerted towards our Lord Jesus Christ. I greatly question whether the equal and the parallel of the dying thief's faith will be readily found outside the Scriptures, or even in the Scriptures.

Observe, that this man believed in Christ *when he literally saw Him dying the death of a felon,* under circumstances of the greatest personal shame. You have never realized what it was to be crucified. None of you could do that, for the sight has never been seen in England in our day. There is not a man or woman here who has ever fully realized what the actual death of Christ was. It stands beyond us. This man saw it with his own eyes,

and for him to call *Him* "Lord" who was hanging on a
gibbet, was no small triumph of faith. For him to ask
Jesus to remember him when He came into His kingdom,
though he saw that Jesus bleeding His life away, and
hounded to the death, was a notable act of reliance.
For him to commit his everlasting destiny into the hands
of One who was, to all appearance, unable even to preserve
His own life, was a noble achievement of faith. I say that
this dying thief leads the van in the matter of faith, for
what he saw of the circumstances of the Saviour was
calculated to contradict rather than help his confidence,
for he saw our Lord in the very extremity of agony and
death, and yet he believed in Him as the King shortly to
come into His kingdom.

Recollect, too, that at that time, when the thief believed
in Christ, *all the disciples had forsaken Him, and fled.*
John might have been lingering at a little distance, and
holy women may have stood farther off; but no one was
present bravely to champion the dying Christ. Judas had
sold him, Peter had denied Him, and the rest had forsaken
Him; and it was then that the dying thief called Him
"Lord", and said, "Remember me when Thou comest into
Thy kingdom." I call that glorious faith. Why, some
of you do not believe, though you are surrounded by
Christian friends—though you are urged on by the testimony of those whom you regard with love; but this man,
all alone, comes out, and calls Jesus his Lord! No one
else was confessing Christ at that moment: no revival was
taking place amid enthusiastic crowds: he was all by himself
as a confessor of his Lord. After our Lord was nailed
to the tree, the first to bear witness for Him was this
thief. The centurion bore witness afterwards, when Jesus

expired; but this thief was a lone confessor, holding on
to the Saviour when nobody would say "Amen" to what
he said.   Even his fellow-thief was mocking at the crucified
Christ, so that this man shone as a lone star in the
midnight darkness.   Oh, sirs, dare you be Daniels?   Dare
you stand alone?   Would you dare to stand out amidst a
ribald crew, and say, "Jesus is my King.   I only ask Him
to remember me when He comes into His kingdom"?
Would you be likely to avow such a faith when priests
and scribes, princes and people, were all mocking at the
Christ, and deriding Him?   Brethren, the dying robber
exhibited marvellous faith, and I beg you to think of this
next time you speak of him.

And it seems to me that another point adds splendour
to that faith, namely, that *he himself was in extreme torture.*
Remember, he was crucified.   It was a crucified man
trusting in a crucified Christ.   Oh, when the whole frame is
racked with pain, when the tenderest nerves are tortured,
when the body is hung up to die by we know not what
length of torment, then to forget the present and live
in the future is a grand achievement of faith!   While
dying, to turn one's eye to Another dying at your side,
and trust your soul with Him, is very marvellous faith.
Blessed thief, because they put thee down at the bottom,
as one of the least of saints, I think that I must bid thee
come up higher, and take one of the uppermost seats
among those who by faith have glorified the Christ of God!

Why, see, dear friends, once more, the speciality of
this man's faith was that *he saw so much,* though his eyes
had been opened for so short a time!   He saw the future
world.   He was not a believer in annihilation, or in the
possibility of a man not being immortal.   He evidently

expected to be in another world, and to be in existence when the dying Lord should come into His kingdom. He believed all that, and it is more than some do nowadays. He also believed that Jesus would have a kingdom, a kingdom after He was dead, a kingdom though He was crucified. He believed that He was winning for Himself a kingdom by those nailed hands and pierced feet. This was intelligent faith, was it not? He believed that Jesus would have a kingdom in which others would share, and therefore he aspired to have his portion in it. But yet he had right views of himself, and therefore he did not say, "Lord, let me sit at Thy right hand;" or, "Let me share the dainties of Thy palace;" but he said only, "Remember me. Think of me. Cast an eye my way. Think of Thy poor dying comrade on the cross by Thy side. Lord, remember me! Lord, remember me!" I see deep humility in the prayer, and yet a sweet, joyous, confident exaltation of the Christ at the time when the Christ was in His deepest humiliation.

Oh, dear sirs, if any of you have thought of this dying thief only as one who put off repentance, I want you now to think of him as one who did greatly and grandly believe in Christ; and oh, that you would do the same! Oh, that you would put great confidence in my great Lord! Never did a poor sinner trust Christ too much. There was never a case of a guilty one, who believed that Jesus could forgive him, and afterwards found that He could not—who believed that Jesus could save him on the spot, and then woke up to find that it was a delusion. No; plunge into this river of confidence in Christ. Here you will find waters to swim in, not to drown in. Never did a soul perish that glorified Christ by a living, loving faith in Him. Come, then, with all your sin, whatever it may be, with all your deep depression of spirit, with all your agony of conscience, and trust in Christ. Come along with you, and grasp my Lord and Master with both the hands of your faith, and He shall be yours, and you shall be His.

> "Turn to Christ your longing eyes,
> View His bloody sacrifice :
> See in Him your sins forgiven ;
> Pardon, holiness, and heaven ;
> Glorify the King of kings,
> Take the peace the gospel brings."

I think that I have shown you something special in the means of the thief's conversion, and in his faith in our dying Lord.

III. But now, thirdly, as God shall help me, I wish to show you another speciality, namely, in THE RESULT OF HIS FAITH.

I have heard people say, "Well, you see, the dying thief was converted; but then he was not baptized. He never went to communion, and never joined the church." He could not do either; and that which God Himself renders impossible to us, He does not demand of us. The poor man was nailed to the cross; how could he be baptized? But he did a great deal more than that; for if he could not carry out the outward signs, he most manifestly exhibited the things which they signified, which, in his condition, was better still.

The dying thief first of all confessed the Lord Jesus Christ; and that is the very essence of baptism. He confessed Christ. Did he not acknowledge Him to his fellow-thief? It was as open a confession as he could make. Did he not acknowledge Christ before all that were gathered around the cross, within hearing of his voice?

It was as public a confession as he could possibly cause
it to be. Yet certain cowardly fellows claim to be
Christians, though they have never confessed Christ to a
single person, and then they quote this poor thief as an
excuse! Are they nailed to a cross? Are they dying in
agony? Oh, no; yet they talk as if they could claim the
exemption which these circumstances would give them.
What a dishonest piece of business!

The fact is, our Lord requires an open confession as
well as a secret faith; and if you will not render it, there
is no promise of salvation for you, but a threat of being
denied at the last. The apostle puts it, "If thou shalt
confess with thy mouth the Lord Jesus, and shalt believe
in thine heart that God hath raised Him from the dead,
thou shalt be saved." It is stated in another place upon
this wise,—"He that believeth and is baptized shall be
saved,"—that is Christ's way for his disciples to confess
Him. If there be a true faith, there must be a declaration
of it. If you are candles, and God has lit you, "Let your
light so shine before men, that they may see your good
works, and glorify your Father which is in heaven." Soldiers
of Christ must, like her Majesty's soldiers, wear their regi-
mentals; and if they are ashamed of their uniform, they
ought to be drummed out of the regiment. They are not
true soldiers who refuse to march in rank with their
comrades. The very least thing that the Lord Jesus Christ
can expect of us is, that we do confess Him to the best of
our power. If you are nailed up to a cross, I will not
invite you to be baptized. If you are fastened up to a tree
to die, I will not ask you to come into this pulpit, and
declare your faith, for you cannot. But you are required
to do what you can do, namely, to make as distinct and

open an avowal of the Lord Jesus Christ as may be suitable to your present condition.

I believe that many Christian people get into a deal of trouble through not being honest to their convictions. For instance, if a man goes into a workshop, or a soldier into a barrack-room, and if he does not fly his flag from the first, it will be very difficult for him to run it up afterwards. But if he immediately and boldly lets all know, "I am a Christian man, and there are certain things that I cannot do to please you, and certain other things that I cannot help doing though they displease you,"—when that is clearly understood, after a while the singularity of the thing will be gone, and the man will be let alone; but if he is a little sneaky, and thinks that he is going to please the world and please Christ too, he is in for a rough time, let him depend upon it. His life will be that of a toad under a harrow, or a fox in a dog-kennel, if he tries the way of compromise. That will never do. Come out boldly on the Lord's side. Show your colours. Let it be known who you are, and what you are; and although your course will not be smooth, it will certainly not be half so rough as if you tried to run with the hare and hunt with the hounds—a very difficult task that.

This man came out, then and there, and made as open an avowal of his faith in Christ as was possible.

The next thing he did was to rebuke his fellow-sinner. He spoke to him in answer to the ribaldry with which he had assailed our Lord. I do not know what the unconverted convict had been blasphemously saying, but his converted comrade spoke very honestly to him: "Dost not thou fear God, seeing thou art in the same condemnation? And we indeed justly; for we receive the due reward of our

deeds : but this Man hath done nothing amiss." It is more
than ever needful in these days that believers in Christ
should not allow sin to go unrebuked; and yet a great
many of them do so. Do you not know that a person who
is silent, when a wrong thing is said or done, may become a
participator in the sin? If you do not rebuke sin—I mean,
of course, on all fit occasions, and in a proper spirit—your
silence will give consent to the sin, and you will be an
aider and abettor in it. A man who saw a robbery, and
who did not cry "Stop, thief!" would be thought to be in
league with the thief; and the man who can hear swearing,
or see impurity, and never utter a word of protest, may well
question whether he is right himself. Our "other men's
sins" make up a great item in our personal guilt unless
we rebuke them as we have opportunity. This our Lord
expects us to do. The dying thief did it, and did it with
all his heart; and therein far exceeded large numbers of
those who hold their heads high in the church.

Next, *the dying thief made a full confession of his guilt.*
He said to him who was hanged with him, "Dost not thou
fear God, seeing thou art in the same condemnation? *And
we indeed justly."* Not many words, but what a world of
meaning was in them—"we indeed justly." "You and I
are dying for our crimes," said he, "and we deserve to die."
When a man is willing to confess that he deserves the wrath
of God—that he deserves the suffering which his sin has
brought upon him—there is evidence of sincerity in him.
In this man's case, his repentance glittered like a holy
tear in the eye of his faith, so that his faith was bejewelled
with the drops of his penitence. As I have often told you,
I suspect the faith which is not born as a twin with repentance; but there is no room for suspicion in the case of this

penitent confessor. I pray God that you and I may have such a thorough work as this in our own hearts as the result of our faith in Christ.

Then, see, *this dying thief defends his Lord right manfully.* He says, "We indeed justly, but this Man hath done nothing amiss." Was not that beautifully said? He did not say, "This Man does not deserve to die," but "This Man hath done nothing amiss." He means that He is perfectly innocent. He does not even say, "He has done nothing wicked," but he even asserts that He has not acted unwisely or indiscreetly: "This Man hath done nothing amiss." This is a glorious testimony of a dying man to One who was numbered with the transgressors, and was being put to death because His enemies falsely accused Him. Beloved, I only pray that you and I may bear as good witness to our Lord as this thief did. He outruns us all. We need not think much of his conversion coming so late in life; we may far rather consider how blessed was the testimony which he bore for his Lord when it was most needed. When all other voices were silent, one suffering penitent spake out, and said, "This Man hath done nothing amiss."

See, again, another mark of this man's faith. He prays; and *his prayer is directed to Jesus:* "Lord, remember me when Thou comest into Thy kingdom." True faith is always praying faith. "Behold, he prayeth," is one of the surest proofs of the new birth. Oh, friends, may we abound in prayer, for thus we shall prove that our faith in Jesus Christ is what it ought to be! This converted robber opened his mouth wide in prayer; he prayed with great confidence as to the coming kingdom, and he sought that kingdom first, even to the exclusion of all else. He might

have asked for life, or for ease from pain; but he preferred
the kingdom.   This is a high mark of grace.

In addition to thus praying, you will see that *he adores
and worships Jesus*, for he says, " Lord, remember me when
Thou comest into Thy kingdom."   The petition is worded
as if he felt, " Only let Christ think of me, and it is enough.
Let Him but remember me, and the thought of His mind
will be effectual for everything that I shall need in the world
to come."   This is to impute Godhead to Christ.   If a
man can cast his all upon the mere memory of a person, he
must have a very high esteem of that person.   If to be
remembered by the Lord Jesus is all that this man asks, or
desires, he pays to the Lord great honour.   I think that
there was about his prayer a worship equal to the eternal
hallelujahs of cherubim and seraphim.   There was in it a
glorification of his Lord which is not excelled even by the
endless symphonies of angelic spirits who surround the
throne.   Thief, thou hast well done !

Oh, that some penitent spirit here might be helped thus
to believe, thus to confess, thus to defend his Master, thus
to adore, thus to worship ; then the age of the convert
would be a matter of the smallest imaginable consequence.

IV. Now, my last remark is this : There was something
very special about the dying thief as to OUR LORD'S
PROMISE TO HIM CONCERNING THE FUTURE.   Jesus said to
him, " To-day shalt thou be with Me in Paradise."   He only
asked the Lord to remember him, but he obtained this
surprising answer : " To-day shalt thou be with Me in
Paradise."   In some respects I envy this dying thief, for
this reason, that, when the Lord pardoned me, and pardoned
the most of you who are present, He did not give us a
place in Paradise that same day.   We are not yet come to

the rest which is promised to us. No, we are waiting here.
Some of us have been waiting very long.   It is thirty years
with many of us.   It is forty years, it is fifty years, with
many others, since the Lord blotted out your sins, and yet
you are not with Him in Paradise. There is a dear member
of this Church who, I suppose, has known the Lord for
seventy-five years, and she is still with us, having long
passed the ninetieth year of her age. The Lord did not
admit her to Paradise on the day of her conversion. He
did not take any one of us from nature to grace, and from
grace to glory, in a single day.

We have had to wait a good while, and some of us
may have to wait much longer.   Why is this?   There is
something for us to do in the wilderness, so we are kept
out of the Heavenly Garden.   I remember that Mr.
Richard Baxter said that he was not in a hurry to go
to heaven; and a friend called upon Dr. John Owen, who
had been writing about the glory of Christ, and asked him
what he thought of going to heaven. That great divine
replied, "I am longing to be there."   "Why!" said the
other, "I have just spoken to holy Mr. Baxter, and he says
that he would prefer to be here, since he thinks that he can
be more useful on earth."   "Oh!" said Dr. Owen, "my
brother Baxter is always full of practical godliness; but for
all that, I cannot say that I am at all desirous to linger in
this mortal state. I would rather be gone."   Each of these
men seems to me to have been the half of Paul. Paul was
made up of the two, for he was desirous to depart, but he
was willing to remain because it was needful for the people.
We would put both together; and, like Paul, have a strong
desire to depart, and to be with Christ, and yet be willing to
wait if we can do service to our Lord and to His Church.

Still, I think he had the best of it who was converted and entered heaven the same night. This robber breakfasted with the devil, but he dined with Christ on earth, and supped with Him in Paradise. This was short work, but blessed work. What a host of troubles he escaped! What a world of temptation he missed! What an evil world he quitted! He was just born, like a lamb dropped in the field, and then he was lifted into the Shepherd's bosom straight away. I do not remember the Lord ever saying this to anybody else. I dare say it may have happened that souls have been converted and have gone home at once; but I never heard of anybody who had, at the time of conversion, such an assurance from Christ as this man had, "Verily I say unto thee;"—such a personal assurance—"*Verily I say unto thee, To-day shalt thou be with Me in Paradise.*" Dying thief, thou wert favoured above many, "to be with Christ, which is far better," and to be with Him so soon!

Why is it that our Lord does not thus emparadise all of us at once? It is because there is something for us to do on earth. My brethren, are you doing it? *Are you doing it?* Some good people are still on earth; but why? What is the use of them? I cannot make it out. If they are indeed the Lord's people, what are they here for? They get up in the morning, and eat their breakfast, and in due course they eat their dinner, and their supper, and go to bed and sleep; at a proper hour they get up the next morning, and do the same as on the previous day. Is this living for Jesus? Is this life? It does not come to much. Can this be the life of God in man? Oh, Christian people, do justify your Lord in keeping you waiting here! How can you justify Him but by serving Him to the utmost of your power?

The Lord help you to do so! Why, you owe as much to Him as the dying thief! I know I owe a great deal more. What a mercy it is to have been converted while you were yet a boy, to be brought to the Saviour while you were yet a girl! What a debt of obligation young Christians owe to the Lord! And if this poor thief crammed a lifetime of testimony into a few minutes, ought not you and I, who have been spared for years after our conversion, to perform good service for our Lord? Come, let us wake up if we have been asleep! Let us begin to live if we have been half dead. May the Spirit of God make something of us yet; so that we may go as industrious servants from the labours of the vineyard to the pleasures of Paradise! To our once-crucified but now glorified Lord be praise for ever and ever! Amen.

"THERE GO THE SHIPS."

"THERE GO THE SHIPS."

Preached at the Metropolitan Tabernacle, in October, 1875.

✗ "There go the ships."—Ps. civ. 26. ✗

I WAS walking the other day by the side of the sea, looking out upon the English Channel. It so happened that there was a bad wind for the vessels going down the Channel, and they were lying in great numbers between the shore and the Goodwins. I should think I counted more than a hundred, all waiting for a change of wind. On a sudden the wind shifted to a more favourable quarter, and it was interesting to see with what rapidity all sails were spread, and the vessels began to disappear like birds on the wing. It was a sight such as one might not often see, but worth travelling a hundred miles to gaze upon, to see them all sail like a gallant squadron, and disappear southward on their voyages. "There go the ships," was the exclamation that naturally rose to one's lips. The psalmist thought it worth his while to pen the fact which he too had noticed, though it is very questionable whether David had ever seen anything like the number of vessels which pass our coasts, certainly he had seen none to be compared with them for tonnage.

The first lesson which may be learned from the ships and the sea is this—*every part of the earth is made with*

some design. The land, of course, yields "grass for the
cattle and herb for the service of man"; but what about
the broad acres of the sea? We cannot sow them, nor turn
them into pasturage. The reaper fills not his arm from the
briny furrows; they give neither seed for the sower nor
bread for the eater; neither do herds of cattle cover them as
they do the thousand hills of earth. Remorselessly swallow-
ing up all that is cast upon it, the thankless ocean makes
no return of fruit or flower. Is not the larger part of the
world given up to waste? "No," says David, and so say
we—"There go the ships." The sea benefits man by
occasioning navigation, and yielding besides an enormous
harvest of fishes of many kinds. Besides which, as the
blood is needful for the body, so is it necessary for this world
that there should be upon its surface a vast mass of water in
perpetual motion. That measureless gathering together of
the waters is an amazing instance of divine wisdom in its
existence, its perpetual ebb and flow, and even in its form
and quantity. In the ocean there is not a drop of water too
much, nor a drop too little. There is not a single mile of
sea more than there ought to be, nor less than there should
be. An exact balance and proportion is maintained; and
we little know how the blooming of the tiny flower or the
flourishing of the majestic cedar would be affected were the
balance disturbed. Between the tiny drop of dew upon
each blade of grass and the boundless main there is a rela-
tion and proportion such as only an Infinite Mind could
have arranged. Remember also that the ocean's freshness
tends to promote life and health among the sons of men.
It is good that there is sea, or the land might devour its
inhabitants by sickness. God has made nothing in vain.
Ignorance gazes on the stormy deep, and judges it to be a

vast disorder, the mother of confusion and the nurse of storms; but better knowledge teaches us, what revelation had before proclaimed, namely, that in wisdom has the Lord made all things.

But does not the ocean grievously separate lovers and friends? Many a wife thinks of her husband on the far-off Pacific; many a mother casts an anxious thought towards her sailor boy; and both are half inclined to think it a mistake to place so vast a portion of the globe as a cruel dividing gulf between loving hearts. Others evidently thought so in years gone by, for among the figurative excellences of the new earth we are told that "there shall be no more sea." But what a mistake it is to think that the sea is only a divider! It is the great uniter of the races of men, for "there go the ships." It is the highway of nations, by which they reach each other far more readily than they could have done had no sea existed, and arid deserts or towering mountains had intervened. This is one instance in which we do not understand God's designs, for we judge them upon the surface. As the sea apparently divides, but really unites nations, so often in providence things look one way, but go another. We say, "All these things are against me," when all things are working together for our good. We judge that to be a curse which, in the deep intent of God, is a rich blessing; and we write that down among the ills of life which, in God's esteem, is reckoned to be amongst its choicest mercies. Judge not according to the sight of the eyes, or the changeful feelings of the heart; but unstaggeringly believe in the infallible goodness of our great Father in heaven. As the child mistakes God's design in the sea, so will you also mistake His designs in providence, if you set up yourself as the measurer of the Infinite.

"Judge not the Lord by feeble sense
    But trust Him for His grace ;
Behind a frowning providence
    He hides a smiling face."

Our subject, however, shall not be the uses of the sea, but this one simple matter—"There go the ships."

I. And, first, WE SEE THAT THE SHIPS GO. "There go the ships." *The ships are made to go.* The ship is not made to lie for ever upon the stocks, or to be shut up in the docks. It is generally looked upon as an old hulk of little service when it has to lie up in ordinary, and rot in the river. But a ship is made to go ; and, as you see that it goes, remember that you also were made to go. Activity in Christian work is the result and design of grace in the soul. How I wish we could launch some of you ! You are, we trust, converted ; but you as yet serve but slender uses. Very quiet, sluggish, and motionless you lie on the stocks by the month together, and we have nearly as much trouble to launch you as Brunel had with *The Great Eastern.* I have tried hard to knock away your blocks, and remove your dogshores, and grease your ways, but you need hydraulic rams to stir you. When will you feel that you must go, and learn to "walk the water as a thing of life" ? Oh, for a grand launch ! Hundreds are lying high and dry, and to them I would give the motto, "Launch out into the deep." The ships go ; when will you go, too ?

The ships in going at last disappear from view. The vessel flies before the wind, and very speedily it is gone : and such is our destiny ere long. Our life is gone as the swift ships. We think ourselves stationary, but we are always moving on. As we sit in these pews so quietly, the angel of time is bearing us between his wings at a speed more rapid than we guess. Every single tick of the clock

is but a vibration of his mighty wings; and he bears us on,
and on, and on, and never stays to rest either by day or night.
Swift as the arrow from the bow we are always speeding
towards the target. How short time is! How very short
our life is! Let each one say, "How short *my* life is!"
No man knows how near he is to his grave. Perhaps if he
could see it, he would be alarmed to find it is just before
him: I almost wish he could see it, for a yawning grave
might make some men start to reason and to thought.
That yawning grave is there, though they perceive it not.

> ✗ "A point of time, a moment's space,
>   Removes me to yon heavenly place,
>   Or shuts me up in hell."

"There go the ships," and there go you also; you are
never in one stay. You are always flying, swift as the eagle
cleaves the air; or, to come back to the text, as the swift
ship flies over the water, you are speeding towards the end
of your life. Yet "all men think all men mortal but
themselves." The oldest man here probably thinks he
will outlive some of the younger ones. The man who
is soonest to die may be the very man who has the
least thought of death of us all; and he that is nearest to
his departure is, perhaps, the man who least thinks of it.
Just as, in that ancient Mediterranean ship, all were
awake, and every man praying to his God except Jonah,
on whose account the storm was raging, so does it often
happen that, in a congregation, every man may be aroused
and made to think of his latter end except the one man,
the marked man, who will never see to-morrow's sun. As
you see the ships, think of your mortality.

The ships as they go are going upon business. Some few
ships go hither and thither upon pleasure; but for the most

1—8

part the ships have something serious to do. They have a
charter, and they are bound for a certain port; and this
teaches us how we should go on the voyage of life with a
fixed, earnest, weighty purpose. May I ask each one of
you—Have you something to do, and is it worth doing?
You are sailing, but are you sailing like a mere pleasure
yacht, whose port is everywhere, which scuds and flies before
every fitful wind, and is a mere butterfly with no serious
work before it? You may be as heavily-laden and dingy as
a collier, there may be nothing of beauty or swiftness about
you; but, after all, the main thing is the practical result of
your voyage. Dear friend, what are you doing? What have
you been doing? And what do you contemplate doing? I
should like every young man here just to look at himself.
Here you are, young man; you certainly were not sent into
this world merely to wear a coat, and to stand so many feet
in your stockings; you must have been sent here with some
intention. A noble creature like man—and man is a noble
creature as compared with the animal creation—is surely
made for something. What were *you* made for? Not
merely to enjoy yourself. That cannot be. You certainly
are not "a butterfly born in a bower," neither were you
made to be creation's blot and blank. Neither can you
have been created to do mischief. It were an evil thing for
you to be a mere serpent in the world, to creep in the grass,
and wound the traveller. No, you must be made for something. What is that something? Are you answering your
end? For God's glory we were made. Nothing short of
this is worthy of immortal beings. Have we sought that
glory? Are we seeking it now? If not, I commend to
your consideration this thought, that, as the ships go on
their business, so ought men to live with a fixed and worthy

purpose. I would say this, not only to young men, but with greater earnestness still to men who may have wasted forty years. Oh, how could I dare to stand before this congregation to-night, and have to say, "Friends, I have had no object : I have lived in this world for myself alone; I have had no grand purpose before me"? I should be utterly ashamed if that were the fact. And if any man is obliged to feel that his purpose is such that he dares not avow it, or that he has only existed to make so much money, or gain a position in life, or to enjoy himself, but he has never purposed to serve his God, I would say to him, "Wake up, wake up, I pray you, to a noble purpose, worthy of a man. May God, the ever-blessed Spirit, set this before you in the light of eternity, and in the light of Jesus' dying love, and may you be aroused to solemn, earnest purpose and pursuit !" " There go the ships," but not idly : they go upon business.

These ships, however, whatever their errand be, *sail upon a changeful sea.* To-day the sea is smooth like glass : the ship, however, makes very small headway. To-morrow there is a breeze, which fills out the sails, and the ship goes merrily before it. Perhaps, before night comes on, the breeze increases to a gale, and then rushes from a gale into a hurricane. Let the mariner see to it when the storm-winds are out, for the ship need be staunch to meet the tempest. Mark how in the tempestuous hour the sea mingles with the clouds, and the clouds with the sea. See how the ship mounts up to heaven on the crest of the wave, and then dives into the abyss in the furrow between the enormous billows, until the mariners reel to and fro, and stagger like drunken men. Anon they have weathered the storm, and perhaps to-morrow it will be calm again. " There go the ships," on an element which is a proverb for fickle-

ness, for we say, "false as the smooth, deceitful sea."
"*They* go," say you, "upon the sea; but I dwell upon the
solid earth." Ah, good sir, there is not much to choose!
There is nothing stable beneath yon waxing and waning
moon. We say "*terra firma*," but where, where is *terra
firma?* What man is he who has found out the rock immovable? Certainly not he who looks to this world for it.
He has it not who thinks he has, for many plunge from
riches into poverty, from honour to disgrace, from power to
servitude. Who says, "My mountain standeth firm, I shall
never be moved"? He speaks as the foolish speak. It is
a voyage, sir, and even with Christ on board it is a voyage
in which storms will occur, a voyage in which you may have
to say, "Master, carest Thou not that we perish?" Expect
changes, then. Do not hold anything on earth too firmly.
Trust in God and be on the watch, for who knoweth what
may be on the morrow? "There go the ships."

II. But now, having spoken upon that, our second point
is, HOW GO THE SHIPS? What makes them go? For there
are lessons here for Christian men. We leave our steam-
ships out of the question, as they were not known in David's
day, and therefore were not intended. But how go the ships?
Well, *they must go according to the wind.* They cannot make
headway without favouring gales. And if our port be
heaven, there is no getting there except by the blessed
Spirit's blowing upon us. He bloweth where He listeth, and
we need that He should breathe upon us. We never steer
out of the port of destruction upon our venturesome voyage
till the heavenly wind drives us out to sea; and when we
are out upon the ocean of spiritual life, we make no progress
unless we have His favouring breath. We are dependent
upon the Spirit of God, even more than the mariners

upon the breeze. Let us all know this, and therefore
cry—

> "Celestial breeze, no longer stay,
> But fill my sails, and speed my way."

It is not possible to insist too much on the humbling truth,
spoken by our Lord to His disciples, " Without Me ye can
do nothing." It helps to check self-confidence, and it
exalts the Holy Ghost. Unless we honour Him, He will
not honour us; therefore let us cheerfully acknowledge our
absolute dependence upon Him.

Still, the mariner does not go by the wind without exertion on his own part, for the sails must be spread and
managed so that the wind may be utilized. One man will
go many knots, while another with the same breeze goes
but few; for there is a good deal of tacking about wanted
sometimes, to use the little wind, or the cross wind, which
may prevail. Sometimes all the sails must be spread, and
at other times only a part. Management is required. If
some were spread, they might take the wind out of others,
and so the ship might lose instead of gaining. There is a
deal of work on board a ship. I believe that some people
have a notion that the ship goes of itself, and that the
sailors have nothing to do but sit down, and enjoy themselves ; but if you have ever been to sea as an able-bodied
seaman, you have discovered that, if you want an easy life,
you must not be one of a ship's crew. So, mark you, we
are dependent upon the Spirit of God ; but He puts us in
motion and action ; and if Christian men sit down and say,
" Oh, the Spirit of God will do the work !" you will find the
Spirit of God will do nothing of the sort. The only operation which He will be likely to perform will be to convince
you that you are a sluggard, and that you will come to

poverty. The Spirit of God makes men earnest, fervent, living, and intense. He "works in us to will and to do of His own good pleasure." We have sails to manage to catch the favouring breeze, and we shall want all the strength we can obtain if we are to make good headway in the voyage of life. Some professors say, "God will save His own people." I am afraid He will never save *them*. They expect there will come good times when a great number of the elect will be gathered in ; but they fold their arms, and do nothing at all to promote the spread of the gospel. When they see others a little busy, they say, " Ah, mere excitement !" and so on, and they tell us God will have His own, to which I generally reply that I know He will, but I do not believe He will have *them*, because if they were His own they would not talk in that fashion, for those who are God's own people have a zeal for God and a love for souls. Do you not remember what God said to David ? "When thou hearest the sound of a going in the tops of the mulberry-trees, then shalt thou bestir thyself." Not, "Then shalt thou sit still, and say, 'God will do it.'" When David heard the angels coming over the tops of the trees to fight the Philistines, and when he heard their soft tread amongst the leaves, like the rustling of the wind, then he was to bestir himself : and so, when God's Spirit comes to work in the Church, the Christian must bestir himself, and not sit still. "There go the ships." They go with the wind ; but they are the scene of great industry, or else the wind would whistle through the yards, and the ship would make no voyages. Thus, brethren, we see dependence and energy united ; faith sweetly showing itself in good works.

"There go the ships." How do they go ? Well, *they have to be guided and steered by the helm.* The helm is a little thing, but yet it rules the vessel. As the helm is turned, so is the vessel guided. Look ye well to it, Christian men, that your _motives_ and purposes are always right. Your love is the helm of the vessel: where your affection is, your thoughts and actions tend. If you love the world, you will drift with the world; but if the love of the Father be in you, then will your vessel go towards God and towards divine things. Oh, see to it that Christ has His hand on the tiller, and that He guides you towards the haven of perfect peace!

The ship being guided by the helm, *he who manages the helm seeks direction from charts and lights.* "There go the ships," but they do not go of themselves, without management and wisdom. Thought is exercised, knowledge and experience are needed. There is an eye on deck which at night looks out for yonder revolving light, or the coloured ray of the lightship just ahead there, and the thoughtful brain says, "I must steer south-west of such a light," or "to the north of such a light, or I shall be upon the sands." Besides mere outlooks upon the sea, that anxious eye also busies itself with the chart, scans the stars, and takes observations of the moon. The captain's mind is exercised to learn exactly where the vessel is, and where she is going, lest the good ship should come to mischief unawares. And so, dear brethren, if we are to get to heaven, we must study the Scriptures, we must look well to every warning and guiding light of the Spirit's kindling, and ask for direction from above; for as the ships go not at haphazard, so neither will any Christian find his way to heaven unless he shall watch and pray, and look up daily, saying, "Teach me Thy way, O Lord, and lead me in a plain path."

The voyage of a ship on the main ocean seems to me to

be an admirable picture of the life of faith. The sailor does
not see a road before him, or any landmark or seamark, yet
he is sure of his course. He relies upon fixed lights in heaven,
for far out he can see no beacon or light on the sea. His
calculations, based on the laws of the heavenly bodies, are
sure guides on a wild wilderness where no keel ever leaves a
furrow to mark the way. The late Captain Basil Hall, one
of the most scientific officers in the navy, tells the following
interesting incident. He once sailed from San Blas, on the
west coast of Mexico; and after a voyage of eight thousand
miles, occupying eighty-nine days, he arrived off Rio de
Janeiro, having in this interval passed through the Pacific
Ocean, rounded Cape Horn, and crossed the South Atlantic,
without making land or seeing a single sail except an
American whaler. When within a week's sail of Rio, he
set seriously about determining by lunar observations the
position of his ship, and then steered his course by those
common principles of navigation which may be safely
employed for short distances between one known station
and another. Having arrived within what he considered
from his computations fifteen or twenty miles of the coast,
he hove to, at four o'clock in the morning, to await the break
of day, and then bore up, proceeding cautiously, on account
of a thick fog. As this cleared away, the crew had the
satisfaction of seeing the great Sugar Loaf Rock, which
stands on one side of the harbour's mouth, so nearly right
ahead, that they had not to alter their course above a point,
in order to hit the entrance of the port. This was the first
land they had seen for nearly three months, after crossing
so many seas, and being carried backwards and forwards by
innumerable currents and foul winds. The effect upon all
on board was electric, and, giving way to their admiration,

the sailors greeted the commander with a hearty cheer. And what a cheer will we give when, after many a year's sailing by faith, we at last see the pearly gates right straight ahead, and enter into the fair havens without needing to shift a point. Glory be to the Captain of our salvation, it will be all well with us when the fog of this life's care shall lift, and we shall see in the light of heaven !

Once more, how go the ships? They not only go according to the wind, guided by the helm and the chart, but some ships will go better than others, *according to their build.* With the same amount of wind, one vessel makes more way than another. Now, it is a blessed thing when the grace of God gives a Christian a good build. There are some Church-members, who are so queerly shaped, that somehow they never seem to cut the water, and even the Holy Spirit does not make much of them. They will get into the harbour at last, but they will need a world of tugging. The snail did get into the ark : I often wonder how he did it; he must have got up very early that morning. However, the snail got in as well as the grey-hound ; and there are many Christian people who will get to heaven, but God alone knows how they will do it, for they are such queer people that they seem to make no progress in the divine life. I would sooner live in heaven with them for ever than be fifteen minutes with them here below. God seems to shape some Christian minds in a more perfect model than others, so that, having simplicity of character, warmth of heart, zealous temperaments, and generous spirits, when the wind of the Spirit comes they cut through the foam like a first-class clipper ; while others lie like logs upon the water.

Now, I suspect that some good people have by degrees

become like *The Great Eastern* was a short time since, when she was covered with barnacles. I know many Christian people—I could point some out to-night, but I will not—who are covered with barnacles. They cannot go, because of some secret inconsistency, or love of the things of this world rather than the love of God. They want laying up and cleaning a bit, so as to get some of the barnacles off. It is a rough process, but it is one to which some of God's vessels have to be exposed. What headway they would make towards heaven if that which hinders were removed! Sometimes, when a man is on a bed of sickness, he is losing his barnacles; and sometimes, when a man has been rich and wealthy, and he has lost all he had, it takes off the barnacles. When we have lost friends we love, of whom we have made idols, we have been sorry to lose them, but it has cleaned off our barnacles; and when we have got out to sea, there has been greater ease about the going, and we have scarcely known how it was; but God knew that He had made us more fit for His service by the trials to which He had exposed us.

That is how the ships go. There are many mysteries about them, and there are many in us. God makes us go by the gales of His Spirit. Oh, that we may be trim for going, buoyant, and swift to be moved, and so may we make a grand voyage to heaven with Christ Jesus at the helm!

III. Thirdly and briefly, when I saw these ships go, I happened to be near a station of Lloyd's, and I noticed that they ran up flags as the vessels went by, to which the vessels replied. I suppose they were *asking questions*—to know their names, and what their cargo was, and where they were going, and so on. Now, I am going to act as Lloyd's agent did, and to hoist some flags, and ask you something about yourselves. The third point will then be—the ships go, LET US SIGNAL THEM.

And, first, *who is your owner?* "There go the ships," but who is your owner? You do not reply, but I think I can make a guess. There are some hypocrites about, who make fine pretensions, but they are not holy-living people; they even dare to come to the Lord's table, and yet they drink of the cup of devils. They will sing pious hymns with us, and then sing lascivious ditties with their familiars. I would say to such a man, "You are a rotten vessel, you do not belong to King Jesus. Every timber is staunch in His vessels. They are not all what we should like them to be, and, as I have said already, they too often are covered with barnacles, but still they are all sincere. The Lord builds His vessels with sound timber, and unless we are sincere, true, and right, Christ is not our owner, but Satan is. The painted hypocrite is known through the disguise he wears.

There is another vessel over there, a fine vessel too. Look, she is newly-painted, and looks spick and span. You can see nothing amiss with her. What white sails! See how many flags she flies? Take the glass, and read the vessel's name, and you will see in bold letters, "*Self-righteousness.*" Ah, I know that the owner is not the Lord Jesus Christ, for all the ships that belong to Him carry the red-cross flag, and cannot endure the flaunting rag of self-righteousness. All God's people own that they must be saved by sovereign grace, and anything like righteousness of their own they pump overboard as so much leakage and bilge-water. I see another vessel over yonder, with her sails all spread, and every bit of her colours flying. There, there, what a show she makes! How proud she seems as she scuds over the water! That vessel is "*The Pride*," from the port of Self-Conceit, Captain Ignorance. I do not know where she is oftenest to be seen, but sometimes she crosses this bit of water. I should not wonder if she is in sight here now, and you may be sure she does not belong to our Lord Jesus. Whether it is pride of money, or person, or rank, or talent, it cometh of evil, and Jesus Christ does not own it. You must get rid of all pride if you belong to Him. God grant us to be humble in heart! I could mention some more vessels that I see here to-night, but I will not. I will rather beg each man to ask himself, "Can I put my hand on my heart, and say, 'I am not my own, I am bought with a price'? Did Jesus buy me with His precious blood, and do I own that there is not a timber, spar, rope, or bolt in this ship but what belongs to Him?" Blessed be His name, some of us can say there is not a hair of our head or a drop of our blood but what belongs to Him! Thine are we, Thou Son of David, and all that we have!

I hope there are vessels here which are owned by the Lord Jesus Christ. Let them never be ashamed to confess their Owner. A vessel on proper business is never ashamed to answer signals. If there should be a smuggler or pirate in the offing, the crews would not be likely to answer signals; but those who are on honest business are ready to reply. And so, brethren, be ye ready to give a reason for the hope that is in you with meekness and fear; never show in your actions that you are ashamed of Jesus, but ever let the broad flag be flying in whatever waters you are—"Christ is mine, and I am His. For Him I live, His reproach would I bear, and His honour would I maintain."

Our next enquiry is, *What is your cargo?* "There go

the ships," but what do they carry? You cannot tell from looking at them far out at sea, except that you can be pretty sure that some of them do not carry much. Look at that showy brig! You can tell by the look of her that she has not much on board; from the fact that she floats so high it is clear that her cargo is light. Big men, very important individuals, very high-floating people are common; but there is nothing in them. If they had more on board, they would sink deeper in the water. The more grace a man has, the lower he will lie before his God. Well, brethren, what cargo have you got? I am afraid some of you, who lie down rather deeply in the water, are not kept down by any very precious cargo, but I fear you are in ballast. I have gone aboard some Christians; I thought there was a good deal in them, but I have not been able to find it. They have a deal of trouble, and they always tell you about it. There is a good old soul I call in to see sometimes: I begin to converse with her, and her talk is always about rheumatism—nothing else: you cannot get beyond rheumatism: that good sister has more ballast than cargo. There is another friend of mine, a farmer. If you talk with him, it is always about the badness of the times: that brother is in ballast, too. There are many tradesmen who, though they are Christians, cannot be made to talk of anything but the present dulness of business. I wish they could get that ballast out, and fill up with something better, for it is not worth carrying. You must have it sometimes, I suppose; but it is infinitely better to carry a load of praises, prayers, good wishes, holy doctrines, charitable actions, and generous encouragements.

Some ships, I think, carry a cargo of *powder*. You cannot go very near them without feeling that you are in danger;

they are so very apt to misjudge and take offence. I wish
that such persons were made to carry a red flag, that we
might give them a wide berth.

It is well to be loaded with good things. Young people,
study the Word of God, ask to be taught by experience, and,
wherever you go, seek to carry the precious commodities
which God has made dear to your own soul, that others
may be enriched thereby. It is an interesting sight to see
those immense ships laden with passengers for the colonies.
I cannot help praying, as I look at them, "God grant that
no harm may come to them, but may they safely reach their
desired haven!" When I look at some of our brethren
whom God is blessing, so that they have a cargo of precious
souls on board, consisting of hundreds who have been
brought to Jesus by them, I would to God we had many
more. Thank God, I have sometimes had my decks crowded
with passengers who have from my ministry received the
gospel! The Lord has brought them on board, and oh, I
trust, before I die, He will give me thousands more who will
have to praise the Lord that they heard the gospel from these
lips! May we be emigrant vessels, bearing souls away into
the glory-land, where the days of their mourning shall be
ended! Of course, we can only be humble instruments; but
still, what honour God puts upon His instruments when He
makes use of them for this object! "There go the ships."
Not ships of war are we, with guns to carry death; but
missionary vessels, carrying tidings of peace and glad news
to the utmost ends of the earth.

Our last signal asks the question—*Where go the ships?*
Where go the ships? Oh yes, they went merrily down the
Channel the other day, but where are they now? In a
year's time, who will report all the good vessels which just

now passed by our coast? I am looking out upon all of
you, anxious to know for what port you are making. Some
of you are bound for the port of peace. Swiftly may the
winds convey you over the waters, and safely may you
voyage under the convoy of the Lord Jesus! I will try and
keep pace with you. I hope that you will sail in company
with others of my Master's vessels; but if you have to sail
alone over a sea in which you cannot see another sail, may
God, the blessed One, protect and guard you! Bound for
the port of peace, with Christ on board, insured for glory,
bound for life eternal, let us bless the name of the Lord.

But alas, alas, many ships, which sailed for the desired
haven, are lost on the rocks! Some soul-destroying sin
causes their swift destruction. Others, equally fair to look
upon, are lost on the sands. They seemed bound for heaven,
but they were not the Lord's. The sands are very dangerous;
but they are only a mass of little atoms, soft and yielding,
yet as many ships are lost on the sands as on the rocks.
Even so, there are ways and habits of evil which are decep-
tive—there is nothing very bad about them apparently;
nothing heart-breaking, like rocks, but oh, the multitudes of
souls that have been sucked in by sandy temptations! Dear
brother, I hope you are not going that way. God grant you
grace to avoid little sins, and I am sure you will keep off
the rocks of great sin! In any case, may we turn out to be
the Lord's own, and so be kept to the end! Woe unto us
if we should prove to be mere adventurers, and perish in our
presumption!

Among the ships that go to sea are some that *founder*.
One does not know always how it happens, but they sail
all right for a time, and then are never heard of more.
They were sighted on such a day, but never more shall we

hear any tidings of them. How is that? I have known
some of the members of this Church go down in mid-ocean.
I never thought it could have happened, but they have gone.
I can only imagine how it was. They seemed seaworthy
vessels; but they were doubtless rotten through and through.
Oh, brethren, may God keep you from foundering, as some
do by some mysterious sin, which seems as if it clasped the
soul, and dragged it down to the deeps of hell!

Some vessels have I known, too, that have become *derelict*
—waifs and strays upon the sea—men that were the hope of
Churches, but who have abandoned themselves to reckless
living. They used to worship with the people of God, and
seemed to be very earnest and zealous; and now, perhaps,
at this very moment they are passing through the gin-palace
door, or spending this evening in vices which we dare not
mention. Oh, it is dreadful! Many start on their voyage,
and look as if they were Christ's own vessels, and yet for
some strange, unreasonable reason they give all up, and they
will be met with, in years to come, drifting about, rudderless,
captainless, crewless, dangerous to others, and miserable to
themselves. God save you from this, young man! And
you, my friend, though you have been a member of this
Church for twenty years, God save you from despairing,
and sinning furiously; for there sometimes come over men
strange moments of insanity, in which they reverse the whole
of their lives, lay violent hands upon an excellent character,
and become castaways. The grace of God will save the
truly regenerate from this; but, alas, how many high professors never were regenerate at all!

Where will some of the vessels I see before me go? It
is a fine fleet I am looking upon. Brothers and sisters, I
hope all of us will be found in that great harbour in heaven

which can accommodate all His Majesty's fleet. Oh, it will be a great day when we all arrive! Will you give me a hail when you get into port? Will you know me? I shall look out for some of you. I cannot help believing that we shall know each other. We have been in rough waters together these twenty years, and we have had some glorious weather too, have we not? We have seen the works of the Lord, and His wonders in the deep : I hope we shall keep together till we reach that blessed haven, where our fellowship will be eternal. How we will glorify Him who gets us there, even Jesus, the Lord High Admiral of the seas! Christ shall never hear the last of it if I get to heaven. I remember preaching once, when half of my congregation quarrelled with me after I had done preaching, because I had said in my sermon—

> "Then loudest of the crowd I'll sing,
> While heaven's resounding mansions ring
> With shouts of sovereign grace."

As I came downstairs, I met one who said, "You will not sing loudest, for I owe more to grace than you do;" and I found that all the Lord's people said the same. Well, we will have it out when we get to heaven : we will try this contention among the birds of Paradise, and see which of us can sing the most loudly to the praise of redeeming grace. Till then, let us trust the Lord Jesus, and obey His orders, for He is our Captain, and it is our duty to do His bidding.

But it would be a dreadful supposition—and yet, mayhap, it may be worse than a supposition—that some of you will have to cast anchor for ever in the Dead Sea, whose waves are fire, where every vessel is a prison, where every passenger feels a hell. What must it be to be in hell an hour! I wish some of you could think it over. What must it be to be

shut up in despair for one single day! If you have the
toothache a few minutes, how wretched you are, and how
anxious to get rid of it ; but what must it be to be in hell
even if it were for a time,—even if it were *but* for a time! Oh,
if it came to an end, still would I say, by all the humanities
that are in my soul, I charge you, brother, do not risk the
wrath of God ; go not down to the pit ! Pull down that black
flag, man : pull it down, and cast off your old owner. Ask
Christ to be your Owner. Run up the red flag of the cross,
and give yourself to Jesus ; for if you do not, your voyage
must lead to the gulf of black despair, where you will suffer
for ever the result of your sin. God have mercy upon us,
and may we never have to pass through the straits of judgment into the gulf of damnation ! May it never be said,
" There goes one of the ships that the Tabernacle pilot
signalled ; it is gone to destruction !" May it rather be said,
of all of us, all in full sail together, as we go towards heaven,
" There go the ships : " not one of them is drifting to the gulf
of destruction ! Believe in the Lord Jesus Christ, and all
will be well with you. Reject Him, and all will go ill with
you. May He, by His grace, enable you to make a right
choice to-night, for His love's sake ! Amen.

"SUPPOSING HIM TO BE THE GARDENER."

"SUPPOSING HIM TO BE THE GARDENER."

Preached at the Metropolitan Tabernacle, December 31, 1882.

"Supposing Him to be the gardener."—JOHN xx. 15.

THIS is the last day of the year, and yet I was sitting a fortnight ago in a very lovely garden, in the midst of all kinds of flowers which were blooming in delightful abundance all around! Screening myself from the heat of the sun under the overhanging boughs of an olive, I cast my eyes upon palms and bananas, roses and camellias, oranges and aloes, lavender and heliotrope. The garden was full of colour and beauty, perfume and fruitfulness. Surely the gardener, whoever he might be, who had framed, and fashioned, and kept in order that lovely spot, deserved great commendation! So I thought, and then it came to me to meditate upon the Church of God as a garden, and to suppose the Lord Jesus to be *the Gardener*, and then to think of what would most assuredly happen if it were so. "Supposing Him to be the Gardener," my mind conceived of a Paradise where all sweet things flourish, and all evil things are rooted up. If an ordinary worker had produced such beauty as I then saw and enjoyed on earth, what beauty and glory must surely be brought forth "supposing *Him* to be the Gardener"!

You know the "Him" to whom we refer, the ever-blessed Son of God, whom Mary Magdalene in our text mistook for the gardener. We will for once follow a saint in her mistaken track; and yet we shall find ourselves going in a right way. She was mistaken when she fell into the error of "supposing Him to be the gardener" of the garden in which He was buried; but if we are under His Spirit's teaching, we shall not make a mistake if now we indulge ourselves in a quiet meditation upon our ever-blessed Lord, "supposing Him to be the Gardener."

It is not an unnatural supposition, surely; for if we may truly sing—

> "We are a garden walled around,
>   Chosen and made peculiar ground,"

that enclosure needs a Gardener. Are we not all the plants of His right-hand planting? Do we not all need watering and tending by His constant and gracious care? He says, "I am the true Vine, and My Father is the Husbandman." That is one view of it; but we may also sing, "My Well-beloved hath a vineyard in a very fruitful hill: and He fenced it, and gathered out the stones thereof, and planted it with the choicest vine;" that is to say, He acted as Gardener to it. Thus has Isaiah taught us to sing a song to the Well-beloved touching His vineyard. We read of our Lord just now under these terms, "Thou that dwellest in the gardens, the companions hearken to Thy voice." To what purpose does He dwell in the vineyards but that He may see how the vines flourish, and care for all the plants? The image, I say, is so far from being unnatural that it is most pregnant with suggestions, and full of useful teaching. We are not going against the harmonies of nature when we are "supposing Him to be the Gardener."

Neither is the figure unscriptural; for in one of His own parables our Lord makes Himself to be the Dresser of the vineyard. We read just now that parable so full of warning. When the "certain man" came in, and saw the fig-tree that brought forth no fruit, He said unto the Dresser of His vineyard, "Cut it down: why cumbereth it the ground?" Who was it that intervened between that profitless tree and the axe but our great Intercessor and Interposer? He it is who continually comes forward with, "Let it alone this year also, till I shall dig about it and dung it." In this case He takes upon Himself the character of the Vine-dresser, and we are not wrong in "supposing Him to be the Gardener."

If we would be supported by a type, our Lord takes the name of "the Second Man." The first man, Adam, was a gardener. Moses tells us that the Lord God placed the man in the garden of Eden, to dress it and to keep it. Man in his best estate was not to live in this world in a paradise of indolent luxury, but in a garden of recompensed toil. Behold, the Church is Christ's Eden, watered by the river of life, and so fertilized that all manner of fruits are brought forth unto God; and He, our second Adam, walks in this spiritual Eden, to dress it and to keep it; and so, by a type, we see that we are right in "supposing Him to be the Gardener." Thus also Solomon thought of Him when He described the royal Bridegroom as going down with His spouse to the garden, when the flowers appeared on the earth, and the fig-tree had put forth her green figs; He went out with His beloved for the preservation of the gardens, saying, "Take us the foxes, the little foxes, that spoil the vines: for our vines have tender grapes." Neither nature, nor Scripture, nor type, nor song forbids us to think of our adorable Lord Jesus as One who careth for the flowers and fruits of His Church. We err not when we speak of Him, "supposing Him to be the Gardener." And so I sat me still, and indulged the suggested line of thought, which I now repeat in your hearing, hoping that I may open many roads of meditation for your hearts also. I shall not attempt to think out such a subject thoroughly, but only to indicate in which direction you may look for a vein of precious ore.

I. "Supposing Him to be the Gardener," we have here THE KEY TO MANY WONDERS in the garden of His Church.

The first wonder is *that there should be a Church at all in the world;* that there should be a garden blooming in the midst of this sterile waste. Upon a hard and flinty rock the Lord has made the Eden of His Church to grow. How came it to be here—an oasis of life in a desert of death? How came faith in the midst of unbelief, and hope where there is servile fear, and love where hate abounds? "Ye are of God, little children, and the whole world lieth in the wicked one." Whence this being "of God" where all beside is fast shut up in the devil? How came there to be a people for God, separated, and sanctified, and consecrated, and ordained to bring forth fruit unto His name? Assuredly, it could not have been so at all if the doing of it had been left to man. We understand its existence, "supposing Him to be the Gardener;" but nothing else can account for it. He can cause the fir-tree to flourish instead of the thorn, and the myrtle instead of the briar; but no one else can accomplish such a change. The garden in which I sat was made on the bare face of the rock, and almost all the earth of which its terraces were composed had been brought up there, from the shore below, by hard labour, and so upon the rock a soil had been created. It was not by its own nature that the garden was found in such a place; but by skill and labour it had been formed: even so the Church of God has had to be constructed by the Lord Jesus, who is the Author as well as the Perfecter of His garden. Painfully, with wounded hands, has He built each terrace, and fashioned each bed, and planted each plant. All the flowers have had to be watered with His bloody sweat, and watched by His tearful eyes: the nail-prints in His hands, and the wound in His side, are the tokens of what it cost Him to make a new Paradise. He has given His life for the life of every plant that is in the garden, and not one of them had been there on any other theory than "supposing Him to be the Gardener."

Besides, there is another wonder. *How comes the Church of God to flourish in such a climate?* This present evil world is very uncongenial to the growth of grace, and the Church is not able by herself alone to resist the evil influences which surround her. The Church contains within itself elements which tend to its own disorder and destruction if left alone; even as the garden has present in its soil all the germs of a tangled thicket of weeds. The best Church that ever Christ had on earth would, within a few years, apostatize from the truth if deserted by the Spirit of God. The world never helps the Church; it is all in arms against it; there is nothing in the world's air or soil that can fertilize the Church even to the least degree. How is it, then, that, notwithstanding all this, the Church is a fair garden unto God, and there are sweet spices grown in its beds, and lovely flowers are gathered by the divine hand from its borders? The continuance and prosperity of the Church can only be accounted for by "supposing Him to be the Gardener." Almighty strength is put to the otherwise

impossible work of sustaining a holy people among men;
almighty wisdom exercises itself upon this otherwise in-
superable difficulty. Hear ye the word of the Lord, and
learn hence the reason for the growth of His Church below:
"I, the Lord, do keep it: I will water it every moment;
lest any hurt it, I will keep it night and day." That is the
reason for the existence of a spiritual people still in the
midst of a godless and perverse generation. This is the
reason for an election of grace in the midst of surrounding
vice, and worldliness, and unbelief. "Supposing Him to
be the Gardener," I can see why there should be fruitfulness,
and beauty, and sweetness even in the centre of the wilderness of sin.

Another mystery is also cleared up by this supposition.
The wonder is *that ever you and I should have been placed
among the plants of the Lord.* Why are *we* allowed to grow
in the garden of His grace? Why me, Lord? Why me?
How is it that we have been kept there, and borne with in
our barrenness, when He might long ago have said, "Cut
it down: why cumbereth it the ground?" Who else would
have borne with such waywardness as ours? Who could
have manifested such infinite patience? Who could have
tended us with such care; and when the care was so ill-
rewarded, who would have renewed it so long from day to
day, and persisted in designs of boundless love? Who
could have done more for His vineyard? Who could or
would have done so much? Any mere man would have
repented of his good intent, provoked by our ingratitude.
None but God could have had patience with some of us!
That we have not long ago been slipped off as fruitless
branches of the vine; that we are left still upon the stem,
in the hope that we may ultimately bring forth fruit, is a

great marvel. I know not how it is that we have been spared, except upon this ground, "supposing Him to be the Gardener;" for Jesus is all gentleness and grace, so slow with His knife, so tardy with His axe, so hopeful if we do but show a bud or two, or, perchance, yield a little sour berry—so hopeful that these may be prognostics of something better by-and-by. Infinite patience! Immeasurable long-suffering! where are ye to be found save in the breast of the Well-beloved? Surely the hoe has spared many of us simply and only because He who is meek and lowly in heart is the Gardener.

Dear friends, there is one mercy with regard to this Church which I have often had to thank God for, namely, *that evils should have been shut out for so long a time.* During the period in which we have been together as Pastor and people, and that is now some twenty-nine years, we have enjoyed uninterrupted prosperity, going from strength to strength in the work of the Lord. Alas! we have seen many other Churches, that were quite as hopeful as our own, rent with strife, brought low by declension, or overthrown by heresy. I hope we have not been apt to judge their faults severely; but we must be thankful for our own deliverance from the evils which have afflicted them. I do not know how it is that we have been kept together in love, helped to abound in labour, and enabled to be firm in the faith, unless it be that special grace has watched over us. We are full of faults; we have nothing to boast of; and yet no Church has been more divinely favoured: I wonder that the blessing should have lasted so long, and I cannot make it out except when I fall into "supposing *Him* to be the Gardener." I cannot trace our prosperity to the Pastor, certainly; nor even to my beloved friends, the elders and deacons, nor even to the best of you, with your fervent love and holy zeal. I think it must be that Jesus has been the Gardener, and He has shut the gate when I am afraid I have left it open; and He has driven out the wild boar of the wood just when he had entered to root up the weaker plants. He must have been about at nights to keep off the prowling thieves, and He must have been here, too, in the noontide heat to guard those of you who have prospered in worldly goods, from the glare of too bright a sun. Yes, *He* has been with us, blessed be His name! Hence all this peace, and unity, and enthusiasm. May we never grieve Him so that He shall turn away from us; but rather let us entreat Him, saying, "Abide with us. Thou that dwellest in the gardens, let this be one of the gardens in which Thou dost deign to dwell, until the day break, and the shadows flee away." Thus our supposition is a key to many wonders.

II. Let your imaginations run along with mine while I say, in the second place, that "supposing Him to be the Gardener" should be A SPUR TO MANY DUTIES.

One of the duties of a Christian is *joy*. That is a blessed religion which among its precepts commands men to be happy. When joy becomes a duty, who would wish to neglect it? Surely it must help every little plant to drink in the sunlight when it is whispered among the flowers that Jesus is the Gardener. "Oh," you say, "I am such a little plant; I do not grow well; I do not put forth so much leafage, nor are there so many flowers on me as on many round about me!" It is quite right that you should think little of yourself: perhaps to droop your head is a part of your beauty: many flowers had not been half so lovely if they had not practised the art of hanging their heads. But "supposing Him to be the Gardener," then He is as much a

Gardener to you as He is to the most lordly palm in the whole domain. In the Mentone garden, right before me grew the orange and the aloe, and others of the finer and more noticeable plants; but on a wall to my left grew common wallflowers and saxifrages, and tiny herbs such as we find on our own rocky places. Now, the gardener had cared for all of these, little as well as great; in fact, there were hundreds of specimens of the most insignificant growths all duly labelled and described. The smallest saxifrage could say, "He is my gardener just as surely as he is the gardener of the Gloire de Dijon or Maréchal Neil." Oh, feeble child of God, the Lord taketh care of you! Your heavenly Father feedeth ravens, and guides the flight of sparrows: should He not much more care for you, O ye of little faith? Oh, little plants, you will grow rightly enough! Perhaps you are growing downward just now rather than upward. Remember that there are plants of which we value the underground root much more than we do the haulm above ground. Perhaps it is not yours to grow very fast; you may be a slow-growing shrub by nature, and you would not be healthy if you were to run to wood. Anyhow, be this your joy, you are in the garden of the Lord, and, "supposing Him to be the Gardener," He will make the best of you. You cannot be in better hands.

Another duty is that of *valuing the Lord's presence, and praying for it.* We ought, whenever the Sabbath morning dawns, to pray our Well-beloved to come into His garden, and eat His pleasant fruits. What can we do without Him? All day long our cry should go up to Him, "O Lord, behold and visit this vine, and the vineyard which Thy right hand hath planted!" We ought to agonize with Him that He would come and manifest Himself to us as He

does not unto the world. For what is a garden if the
gardener never comes near it? What is the difference
between it and the wilderness if he, to whom it belongs, never
lifts up spade or pruning-hook upon it? So that it is our
necessity that we have Christ with us, "supposing Him to
be the Gardener;" and it is our bliss that we have Christ
walking between our beds and borders, watching every
plant, training, tending, maturing all. "Supposing Him to
be the Gardener," it is well, for from Him is our fruit found.
Divided from Him, we are nothing; only as He watches
over us can we bring forth fruit. Let us have done with
confidence in man; let us forego all attempts to supply the
loss of His spiritual presence by routine or rant, ritualism or
rowdyism; but let us pray our Lord to be ever present with
us, and by that presence to make our garden grow.

"Supposing Him to be the Gardener," there is another
duty, and that is, *let each one of us yield himself up entirely
to Him.* A plant does not know how it ought to be treated;
it knows not when it should be watered, or when it should
be kept dry: a fruit-tree is no judge of when it needs to be
pruned, or digged, or dunged. The wit and wisdom of
the garden lie not in the flowers and shrubs, but in the
gardener. Now, then, if you and I are here to-day with
any self-will and carnal judgment about us, let us seek to
lay it all aside that we may be absolutely at our Lord's
disposal. You might not be willing to put yourself implicitly
into the hand of any mere man (pity that you should); but,
surely, thou plant of the Lord's right-hand planting, thou
mayest put thyself without a question into His dear hand.
"Supposing Him to be the Gardener," thou mayest well say,
"I would neither have will, nor wish, nor wit, nor whim,
nor way; but I would be as nothing in the Gardener's hands,

that He may be to me my wisdom and my all. Here, kind
Gardener, thy poor plant bows itself to Thy hand ; train me
as Thou wilt." Depend upon it, happiness lives next door
to the spirit of complete acquiescence in the will of God,
and it will be easy to exercise that perfect acquiescence
when we suppose the Lord Jesus to be the Gardener. If
the Lord hath done it ; what has a saint to say? Oh, thou
afflicted one, the Lord hath done it : wouldest thou have it
otherwise? Nay, art thou not thankful that it is even so,
because it is the will of Him in whose hand thy life is, and
whose are all thy ways? The duty of submission is very
plain, "supposing Him to be the Gardener."

One more duty I would mention, though others suggest
themselves. "Supposing Him to be the Gardener," then
let us bring forth fruit to Him. I do not address a people
this morning who feel no care as to whether they serve God
or not. I believe that most of you do desire to glorify
God ; for being saved by grace, you feel a holy ambition to
show forth His praises who has called you out of darkness
into His marvellous light. You wish to bring others to
Christ, because you yourselves have been brought to life and
liberty in Him. Now, let this fact that Jesus is the Gardener be a stimulus to your fruit-bearing. Where you have
brought forth a single cluster, bring forth a hundred, "supposing Him to be the Gardener." If He is to have the
honour of it, then labour to do that which will give Him
great renown. If our spiritual state were to be attributed
to ourselves, or to our minister, or to some of our fellow-
Christians, we might not feel that we were under a great
necessity to be fruitful ; but if Jesus be the Gardener, and
is to bear the blame or the honour of what we produce, then
let us use up every drop of sap, and strain every fibre, that,

to the utmost of which our manhood is capable, we may
produce a fair reward for our Lord's travail. Under such
tutorship and care we ought to become eminent scholars.
Doth Christ train us? Oh, let us never cause the world to
think meanly of our Master! Students feel that their *alma
mater* deserves great things of them, so they labour to
make their university renowned. And so, since Jesus is
Tutor and University to us, let us feel that we are bound to
reflect credit upon so great a Teacher, upon so divine a
name. I do not know how to put it, but surely we ought
to do something worthy of such a Lord. Each little flower
in the garden of the Lord should wear its brightest hues,
and put forth its rarest perfume, because Jesus cares for it.
The best of all possible good should be yielded by every
plant in our Father's garden, supposing Jesus to be the
Gardener.

Thus much, then, on those two points—a key to many
wonders, and a spur to many duties.

III. Thirdly, I have found in this supposition A RELIEF
FROM CRUSHING RESPONSIBILITY. One has a work given
him of God to do, and if he does it rightly, he cannot do it
carelessly. The first thing when he wakes, he asks, " How
is the work prospering?" and the last thought at night is,
" What can I do to fulfil my calling?" Sometimes the
anxiety even troubles his dreams, and he sighs, "O Lord,
send now prosperity!" How is the garden prospering which
we are set to tend? Are we broken-hearted because
nothing appears to flourish? Is it a bad season; or is the
soil lean and hungry? It is a very blessed relief to an
excess of care if we can fall into the habit of "supposing
Him to be the Gardener." If Jesus be the Master and
Lord in all things, it is not mine to keep all the Church in

order. I am not responsible for the growth of every Christian, nor for every backslider's errors, nor for every professor's faults of life. This burden must not lie on me so that I shall be crushed thereby. "Supposing Him to be the Gardener," then the Church enjoys a better oversight than mine; better care is taken of the garden than could be taken by the most vigilant watchers, even though by night the frost devoured them, and by day the heat.

"Supposing Him to be the Gardener," *then all must go well.* He that keepeth Israel doth neither slumber nor sleep; we need not fret and despond. I beg you earnest workers, who are becoming depressed, to think this out a little. You see it is yours to work under the Lord Jesus; but it is not yours to take the anxiety of His office into your souls as though you were to bear His burdens. The under-gardener, the workman in the garden, needs not fret about the whole garden as though it were all left to him. No, no; let him not take too much upon himself. I pray you, bound your anxiety by the facts of the case. So you have a number of young people around you, and you are watching for their souls as they that must give account. This is well; but do not be worried and wearied; for, after all, the saving and the keeping of those souls is not in your hands; but it rests with One far more able than yourself. Just think that the Lord is the Gardener. I know it is so in matters of providence. A certain man of God, in troublous times, became quite unable to do his duty because he laid to heart so much the ills of the age; he became depressed and disturbed, and he went on board a vessel, wanting to leave the country, which was getting into such a state that he could no longer endure it. Then one said to him, "Mr. White-lock, are you the manager of the world?" No, he was not quite that. "Did not God get on pretty well with it before you were born, and don't you think He will do very well with it when you are dead?" That reflection helped to relieve the good man's mind, and he went back to do his duty. I want you thus to perceive the limit of your responsibility : you are not the Gardener himself; you are only one of the Gardener's boys, set to run on errands, or to do a bit of digging, or to sweep the paths. The garden is well enough managed even though you are not head manager in it.

While this relieves us of anxiety, *it makes labour for Christ very sweet*, because, if the garden does not seem to repay us for our trouble, we say to ourselves, "It is not my garden, after all. 'Supposing Him to be the Gardener,' I am quite willing to work on a barren piece of rock, or tie up an old withered bough, or dig in worthless soil; for if it only pleases Jesus, the work is for that one sole reason profitable to the last degree. It is not mine to question the wisdom of my task, but to set about it in the name of my Master and Lord. 'Supposing Him to be the Gardener' lifts the ponderous responsibility of it from me, and my work becomes pleasant and delightful."

In dealing with the souls of men, *we meet with cases which are extremely difficult.* Some persons are so timid and fearful that you do not know how to comfort them ; others are so fast and presumptuous that you hardly know how to help them. A few are so double-faced that you cannot understand them, and others so fickle that you cannot hold them. Some flowers puzzle the ordinary gardener: we meet with plants which are covered with prickles, and when you try to train them, they wound the hand that would help them. These strange growths would make a great muddle for you if you were the gardener; but "supposing Him to be the Gardener," you have the happiness of being able to go to Him constantly, saying, "Good Lord, I do not understand this singular creature; it is as odd a plant as I am myself. Oh, that Thou wouldest manage it, or tell me how to do so! I have come to tell Thee of it."

Constantly our trouble is that *we have so many plants to look after* that we have not time to cultivate any one in the best manner, because we have fifty more all wanting attention at the time; and then, before we have done with the watering-pot, we have to fetch the hoe and the rake and the spade, and we are puzzled with these multitudinous cares, even as Paul was when he said, "That which cometh upon me daily, the care of all the churches." Ah! then it is a blessed thing to do the little we can do, and leave the rest to Jesus, "supposing Him to be the Gardener."

In the Church of God *there is a discipline which we cannot exercise.* I do not think it is half so hard to exercise discipline as it is not to be able to exercise it when yet you feel that it ought to be done. The servants of the householder were perplexed when they might not root up the tares. "Didst Thou not sow good seed in Thy field? From whence then hath it tares?" "An enemy hath done this." "Wilt Thou, then, that we go and gather them up?" "Not so," said He, "lest ye root up the wheat with them." This afflicts the Christian minister when he must not remove a pestilent, hindering weed. Yes, but "supposing *Him* to be the Gardener," and it is His will to let that weed remain, what have you and I to do but to hold our peace? He has a discipline more sure and safe than ours, and in due time the tares shall know it. In patience let us possess our soul.

And then, again, *there is that succession in the garden which we cannot keep up.* Plants will die down, and others must be put into their places, or the garden will grow bare; but we know not where to find these fresh flowers. We say, "When yonder good man dies, who will succeed him?" That is a question I have heard many a time, till I am rather weary of it. Who is to follow such a man? Let us wait till he is gone and needs following. Why sell the man's coat when he can wear it himself? We are apt to think, when this race of good brethren shall die out, that none will arise worthy to unloose the latchets of their shoes. Well, friend, I could suppose a great many things; but this morning my text is, "Supposing Him to be the Gardener," and on that supposition I expect that the Lord has other plants in reserve which you have not yet seen, and these will exactly fit into our places when they become empty, and the Lord will keep up the true apostolical succession till the day of His Second Advent. In every time of darkness and dismay, when the heart sinks and the spirits decline, and we think it is all over with the Church of God, let us fall back on this, "Supposing Him to be the Gardener," and expect to see greater and better things than these. We are at the end of *our* wits, but He is not at the beginning of His yet: we are nonplussed, but He never will be; therefore let us wait and be tranquil, "supposing Him to be the Gardener."

IV. Fourthly, I want you to notice that this supposition will give you A DELIVERANCE FROM MANY GLOOMY FEARS. I walked down the garden, and I saw a place where all the path was strewn with leaves, and broken branches, and stones, and I saw the earth upon the flower-beds tossed about, and roots lying quite out of the ground: all was in disorder. Had a dog been amusing himself; or had a mischievous child been at work? If so, it was a great pity. But no; in a minute or two I saw the gardener come back, and I perceived that *he* had been making all this disarrangement. He had been cutting, and digging, and hacking, and mess-making; and all for the good of the garden. It may be it has happened to some of you that you have been a good deal clipped lately, and in your domestic affairs things have not been in so fair a state as you could have wished: it may be in the Church we have seen ill weeds plucked up, and barren branches lopped, so that everything is *en deshabille.* Well, if the Lord has done it, our gloomy fears are idle. "Supposing Him to be the Gardener," all is well.

As I was talking over this theme with my friend, I said to him, "Supposing Him to be the Gardener," then *the serpent will have a bad time of it.* Supposing Adam to be the gardener, then the serpent gets in, and has a chat with his wife, and mischief comes of it; but supposing Jesus to be the Gardener, woe to thee, serpent: there is a blow for thy head within half a minute if thou dost but show thyself within the boundary! So, if we are afraid that the devil should get in among us, let us always in prayer entreat that there may be no space for the devil, because the Lord Jesus Christ fills all, and keeps out the adversary. Other creatures besides serpents intrude into gardens; caterpillars and palmerworms, and all sorts of destroying creatures are apt to devour our Churches. How can we keep them out? The highest wall cannot exclude them: there is no protection except one, and that is, "supposing Him to be the Gardener." Thus it is written, "I will rebuke the devourer for your sakes, and he shall not destroy the fruits of your ground; neither shall your vine cast her fruit before the time in the field, saith the Lord of hosts."

I am sometimes troubled by the question, *What if roots of bitterness should spring up among us to trouble us?* We are all such fallible creatures, supposing some brother should permit the seed of discord to grow in his bosom, then there may be a sister in whose heart the seeds will also spring up, and from her they will fly to another sister, and be blown about till brethren and sisters are all bearing rue and wormwood in their hearts. Who is to prevent this? Only the Lord Jesus by His Spirit. He can keep out this evil, "supposing Him to be the Gardener." The root which beareth wormwood will grow but little where Jesus is. Dwell with us, Lord, as a Church and people: by Thy Holy Spirit reside with us and in us, and never depart from us, and then no root of bitterness shall spring up to trouble us!

Then comes another fear. *Suppose the living waters of God's Spirit should not come to water the garden*, what then? We cannot make them flow, for the Spirit is a Sovereign, and He flows where He pleases. Ah! but the Spirit of God will be in our garden, supposing our Lord to be the Gardener. There is no fear of our not being watered when Jesus undertakes to do it. "He will pour water on him that is thirsty, and. floods upon the dry ground." But what if the sunlight of His love should not shine on the garden? If the fruits should never ripen, if there should be no peace, no joy in the Lord? That cannot happen "supposing Him to be the Gardener;" for His face is the sun, and His countenance scatters those health-giving beams, and nurturing warmths, and perfecting influences which are needful for maturing the saints in all the sweetness of grace to the glory of God. So, "supposing Him to be the Gardener" at this the close of the year, I fling away my doubts and fears, and invite you who bear the Church upon your heart to do the same. It is all well with Christ's cause because it is in His own hands. "He shall not fail nor be discouraged;" "The pleasure of the Lord shall prosper in His hand."

V. Fifthly, here is A WARNING FOR THE CARELESS,— "supposing Him to be the Gardener." In this great congregation, many are to the Church what weeds are to a garden. They are not planted by God; they are not growing under His nurture, they are bringing forth no fruit to His glory. My dear friend, I have often tried to get at you, to impress you, but I cannot. Take heed; for one of these days, "supposing Him to be the Gardener," He will reach you, and you shall know what that word meaneth, "Every plant which My heavenly Father hath not planted shall be rooted up." Take heed to yourselves, I pray.

Others among us are like the branches of the Vine which bear no fruit. We have often spoken very sharply to these, speaking honest truth in unmistakable language, and yet we have not touched their consciences. Ah! but, "supposing Him to be the Gardener," He will fulfil that sentence: "Every branch in Me that beareth not fruit He taketh away." He will get at you, if *we* cannot. Would God, ere this old year were quite dead, you would turn unto the Lord with full purpose of heart; so that, instead of being a weed, you might become a choice flower; that, instead of a dry stick, you might be a sappy, fruit-bearing branch of the Vine! The Lord make it to be so; but if any here need the caution, I pray them to take it to heart at once! "Supposing Him to be the Gardener," there

will be no escaping from His eye; there will be no deliverance from His hand. As "He will throughly purge His
floor, and burn up the chaff with unquenchable fire," so
He will throughly cleanse His garden, and cast out every
worthless thing.

VI. Another set of thoughts may well arise as A QUIETUS
TO THOSE WHO COMPLAIN,—"supposing Him to be the
Gardener." Certain of us have been made to suffer much
physical pain, which often bites into the spirits, and makes
the heart to stoop; others have suffered heavy *temporal
losses*, having had no success in business, but, on the contrary,
having had to endure privation, perhaps even to penury.
Are you ready to complain against the Lord for all this?
I pray you, do not so. Take the supposition of the text
into your mind this morning. The Lord has been pruning
you sharply, cutting off your best boughs, and you seem to
be like a thing despised, that is constantly tormented with
the knife. Yes, but "supposing Him to be the Gardener,"
suppose that your loving Lord has wrought it all, that from
His own hand all your grief has come, every cut, and every
gash, and every slip: does not this alter the case? Hath
not the Lord done it? Well, then, if it be so, put your
finger to your lip, and be quiet, until you are able from your
heart to say, "The Lord gave, and the Lord hath taken
away; blessed be the name of the Lord." I am persuaded that the Lord hath done nothing amiss to any one
of His people; that no child of His can rightly complain
that he has been whipped with too much severity; and that
no one branch of the Vine can truthfully declare that it has
been pruned with too sharp an edge. No; what the Lord
has done is the best that could have been done, the very
thing that you and I, if we could have possessed infinite

wisdom and love, would have wished to have done; therefore let us stop each thought of murmuring, and say, " The
Lord hath done it," and be glad.

Especially I speak to those who have suffered *bereave-
ment.* I can hardly express to you how strange I feel at
this moment when my sermon revives a memory so sweet,
dashed with such exceeding bitterness. I sat with my friend
and secretary in that garden some fifteen days ago, and we
were then in perfect health, rejoicing in the goodness of the
Lord. We returned home, and within five days I was
smitten with disabling pain; and worse, far worse than that,
he was called upon to lose his wife. We said to one
another, as we sat there reading the Word of God and
meditating, " How happy we are! Dare we think of continuing so? Must it not speedily end?" I little thought
I should have to say to him, "Alas, my brother, thou art
brought very low, for the delight of thine eyes is taken from
thee!" But here is our comfort: the Lord hath done it.
The best rose in the garden is gone. Who has taken it?
The Gardener came this way, and gathered it. He planted
it, and watched over it, and now He has taken it. Is not
this most natural? Does anybody weep because of that?
No; everybody knows that it is right, and according to the
order of nature, that He should come and gather the best
in the garden. If you are sore troubled by the loss of your
beloved, yet dry your grief by " supposing Him to be the
Gardener." Kiss the hand that has wrought you such grief.
Brethren beloved, remember, the next time the Lord comes
to your part of the garden, and He may do so within the
next week, He will only gather His own flowers, and would
you prevent His doing so even if you could?

VII. "Supposing Him to be the Gardener," then there

IS AN OUTLOOK FOR THE HOPEFUL. "Supposing Him to be the Gardener," then I expect to see in the garden where He works the best possible prosperity; I expect to see no flower dried up, no tree without fruit: I expect to see the richest, rarest fruit with the daintiest bloom upon it, daily presented to the great Owner of the garden. Let us expect that in this Church, and pray for it. Oh, if we have but faith, we shall see great things! It is our unbelief that straitens God. Let us believe great things from the work of Christ by His Spirit in the midst of His people's hearts, and we shall not be disappointed.

"Supposing Him to be the Gardener," then, dear friends, we may expect divine intercourse of unspeakable preciousness. Go back to Eden for a minute. When Adam was the gardener, what happened? The Lord God walked in the garden in the cool of the day. But "supposing HIM to be the Gardener," then we shall have the Lord God dwelling among us, and revealing Himself in all the glory of His power and the plenitude of His Fatherly heart; making us to know Him, that we may be filled with all the fulness of God. What joy is this!

One other thought: "Supposing Him to be the Gardener," and God to come and walk among the trees of the garden, then I expect He will remove the whole of the garden upward with Himself to fairer skies; for He rose, and His people must rise with Him. I expect a blessed transplantation of all these flowers below to a clearer atmosphere above, away from all this smoke and fog and damp, up where the sun is never clouded, where flowers never wither, where fruits never decay. Oh, the glory we shall then enjoy up yonder, on the hills of spices in the garden of God! "Supposing Him to be the Gardener," what a garden will He form above, and how shall you and I grow therein, developing beyond imagination! "It doth not yet appear what we shall be: but we know that, when He shall appear, we shall be like Him; for we shall see Him as He is." Since He is the Author and Finisher of our faith, to what perfection will He conduct us, and to what glory will He bring us! Oh, to be found in Him! God grant that we may be! To be plants in His garden, "supposing Him to be the Gardener," is all the heaven we can desire.

CHRIST PUT ON.

CHRIST PUT ON.

Preached at the Metropolitan Tabernacle, February 23, 1890.

"But put ye on the Lord Jesus Christ, and make not provision for the flesh, to fulfil the lusts thereof."—ROM. xiii. 14.

CHRIST must be in us before He can be on us. Grace puts Christ within, and enables us to put on Christ without. Christ must be in the heart by faith, before He can be in the life by holiness. If you want light from a lantern, the first business is to light the candle inside it; and then, as a consequence, the light shines through, to be seen of men. When Christ is formed in you, the hope of glory, do not conceal your love to Him; but put Him on in your conduct as the glory of your hope. As you have Christ within as your Saviour, the secret of your inner life, so put on Christ to be the beauty of your daily life. Let the external be brightened by the internal; and this shall be to you that "armour of light" which all the soldiers of the Lord Jesus are privileged to wear. As Christ is your food, nourishing the inner man, so put Him on as your dress, covering the outer man.

"Put ye on the Lord Jesus Christ." It is a very wonderful expression. It is most condescending on our Lord's part to allow of such an exhortation. Paul speaks

the mind of the Holy Spirit, and the word is full of meaning. Oh, for grace to learn its teaching! It is full of very
solemn warning to us, for we need a covering thus divinely
perfect. Oh, for grace to practise the command to put it
on! The apostle does not so much say, "Take up the
Lord Jesus Christ, and *bear* Him with you;" but, "'Put on
the Lord Jesus Christ,' and thus *wear* Him as the garment
of your life." A man takes up his staff for a journey, or
his sword for a battle; but he lays these down again after
a while: you are to put on the Lord Jesus as you put
on your garment; and thus He is to cover you, and to
become part and parcel of your outward appearance,
surrounding your very self, as a visible part of your manifest
personality.

"Put ye on the Lord Jesus Christ." This we do when
we believe in Him: then we put on the Lord Jesus Christ
as our robe of righteousness. It is a very beautiful picture
of what faith does. Faith finds our manhood naked to its
shame; faith sees that Christ Jesus is the robe of righteousness provided for our need; and faith, at the command of
the gospel, appropriates Him, and gets the benefit of Him
for it. By faith the soul covers her weakness with His
strength, her sin with His atonement, her folly with His
wisdom, her failure with His triumphs, her death with
His life, her wanderings with His constancy. By faith, I
say, the soul hides itself within Jesus; till Jesus only is
seen, and the man is seen in Him. We take not only His
righteousness as being imputed to us, but we take Himself
to be really ours; and so His righteousness becomes ours
as a matter of fact. "By the obedience of One shall many
be made righteous." His righteousness is set to our account,
and becomes ours because *He* is ours. I, though long

unrighteous in myself, believe in the testimony of God
concerning His Son Jesus Christ, and I am accounted
righteous, even as it is written, "Abraham believed God,
and it was counted to him for righteousness." The riches
of God in Christ Jesus become mine as I take the Lord
Jesus Christ to be everything to me.

But, you see, the text does not distinctly refer to this
great matter, for the apostle is not referring to the imputed
righteousness of Christ. The text stands in connection
with precepts concerning matters of every-day practical life,
and to these it must refer. It is not justification, but
sanctification that we have here. Moreover, we cannot be
said to put on the imputed righteousness of Christ after we
have believed, for that is upon us as soon as we believe,
and needs no more putting on. The command before us
is given to those who have the imputed righteousness of
Christ, who are justified, who are accepted in Christ Jesus.
"Put ye on the Lord Jesus Christ," is a word to you that
are saved by Christ, and justified by His righteousness.
You are to put on Christ, and keep on putting Him on
in the sanctifying of your lives unto your God. You are
every day continually more and more to wear as the dress
of your lives the character of your Lord.

I will handle this subject by answering questions. First,
Where are we to go for our daily dress? "Put ye on the
Lord Jesus Christ." Secondly, *What is this daily dress?*
"Put ye on the Lord Jesus Christ." Thirdly, *How are we
to act towards evil when we are thus clad?* "And make not
provision for the flesh, to fulfil the lusts thereof." And
then I will finish with the consideration of the question,
Why should we hasten to put on this matchless dress? The
twelfth verse answers that question : "The night is far spent,

the day is at hand : let us therefore cast off the works of darkness, and let us put on the armour of light."

I. May the Holy Spirit help us while we, in the first place, answer the inquiry, WHERE ARE WE TO GO FOR DAILY DRESS? Beloved, there is but one answer to all questions as to our necessities. We go to the Lord Jesus Christ for everything. To us "Christ is all." "He is made of God unto us wisdom, and righteousness, and sanctification, and redemption." When you have come to Christ for pardon and justification, you are not to go elsewhere for the next thing. Having begun with Jesus, you are to go on with Him, even to the end, "for ye are complete in Him," perfectly stored in Christ, fully equipped in Him. "It pleased the Father that in Him should all fulness dwell." Every necessity that can ever press upon you, between this Marah in the wilderness and yonder sea of glass before the throi e, will be found to be met in Christ Jesus. You ask, "What am I to do for a vesture which will befit the courts of the Lord? for armour that will protect me from the assaults of the foe? for a robe that will enable me to act as a priest and king unto God?" The one answer to the much-including question is, "Put ye on the Lord Jesus Christ." You have no further need. You need not look elsewhere for a thread or a shoe-latchet.

So, dear friends, I gather from this, that if we seek *an example*, we may not look elsewhere than to our Lord Jesus Christ. It is not written, "Put ye on this man or that ; " but "Put ye on the Lord Jesus Christ." The model for a saint is his Saviour. We are very apt to select some eminently gracious or useful man to be a pattern to us. A measure of good may result from such a course; but a degree of evil may also come of it. There will always be

some fault about the most excellent of our fellow-mortals ;
and as our tendency is to caricature virtues till we make
them faults, so is it our greater folly to mistake faults for
excellences, and copy them with careful exactness, and
generally with abundant exaggeration. By this plan, with
the best intentions, we may reach very sad results. Follow
Jesus in the way, and thou wilt not err : let thy feet go down
exactly in His footprints, and thou canst not slide. As His
grace enables us, let us make it true, that "as He was, so are
we in this world." You need not look beyond your Lord
for example under any circumstances. Of Him you may
enquire as of an unfailing oracle. You need never enquire
what is the general custom of those about you : the broad
road of the many is no way for you. You may not ask,
"What are the rulers of the people doing?" You follow
not the fashion of the great, but the example of the Greatest
of all. "Put ye on the Lord Jesus Christ," will apply to
each one of us. If I am a tradesman, I am not to ask myself,—On what principles do other traders conduct their
business? Not so. What the world may do is no rule for
me. If I am a student, I should not enquire,—How do others
feel towards religion? Let others do as they will, it is for
us to serve the Lord. In every relationship, in the domestic
circle, in the literary world, in the sphere of friendship, or
in business connections, I am to "put on the Lord Jesus
Christ." If I am perplexed, I am bound to ask—What
would Jesus do? and His example is to guide me. If I
cannot conceive of His acting in a certain way, neither must
I allow myself to do so ; but if I perceive, from His precept,
His spirit, or His action, that He would follow such and
such a course, to that line I must keep. I am not to put
on the philosopher, the politician, the priest, or the popu-

larity hunter ; but I am to put on the Lord Jesus Christ, by taking His life to be the model upon which I fashion my own life.

From our text I should also gather that we are to go to the Lord Jesus Christ for *stimulus*. We want not only an example, but a motive, an impulse and constraining power to keep us true to that example. We need to put on zeal as a cloak, and to be covered with a holy influence which will urge us onward. Let us go to the Lord Jesus for motives. Some fly to Moses, and would drive themselves to duty by the thunders of Sinai. Their design in service is to earn eternal life, or prevent the loss of the favour of God. Thus they come under law, and forsake the true way of the believer, which is faith. Not from dread of punishment, or hope of hire, do believers serve the living God ; but we put on Christ, and the love of Christ con-straineth us. Here is the spring of true holiness : "Sin shall not have dominion over you, for ye are not under the law, but under grace." A stronger force than law has gripped you : you serve God, not as servants, whose sole thought is the wage, but as children, whose eye is on the father and his love. Your motive is gratitude to Him by whose precious blood you are redeemed. He has put on *your* cause, and therefore you would take up *His* cause. I pray you, go not to the steep sides of Sinai to find motives for holiness ; but hasten to Calvary, and there find those sweet herbs of love, which shall be the medicine of your soul. "Put ye on the Lord Jesus Christ." Covered with a consciousness of His love, fired with love to Him in return, you will be strong to be, to do, or to suffer, as the Lord God may appoint.

Need I say,—Never find a reason for doing right in a desire to win the approbation of your fellow-men? Do not say, "I must do this or that in order to please my company." That is poor life which is sustained by the breath of other men's nostrils. Followers of Jesus will not wear the livery of custom, or stand in awe of human censure. Love of commendation, and fear of disapprobation, are low and beggarly motives: they sway the feeble many, but they ought not to rule the man in Christ. You must be moved by a far higher consideration: you serve the Lord Christ, and must not, therefore, become the lackey of men. His glory is to be your one aim; and for the joy of this you must treat all else as a light thing. Here we find our spur,—"The love of Christ constraineth us."

Beloved, the text means more than this. "Put ye on the Lord Jesus Christ;" that is, find in Jesus your *strength*. Although you are saved, and are quickened by the Holy Spirit, so as to be a living child of the living God, yet you have no strength for heavenly duty, except as you receive it from above. Go to Jesus for power. I charge you, never say, "I shall do the right because I have resolved to do it. I am a man of strong mind; I am determined to resist this evil, and I know I shall not yield. I have made up my mind, and there is no fear of my turning aside." Brother, if you rely upon yourself in that way, you will soon prove to be a broken reed. Failure follows at the heels of self-confidence. "Put ye on the Lord Jesus Christ."

I charge you, do not rely upon what you have acquired in the past. Say not in your heart, "I am a man of experience, and therefore I can resist temptation, which would crush the younger and greener folk. I have now spent so many years in persistent well-doing that I may reckon myself out of danger. Is it likely that I should ever be led astray?" Oh, sir, it is more than likely! It is a fact already.

The moment that a man declares he cannot fall, he has
already fallen from sobriety and humility. Your head is
turned, my brother, or you would not talk of your inward
perfection ; and when the head turns, the feet are not very
safe.   Inward conceit is the mother of open sin.   Make
Christ your strength, and not yourself; nor your acquire-
ments or experiences.   " Put ye on the Lord Jesus Christ,"
day by day, and make not the rags of yesterday to be the
raiment of the future.   Get grace fresh and fresh.   Say with
David, " All my fresh springs are in thee." Get all your
power for holiness and usefulness from Jesus, and from Him
alone.   " In the Lord have I righteousness and strength."
Rely not on resolves, pledges, methods, prayers ; but lean
on Jesus only as the strength of your life.

   " Put ye on the Lord Jesus Christ."   This is a wonderful word to me, because it indicates that in the Lord Jesus
we have *perfection*.   I shall, in a moment or two, show you
some of the virtues and graces which are resplendent in the
character of our Lord Jesus Christ.   These may be likened
to different parts of our armour or dress—the helmet, the
shoes, the breastplate.   But the text does not say, " Put on
this quality or virtue of the Lord Christ," but " Put ye on
the Lord Jesus Christ."   He Himself, as a whole, is to be
our array ; not this excellence or that, but Himself.   He
must be to us a sacred over-all.   I know not by what other
means to bring out my meaning : he is to cover us from
head to foot.   We do not so much copy His humility, His
gentleness, His love, His zeal, His prayerfulness, as Himself.   Endeavour to come into such communion with Jesus
Himself that His character is reproduced in you.   Oh, to
be wrapped about with Himself : feeling, desiring, acting,
as He felt, desired, and acted !   What a raiment for our

spiritual nature is our Lord Jesus Christ! What an honourable robe for a man to wear! Why, in that case, our life would be hid in Christ, and He would be seen over us in a life quickened by His Spirit, swayed by His motives, sweetened with His sympathy, pursuing His designs, and following in His steps! When we read, "Put ye on the Lord Jesus Christ," it means, Receive the whole character of Christ, and let your whole character be conformed to His will. Cover your whole being with the whole of the Lord Jesus Christ. What a wonderful precept! Oh, for grace to carry it out! May the Lord turn the command into an actual fact! Throughout the rest of our lives may we be more and more like Jesus, that the purpose of God may be fulfilled wherein we are "predestinated to be conformed to the image of His Son."

Once more, observe the *speciality* which is seen in this dress. It is specially adapted to each individual believer. Paul does not say merely to one person, "Put *thou* on the Lord Jesus Christ," but to all of us, "Put *ye* on the Lord Jesus Christ." Can all the saints put on Christ, whether babes, young men, or fathers? You could not all of you wear my coat, I am quite certain; and I am equally certain that I could not wear the garments of many of the young people now present; but here is a matchless garment, which will be found suitable for every believer, without expansion or contraction. Whoever puts on the Lord Jesus Christ has put on a robe which will be his glory and beauty. In every case the example of Jesus is admirably suited for copying. Suppose a child of God should be a king; what better advice could I give to him, when about to rule a nation, than this, "Put on the Lord Jesus Christ"? Be such a king as Jesus would have been. Nay, copy His

royal character. Suppose, on the other hand, that the person
before us is a poor woman from the workhouse; shall I say
the same to her?   Yes, and with equal propriety; for Jesus
was very poor, and is a most suitable example for those
who have no home of their own.   O worker, put on Christ,
and be full of zeal!   O sufferer, put on the Lord Jesus
Christ, and abound in patience !   Yonder friend is going
to the Sunday-school this afternoon.   Well, in order to win
those dear children to the Saviour, " put on the Lord Jesus
Christ," who said, " Suffer the little children to come unto
Me, and forbid them not."   In His sacred raiment you will
make a good teacher.   Are you a preacher, and about to
address thousands of grown-up persons?   How better can
I advise you than that you put on Christ, and preach the
gospel in His own loving, pleading, earnest style?   The
preacher's model should be his Lord.   This is our preaching gown, our praying surplice, our pastoral robe—the
character and spirit of the Lord Jesus ; and it admirably
suits each form of service.

No man's example will precisely fit his fellow-man ; but
there is this strange virtue about the character of Christ,
that you may all imitate it, and yet be none of you mere
imitators.   He is perfectly natural who is perfectly like
Christ.   There need be no affectation, no painful restraint,
no straining.   In a life thus fashioned there will be nothing
grotesque or disproportionate, unmanly or romantic.   So
wonderfully is Jesus the Second Adam of the new-born race,
that each member of that family may bear a likeness to
Him, and yet exhibit a clear individuality.   A man advanced
in years and wisdom may put Him on, and so may the least-
instructed, and the freshest comer among us.   Please remember this : we may not choose examples, but each one

is bound to copy the Lord Jesus Christ. You, dear friend, have a special personality; you are such a person that there is not another exactly like you, and you are placed in circumstances so peculiar that no one else is tried exactly as you are;—to you, then, is this exhortation sent : " Put on the Lord Jesus Christ." It is absolutely certain that, for you, with your personal singularity and peculiar circumstances, there can be nothing better than that you array yourself in this more than royal robe. You, too, who live in ordinary circumstances, and are only tried by common temptations, you are to "put on the Lord Jesus Christ;" for He will be suitable for you also. "Oh," cries one, "but the Lord Jesus never was exactly where I am!" You say this from want of knowing better, or from want of thought. He has been tempted in all points like as you are. There are certain relationships which the Lord Jesus could not literally occupy; but then, He took their spiritual counterpart. For instance, Jesus could not be a husband after the flesh. Does any one demand how He could be an example for husbands? Hearken! "Husbands, love your wives, even as Christ also loved the Church, and gave Himself for it." He is your model in a relationship which, naturally, He never sustained, but which, in very deed, He has more than fulfilled. Wherever you may be, you find that the Lord Jesus has occupied the counterpart of your position, or else the position is sinful, and ought to be quitted. In any place, at any hour, under any circumstances, in any matter, you may put on the Lord Jesus Christ, and never fear that your array will be unsuitable. Here you have a summer and winter garment—good in prosperity as well as in adversity. Here you have a garment for the private chamber or the public forum, for

sickness or for health, for honour or for reproach, for life
or for death. "Put ye on the Lord Jesus Christ," and
in this raiment of wrought gold you may enter into the
King's palace, and stand among the spirits of just men
made perfect.

II. Secondly, trusting to the Holy Spirit, let us enquire
WHAT IS THIS DAILY DRESS? The Lord Jesus Christ is to
be put on. May the Spirit of God help us to do so!

We see how *the sacred dress is here described in three
words.* The sacred titles of the Son of God are spread out
at length : "Put ye on the Lord—Jesus—Christ." Put Him
on as *Lord.* Call Him your Master and Lord, and you will
do well. Be you His servant in everything. Submit every
faculty, every capacity, every talent, every possession, to His
government. Submit all that you have and are to Him,
and delight to own His superior right and His royal claim
to you. Be Christ's man ; His servant, under bonds to His
service for ever, finding therein life and liberty. Let the
dominion of your Lord cover the kingdom of your nature.
Then put on *Jesus.* Jesus means a Saviour : in every part
be covered by Him in that blessed capacity. You, a sinner,
hide yourself in Jesus, your Saviour, who shall save you
from your sins. He is your Sanctifier driving out sin, and
your Preserver keeping sin from returning. Jesus is your
armour against sin. You overcome through His blood. In
Him you are defended against every weapon of the enemy :
He is your shield keeping you from all evil. He covers you
all over like a complete suit of armour, so that when arrows
of temptation fly like a fiery shower, they may be quenched
upon heavenly mail, and you may stand unharmed amid a
shower of deaths. Put on Jesus, and then put on *Christ.*
You know that Christ signifies "anointed." Now, our Lord

is anointed as Prophet, Priest, and King, and as such we put Him on. What a splendid thing it is to put on Christ as the anointed *Prophet*, and to accept His teaching as our creed! I believe it. Why? Because He said it. This is argument enough for me; mine not to argue, or doubt, or criticize; the Christ has said it, and I, putting Him on, find in His authority the end of all strife. What Christ declares, I believe; discussion ends where Christ begins. Put Him on also as your *Priest*. Notwithstanding your sins, your unworthiness, your defilement, go to the altar of the Lord by Him who, as Priest, has taken away your sin, clothed you with His merit, and made you acceptable to God. In our great High Priest we enter within the veil. We are in Him; by faith we realize this, and so put Him on as our Priest, and lose ourselves in His accepted sacrifice. Our Lord Jesus is also anointed to be *King*. Oh, put Him on in all His imperial majesty, by yielding your every wish and thought to His sway! Set Him on the throne of your heart. As you have submitted your thought and understanding to His prophetic instruction, submit your action and your practical life to His kingly government. As you put on His priesthood, and find atonement in Him, so put on His royalty, and find holiness in Him.

I now wish you to *note the description given in Colossians iii. from the twelfth verse.* I will take you to the wardrobe for a minute, and ask you to look over the articles of our outfit. See here, "Put on therefore;" you see everything is to be put on; nothing is to be left on the pegs for the moth to eat, nor in the window to be idly stared at : you are to *put on* the whole armour of God. In true religion everything is designed for practical use. We keep no garments in the drawer; we have to put on all that is provided. "Put on therefore, as the elect of God, holy and beloved, bowels of mercies, kindness." Here are two choice things: mercy and kindness—silken robes indeed! Have you put them on? I am to be as merciful, as tender-hearted, as kind, as sympathetic, as loving to my fellow-men as Christ Himself was. Have I reached this point? Have I ever aimed at it? Who among us has put on these royal gloves?

See what follows—these choice things come in pairs—"humbleness of mind, meekness." These choice garments are not so much esteemed as they should be. The cloth of one called "Proud-of-heart" is very fashionable, and the trimmings of Mr. Masterful are much in request. It is a melancholy thing to see what great men some Christians are. Truly, the footman is bigger than his Master. How some who would be thought saints can bluster and bully! Is this to put on the Lord Jesus Christ? Point me to a word of our Lord's in which He scolded, and tyrannized, and overrode any man. He was meek and lowly, even He, the Lord of all: what ought we to be, who are not worthy to loose the latchets of his shoes? Permit me to say to any dear brother who has not a very tender nature, who is naturally hard and rasping, "Put on the Lord Jesus Christ," my brother, and make not provision for that unfeeling nature of yours. Endeavour to be lowly in mind, that you may be gentle in spirit.

See, next, we are to put on "longsuffering" and "forbearance." Some men have no patience with others: how can they expect God to have patience with them? If everything is not done to their mind, they are in a fine fury. Dear me! whom have we here? Is this a servant of Mars, or of the Fire-god? Surely, this fighting man does not profess to be a worshipper of Christ! Do not tell me that the man lost his temper. It would be a mercy if he had lost it, so as never to find it again. He is selfish, petulant, exacting, and easily provoked. Has this man the spirit of Christ? If he be a Christian, he is a naked Christian, and I would urge him to " put on the Lord Jesus Christ," that he may be fitly clothed. Our Lord was full of forbearance. "Consider Him that endured such contradiction of sinners against Himself, lest ye be wearied, and faint in your minds." Put on the Lord Jesus Christ, and bear and forbear. Put up with a great deal that really ought not to be inflicted upon you, and be ready to bear still more rather than give or take offence.

" Forgiving one another, if any man have a quarrel against any; even as Christ forgave you, so also do ye." Is not this heavenly teaching? Put it in practice. Put ye on your Lord. Have you fallen to loggerheads with one another, and did I hear one of you growling, " I'll, I'll, I'll——"? Stop, brother! What will you do? If you are true to the Lord Jesus Christ, you will not avenge yourself, but give place unto wrath. Put the Lord Jesus on your tongue, and you will not talk so bitterly; put Him on your heart, and you will not feel so fiercely; put Him on your whole character, and you will readily forgive, not only this once, but unto seventy times seven. If you have been unjustly treated by one who should have been your friend, lay aside wrath, and begin again; and perhaps your brother will begin again also, and both of you by love will overcome evil. "Put ye on the Lord Jesus Christ."

" And above all these things put on charity, which is the bond of perfectness." Love is the girdle which binds up the other garments, and keeps all the other graces well braced, and in their right places. Put on love—what a golden girdle! Are we all putting on love? We have been baptized into Christ, and we profess to have put on Christ; but do we daily try to put on love? Our baptism was not true if we are not buried to all old enmities. We may have a great many faults, but God grant that we may be full of love to Jesus, to His people, and to all mankind!

How much I wish that we could all put on, and keep on, the next article of this wardrobe! "And let the peace of God rule in your hearts, to the which also ye are called in one body; and be ye thankful." Oh, for a peaceful mind! Oh, to rest in the Lord! I recommend that last little word, "Be ye thankful," to farmers and others whose interests are depressed. I might equally recommend it to certain tradespeople, whose trade is quite as good as they could expect. "Things *are* a little better," said one to me; and at that time he was heaping up riches. When things are extremely well, people say they are "middling," or a "little better;" but when there is a slight falling off, they cry out about "nothing doing, stagnation, universal ruin." Thankfulness is a rare virtue; but let the lover of the Lord Jesus abound in it. The possession of your mind in peace, keeping yourself quiet, calm, self-possessed, content—this is a blessed state; and in such a state Jesus was; therefore, "put ye on the Lord Jesus Christ." He was never in a fret or fume. He was never hurried or worried; He never repined or coveted. Had He nothing to worry Him? More than you have, brother. Had He not many things to distress Him? More than all of us put together. Yet He was not ruffled, but showed a prince-like calm, a divine serenity. This our Lord would have us wear. His peace He leaves with us, and His joy He would have fulfilled in us. He wishes us to go through life with

the peace of God keeping our hearts and minds from the
assaults of the enemy. He would have us quiet and strong
—strong because quiet, quiet because strong.

I have read of a great man, that he took two hours and
a half to dress himself every morning. In this he showed
rather littleness than greatness; but if any of you put on
the Lord Jesus Christ, you may take what time you will in
making such a toilet. It will take you all your lives, my
brothers and sisters, fully to put on the Lord Jesus Christ,
and to keep Him on; for let me again say, that you are
not only to put on all these garments which I have shown
to you in the wardrobe of the Colossians, but, more than
this, you are to put on all else that makes up Christ Himself. What a dress is this! "Put ye on the Lord Jesus
Christ," says the text.

Put on the Lord Jesus Christ for daily wear; not for
high days and holy days only, but for all time, and every
time. Put on the Lord Jesus Christ on the Lord's-day;
but do not lay Him aside during the week. Ladies have
ornaments which they put on occasionally for display on
grand occasions: as a rule, these jewels are hidden away in
a jewel-case. Christians, you must wear your jewels always.
Put on the Lord Jesus Christ, and have no casket in which
to conceal any part of Him. Put on Christ to keep Him
on. I saw a missionary from the cold north the other day,
and he was wearing a coat of moose-skin, which he had
worn among the Red Indians. "It is a capital coat," he
said; "there's nothing like leather. I have worn it for
eleven years." In the Arctic region, through which he had
travelled, he had worn this garment both by night and by
day; for the climate was much too cold to allow the taking
off of anything. Brethren, the world is far too cold to

allow of our taking off Christ even for an hour. So many arrows are flying about, that we dare not remove a single piece of our armour even for an instant. Thank God, we have in our Lord a dress which we may always wear! We can live in it, and die in it; we can work in it, and rest in it; and, like the raiment of Israel in the wilderness, it will never wax old. Put on the Lord Jesus Christ more and more.

If you have put on something of Christ, put on more of Christ. I dare not say much in commendation of apparel, here in England, for the tendency is to excess in that direction; yet I noticed, the other day, the remark of a missionary in the South Sea Islands, that as the heathen people became converted, they began to clothe themselves, and as they acquired tenderness of conscience, and delicacy of feeling, they gave more attention to dress—wearing more clothes, and of a better sort. However that may be as to dress for the body, it is certainly so as to the arraying of the soul. As we make spiritual progress, we have more graces and more virtues than in the beginning. Once we were content to wear faith only, but now we put on hope and love. Once, if we wore humbleness, we failed to wear thankfulness; but our text exhorts us to wear a full dress, a court suit; for we are to "put on the Lord Jesus Christ." You cannot wear too much of Him. Be covered from head to foot with Him.

Put on the Lord in every time of trial. Do not take Him off when it comes to the test. Quaint Henry Smith says that some people wear the Lord Jesus as a man wears his hat, which he takes off to everybody he meets. I am afraid I know persons of that kind, who wear Christ in private; but they off with Him in company, especially in the

company of the worldly, the sarcastic, and the unbelieving,
Put on Christ, intending never to put Him off again.
When tempted, tried, ridiculed, hear in your ear this voice,
"Put ye on the Lord Jesus Christ." Put Him on the more
as others tempt you to put Him off.

III. My time fails me, and I must hurriedly notice, in
the third place, HOW WE ARE TO ACT TOWARDS EVIL IN
THIS DRESS. The text says, "Put ye on the Lord Jesus
Christ, and make not provision for the flesh, to fulfil the
lusts thereof." By "the flesh" is here meant the evil part of
us, which is so greatly aided by the appetites and desires of
the body. When a man puts on Christ, has he still the flesh
about him? Alas! it is even so. I hear some brethren
say that they have no remaining corruptions. I claim
liberty to believe as much as I like of a man's statements as
to his own personal character. When he bears witness concerning himself, his witness may or may not be true. When
a man tells me that he is perfect, I hear what he has to say,
but I quietly think within myself that, if he had been so, he
would not have felt the necessity of spreading the information. "Good wine needs no bush;" and when our town
once holds a perfect man within its bounds, there will be no
need to advertise him. Goods that are puffed probably
need puffery. Brethren, I fear we have all very much of
the flesh about us, and therefore we need to be on our
guard against it. What does the apostle say? "Make not
provision for the flesh." By this, he means several things.

First, give *no tolerance* to it. Do not say, "Christ has
sanctified me so far; but you see I have a bad temper
naturally, and you cannot expect it to be removed." Dear
brother, do not make provision for thus sheltering and
sparing one of your soul's enemies. Another cries, "You

know I always was a good deal desponding ; and therefore I can never have much joy in the Lord." Don't make room for your unbelief. If you find a kennel for this dog, it will always lie in it. "But," says another, " I was always rather fond of gaiety, and so I must mix up with the world." Well, if you cook a dinner for the devil, he will take a seat at your table. This is to make provision for the flesh, to fulfil the lusts of it. Do not so ; but slay the Canaanites, break their idols, throw down their altars, and fell their groves.

Moreover, give sin *no time*. Allow no furlough to your obedience. Do not say to yourself, "At all other times I am exact, but once in a year, at a family meeting, I take a little liberty." Is it liberty to you to sin ? I am afraid there is something rotten in your heart. " Ah ! " cries one, " I only allow myself an hour or two occasionally with questionable company. I know it does me harm ; but we must all have a little relaxation, and the talk is very amusing, though rather loose." Is evil a relaxation to you ? It ought to be worse than slavery. What a trial is foolish talking to a child of God ! How can you find pleasure in it ? Give no license to the flesh ; you cannot tell how far it will go. Keep it always under subjection, and make no space for its indulgence.

Provide *no food* for it. Carve it no rations. Starve it out ; at any rate, if it wants fodder, let it look elsewhere. When you are allotting your provision to the body, the soul, the spirit, allot nothing to the depraved passions. If the flesh says, "What is for me ?" say, "Nothing." Some people like a little bit of reading for the flesh. As some people like a little bit of what they call "rather high" meat, so do these folk enjoy a portion of tainted doctrine, or questionable morality. Thus they make provision for the flesh, and the flesh takes care to feed thereon, and to give its lusts a meal. I have known professors, whom I would not dare to judge, dabble just a little in matters which they would forbid to others, but they think them allowable to themselves, if done in secret. "You must not be too exact," they say. But the apostle says, "Make not provision for the flesh." Do not give it a morsel; do not even allow it the crumbs that fall from your table. The flesh is greedy, and never hath enough; and if you give it some provision, it will steal much more.

"Put ye on the Lord Jesus Christ," and then you will leave *no place* for the lusts of the flesh. That which Christ does not cover is naked unto sin. If Christ be my livery, and I wear Him, and so am known to be His avowed servant, then I place myself entirely in His hands always and for ever, and the flesh has no claim whatsoever upon me. If, before I put on Christ, I might make some reserve, and duty did not call, yet now that the Lord Jesus Christ is upon me, I have done with reserves, and am openly and confessedly my Lord's. "Know ye not," saith the apostle, "that as many of you as were baptized into Christ have put on Christ?" Being buried with Him, we are dead to the world, and live only unto Him. The Lord bring us up to this mark by His mighty Spirit; and He shall have the glory of it!

IV. If this be the case, and we have indeed "put on the Lord Jesus Christ," we will thank God evermore; but if it be not so, let us not delay to be arrayed in this dress. WHY SHOULD WE HASTEN TO PUT ON CHRIST? A moment is all that remains. It is dark. Here is armour made of solid light; let us put on this attire at once; then the night will be light about us, and others beholding us will glorify God, and ask for the same raiment. With so dense a night round about us, a man needs to be dressed in luminous robes; he needs to wear the light of God, he needs thus to be practically protected from the darkness around him.

"Put on the Lord Jesus Christ," moreover, for the night will soon be over, the morning will soon dawn. The rags of sin, the sordid robes of worldliness, are not fit attire for the heavenly morning. Let us dress for the sun-rising. Let us go forth to meet the dawn with garments of light about us.

"Put on the Lord Jesus Christ," for He is coming, the Beloved of our souls! Over the hills we hear the trumpet sounding; the heralds are crying aloud, "The Bridegroom cometh! The Bridegroom cometh!" Though He has seemed to tarry, He has been always coming post haste. To-day we hear His chariot-wheels in the distance. Nearer and nearer is His Advent. Let us not sleep as do others. Blessed are they who will be ready for the wedding when the Bridegroom cometh. What is that wedding-dress that shall make us ready? Nothing can make us more fit to meet Christ, and to be with Him in His glory, than for us to put on Christ to-day. If I wear Christ as my dress, I do great honour to Christ as my Bridegroom. If I take Him for my glory and my beauty while I am here, I may be sure that He will be all that and more to me in eternity. If I take pleasure in Jesus here, Jesus will take pleasure in me when He shall meet me in the air, and take me up to dwell with Himself for ever. Put on the wedding-dress, ye beloved of the Lord! Put on the wedding-dress, ye brides of the Lamb, and put it on at once, for behold He cometh! Haste, haste, ye slumbering virgins! Arise, and trim your lamps! Put on your robes, and be ready to behold His glory, and to take part in it. O ye virgin souls, go forth to meet Him; with joy and gladness go forth, wearing Himself as your gorgeous apparel, fit for the daughters of a King. The Lord bless you, for Christ's sake! Amen.

LIFTING UP THE BRAZEN SERPENT.

LIFTING UP THE BRAZEN SERPENT.

Preached at the Metropolitan Tabernacle, October 19, 1879; *being the Fifteen Hundredth published Sermon.*

" And Moses made a serpent of brass, and put it upon a pole, and it came to pass, that if a serpent had bitten any man, when he beheld the serpent of brass, he lived."—NUMB. xxi. 9.

THIS discourse, when it shall be printed, will make fifteen hundred of my sermons which have been published regularly week by week. This is certainly a remarkable fact. I do not know of any instance, in modern times, in which fifteen hundred sermons have thus followed each other from the press from one person, and have continued to command a large circle of readers. I desire to utter most hearty thanksgivings to God for divine help in thinking out and uttering these sermons,—sermons which have not merely been printed, but have been *read* with eagerness, and have also been translated into many foreign tongues ; sermons which are publicly read on this very Sabbath day in hundreds of places where a minister cannot be found ; sermons which God has blessed to the conversion of multitudes of souls. I may and I must joy and rejoice in this great blessing which I most heartily ascribe to the undeserved favour of the Lord.

I thought the best way in which I could express my thankfulness would be to preach Jesus Christ again, and set Him forth in a sermon in which the simple gospel should be made as clear as a child's alphabet. I hope that, in closing the list of fifteen hundred discourses, the Lord will give me a word which will be blessed more than any which have preceded it, to the conversion of those who hear it or read it. May those who sit in darkness, because they do not understand the freeness of salvation, and the easy method by which it may be obtained, be brought into the light by discovering the way of peace through believing in Christ Jesus! Forgive this prelude; my thankfulness would not permit me to withhold it.

Concerning our text and the serpent of brass. If you turn to John's Gospel, you will notice that its commencement contains a sort of orderly list of types taken from Holy Scripture. It begins with the creation. God said, "Let there be light," and John begins by declaring that Jesus, the eternal Word, is "the true Light, which lighteth every man that cometh into the world." Before he closes his first chapter, John has introduced a type supplied by Abel; for when the Baptist saw Jesus coming to him, he said, "Behold the Lamb of God, which taketh away the sin of the world!" Nor is the first chapter finished before we are reminded of Jacob's ladder; for we find our Lord declaring to Nathanael, "Hereafter ye shall see heaven open, and the angels of God ascending and descending upon the Son of man." By the time we have reached the third chapter, we have come as far as Israel in the wilderness, and we read the joyful words, "As Moses lifted up the serpent in the wilderness, even so must the Son of man be lifted up : that whosoever believeth in Him should not perish, but have everlasting life." We are going to speak of this act of Moses this morning, that we may all of us behold Him of whom the brazen serpent was a notable type ; and may find the promise true, "every one that is bitten, when he looketh upon the serpent of brass, shall live." It may be that you who have looked before will derive fresh benefit from looking again, while some who have never turned their eyes in that direction may gaze upon the uplifted Saviour, and this morning be saved from the burning venom of the serpent, that deadly poison of sin which now lurks in their nature, and breeds death to their souls. May the Holy Spirit make the Word effectual to that gracious end !

I. I shall invite you to consider the subject, first, by noticing THE PERSON IN MORTAL PERIL, for whom the brazen serpent was made and lifted up. Our text saith, "It came to pass, that if a serpent had bitten any man, when he beheld the serpent of brass, he lived."

Let us notice that the fiery serpents first of all came among the people because *they had despised God's way and God's bread.* "The soul of the people was much dis-couraged because of the way." It was God's way, He had chosen it for them, and He had chosen it in wisdom and mercy ; but they murmured at it. As an old divine says, "It was lonesome and longsome," but still it was God's way, and therefore it ought not to have been loathsome : His pillar of fire and cloud went before them, and His servants Moses and Aaron led them like a flock, and they ought to have followed cheerfully. Every step of their previous journey had been rightly ordered, and they ought to have been quite sure that this compassing of the land of

Edom was rightly ordered too. But no; they quarrelled
with God's way, and wanted to have their own way. This
is one of the great standing follies of men ; they cannot be
content to wait on the Lord, and keep His way ; but they
prefer a will and way of their own.

The people, also, quarrelled with God's food. He gave
them the best of the best, for " men did eat angels' food ;"
but they called the manna by an opprobrious title, which
in the Hebrew has a sound of ridicule about it, and even
in our translation conveys the idea of contempt. They
said, " Our soul loatheth this light bread," as if they thought
it unsubstantial, and only fitted to puff them out, because
it was easy of digestion, and did not breed in them that
heat of blood and tendency to disease which a heavier diet
would have brought with it. Being discontented with their
God, they quarrelled with the bread which He set upon their
table, though it surpassed any that mortal man has ever
eaten before or since. This is another of man's follies ;
his heart refuses to feed upon God's Word, or believe God's
truth. He craves for the flesh-meat of carnal reason, the
leeks and the garlic of superstitious tradition, and the
cucumbers of speculation ; he cannot bring his mind down
to believe the Word of God, or to accept truth so simple,
so fitted to the capacity of a child. Many demand something deeper than the divine, more profound than the
infinite, more liberal than free grace. They quarrel with
God's way, and with God's bread, and hence there come
among them the fiery serpents of evil lusting, pride, and
sin. I may be speaking to some who have up to this
moment quarrelled with the precepts and the doctrines of
the Lord, and I would affectionately warn them that their
disobedience and presumption will lead to sin and misery.

Rebels against God are apt to wax worse and worse.   The
world's fashions and modes of thought lead on to the
world's vices and crimes.   If we long for the fruits of Egypt,
we shall soon feel the serpents of Egypt.   The natural
consequence of turning against God, like serpents, is to find
serpents waylaying our path.   If we forsake the Lord in
spirit or in doctrine, temptation will lurk in our path, and
sin will sting our feet.

I beg you carefully to observe, concerning those persons
for whom the brazen serpent was specially lifted up, that
they had been actually bitten by the serpents.   The Lord sent
fiery serpents among them; but it was not the serpents
being *among* them that involved the lifting up of a brazen
serpent; it was the serpents having actually poisoned them
which led to the provision of a remedy.   "It shall come
to pass, that *every one that is bitten,* when he looketh upon
it, shall live."   The only people who did look, and derive
benefit from the wonderful cure uplifted in the midst of
the camp, were those who had been stung by the vipers.
The common notion is that salvation is for good people,
salvation is for those who fight against temptation, salvation
is for the spiritual healthy; but how different is God's
Word !   God's medicine is for the sick, and His healing is
for the diseased.   The grace of God, through the atonement
of our Lord Jesus Christ, is for men who are actually and
really guilty.   We do not preach a sentimental salvation from
fancied guilt, but real and true pardon for actual offences.   I
care nothing for sham sinners : you who never did anything
wrong, you who are so good in yourselves that you are all
right—I leave you, for I am sent to preach Christ to those
who are full of sin, and worthy of eternal wrath.   The
serpent of brass was a remedy for those who had been bitten.

What an awful thing it is to be bitten by a serpent! I dare say some of you recollect the case of Gurling, one of the keepers of the reptiles in the Zoological Gardens. It happened in October, 1852, and therefore some of you will remember it. This unhappy man was about to part with a friend who was going to Australia, and according to the wont of many he must needs drink with him. He drank considerable quantities of gin, and though he would probably have been in a great passion if any one had called him drunk, yet reason and common-sense had evidently become overpowered. He went back to his post at the gardens in an excited state. He had some months before seen an exhibition of snake-charming, and this was on his poor muddled brain. He must emulate the Egyptians, and play with serpents. First he took out of its cage a Morocco venom-snake, put it round his neck, twisted it about, and whirled it round about him. Happily for him it did not arouse itself so as to bite. The assistant-keeper cried out, "For God's sake put back the snake!" but the foolish man replied, "I am inspired." Putting back the venom-snake, he exclaimed, "Now for the cobra." This deadly serpent was somewhat torpid with the cold of the previous night, and therefore the rash man placed it in his bosom till it revived, and glided downward till its head appeared below the back of his waistcoat. He took it by the body, about a foot from the head, and then seized it lower down by the other hand, intending to hold it by the tail, and swing it round his head. He held it for an instant opposite to his face, and like a flash of lightning the serpent struck him between the eyes. The blood streamed down his face, and he called for help, but his companion fled in horror; and, as he told the jury, he did

not know how long he was gone, for he was "in a maze."
When assistance arrived, Gurling was sitting on a chair,
having restored the cobra to its place. He said, "I am a
dead man." They put him in a cab, and took him to the
hospital. First his speech went—he could only point to
his poor throat, and moan; then his vision failed him, and
lastly his hearing. His pulse gradually sank, and in one
hour from the time at which he had been struck he was a
corpse. There was only a little mark upon the bridge of
his nose, but the poison spread over the body, and he was
a dead man. I tell you that story that you may use it as
a parable, and learn never to play with sin, and also in
order to bring vividly before you what it is to be bitten by
a serpent. Suppose that Gurling could have been cured
by looking at a piece of brass, would it not have been good
news for him? There was no remedy for that poor in-
fatuated creature, but there is a remedy for you. For men
who have been bitten by the fiery serpents of sin, Jesus
Christ is lifted up: not for you only who are as yet playing
with the serpent, not for you only who have warmed it in
your bosom, and felt it creeping over your flesh, but for
you who are actually bitten, and are mortally wounded. If
any man be bitten so that he has become diseased with sin,
and feels the deadly venom in his blood, it is for him that
Jesus is set forth to-day. Though he may think his to
be an extreme case, it is for such that sovereign grace
provides a remedy.

The bite of the serpent was painful. We are told in the
text that these serpents were "fiery" serpents, which may
perhaps refer to their colour, but more probably has
reference to the burning effects of their venom. It heated
and inflamed the blood so that every vein became a boiling

river, swollen with anguish. In some men that poison of
asps which we call sin has inflamed their minds. They
are restless, discontented, and full of fear and anguish.
They write their own damnation; they are sure that they
are lost; they refuse all tidings of hope. You cannot get
them to give a cool and sober hearing to the message of
grace. Sin works in them such terror that they give
themselves over as dead men. They are in their own
apprehension, as David says, "free among the dead, like
the slain that lie in the grave, whom God remembers no
more." It was for men bitten by the fiery serpents that
the brazen serpent was lifted up, and it is for men actually
envenomed by sin that Jesus is preached. Jesus died for
such as are at their wits' end: for such as cannot think
straight, for those who are tumbled up and down in their
minds, for those who are condemned already—for such was
the Son of man lifted up upon the cross. What a comforting thing that we are able to tell you this!

The bite of these serpents was, as I have told you, mortal.
The Israelites could have no question about that, because
in their own presence "much people of Israel died." They
saw their own friends die of the snake-bite, and they helped
to bury them. They knew why they died, and were sure
that it was because the venom of the fiery serpents was in
their veins. They were left without an excuse for imagining
that they could be bitten and yet live. Now, we know that
many have perished as the result of sin. We are not in
doubt as to what sin will do, for we are told by the infallible
Word that "the wages of sin is death," and yet again,
"Sin, when it is finished, bringeth forth death." We know,
also, that this death is endless misery, for the Scripture
describes the lost as being cast into outer darkness, "where

their worm dieth not, and their fire is not quenched." Our Lord Jesus speaks of the condemned going away into everlasting punishment, where there shall be weeping, and wailing, and gnashing of teeth. We ought to have no doubt about this, and the most of those who profess to doubt it are those who fear that it will be their own portion, who know that they are going down to eternal woe themselves, and therefore try to shut their eyes to their inevitable doom. Alas, that they should find flatterers in the pulpit who pander to their love of sin by piping to the same tune ! We are not of their order. We believe in what the Lord has said in all its solemnity of dread; and, knowing the terrors of the Lord, we persuade men to escape therefrom. But it was for men who had endured the mortal bite, for men upon whose pallid faces death began to set his seal, for men whose veins were burning with the awful poison of the serpent within them—for them it was that God said to Moses, " Make thee a fiery serpent, and set it upon a pole : and it shall come to pass, that every one that is bitten, when he looketh upon it, shall live."

There is no limit set to the stage of poisoning. However far gone, the remedy still had power. If a person had been bitten a moment before, though he only saw a few drops of blood oozing forth, and only felt a little smart, he might look and live ; and if he had waited, unhappily waited, even for half an hour, and speech failed him, and the pulse grew feeble, yet if he could but look, he would live at once. No bound was set to the virtue of this divinely-ordained remedy, or to the freedom of its application to those who needed it. The promise had no qualifying clause. " It shall come to pass, that every one that is bitten, when he looketh upon it, shall live ;" and our text tells us that God's promise came to pass in every case, without exception, for we read, "It came to pass, that if a serpent had bitten *any man*, when he beheld the serpent of brass, he lived." Thus, then, I have described the person who was in mortal peril.

II. Secondly, let us consider THE REMEDY PROVIDED FOR HIM. This was as singular as it was effectual. *It was purely of divine origin*, and it is clear that the invention of it, and the putting of power into it, was entirely of God. Men have prescribed several fomentations, decoctions, and operations for serpent-bites: I do not know how far any of them may be depended upon, but this I know, I would rather not be bitten in order to try any of them, even those that are most in vogue. For the bites of the fiery serpents in the wilderness there was no remedy whatever, except this which God had provided, and at first sight that remedy must have seemed to be a very unlikely one. A simple look to the figure of a serpent on a pole—how unlikely to avail! How and by what means could a cure be wrought through merely looking at twisted brass? It seemed, indeed, to be almost a mockery to bid men look at the very thing which had caused their misery. Shall the bite of a serpent be cured by looking at a serpent? Shall that which brings death also bring life? But herein lay the excellence of the remedy, that it was of divine origin; for when God ordains a cure, He is by that very fact bound to put potency into it. He will not devise a failure, nor prescribe a mockery. It should always be enough for us to know that God ordains a way of blessing us; for if He ordains, it must accomplish the promised result. We need not know *how* it will work; it is quite sufficient for us that God's mighty grace is pledged to make it bring forth good to our souls.

This particular remedy of a serpent lifted on a pole was *exceedingly instructive*, though I do not suppose that Israel understood it. We have been taught by our Lord, and know the meaning. It was a serpent impaled upon a pole. As you would take a sharp pole, and drive it through a serpent's head to kill it, so this brazen serpent was exhibited as killed, and hung up as dead before all eyes. It was the image of a dead snake. Wonder of wonders that our Lord Jesus should condescend to be symbolized by a dead serpent! The instruction to us after reading John's Gospel is this: our Lord Jesus Christ, in infinite humiliation, deigned to come into the world, and to be made a curse for us. The brazen serpent had no venom of itself, but it took the form of a fiery serpent. Christ is no sinner, and in him is no sin. But the brazen serpent was in the form of a serpent; and so was Jesus sent forth by God "in the likeness of sinful flesh." He came under the Law, and sin was imputed to Him, and therefore He came under the wrath and curse of God for our sakes. In Christ Jesus, if you will look at Him upon the cross, you will see that sin is slain and hung up as a dead serpent: there too is death put to death, for "He hath abolished death, and brought life and immortality to light:" and there also is the curse for ever ended, because He has endured it, being "made a curse for us; as it is written, Cursed is every one that hangeth on a tree." Thus are these serpents hung up upon the cross as a spectacle to all beholders, all slain by our dying Lord. Sin, death, and the curse are as dead serpents now. Oh, what a sight! If you can see it, what joy it will give you! Had the Hebrews understood it, that dead serpent, dangling from a pole, would have prophesied to them the glorious sight

which this day our faith gazes upon—Jesus slain, and sin,
death, and hell slain in Him. The remedy, then, to be
looked to was exceedingly instructive, and we know the
instruction it was intended to convey to us.

Please to recollect that in all the camp of Israel *there
was but one remedy* for serpent-bite, and that was the
brazen serpent; and there was but one brazen serpent, not
two. Israel might not make another. If they had made
a second, it would have had no effect : there was one, and
only one, and that was lifted high in the centre of the
camp, that if any man was bitten by a serpent he might
look to it and live. There is one Saviour, and only one.
" There is none other name under heaven given among
men, whereby we must be saved." All grace is concen-
trated in Jesus, of whom we read, " It pleased the Father
that in Him should all fulness dwell." Christ's bearing
the curse and ending the curse, Christ's being slain by sin
and destroying sin, Christ bruised as to His heel by the
old serpent, but breaking the serpent's head,—it is Christ
alone that we must look to if we would live. O sinner,
look to Jesus on the cross, for He is the one remedy for
all forms of sin's poisoned wounds !

There was but one healing serpent, and that one was
bright and lustrous. It was a serpent of brass, and brass
is a shining metal. This was newly-made brass, and therefore not dimmed; and whenever the sun shone, there
flashed forth a brightness from this brazen serpent. It
might have been a serpent of wood, or of any other metal,
if God had so ordained; but He commanded that it must
be of brass, that it might have a brightness about it. What
a brightness there is about our Lord Jesus Christ ! If we
do but exhibit Him in His own true metal, He is lustrous

in the eyes of men. If we will but preach the gospel simply, and never think to adorn it with our philosophical thought, there is enough brightness in Christ to catch a sinner's eye; ay, and it does catch the eyes of thousands! From afar the everlasting gospel gleams in the person of Christ. As the brazen standard reflected the beams of the sun, so Jesus reflects the love of God to sinners, and seeing it, they look by faith and live.

Once more, this remedy was *an enduring one*. It was a serpent of brass, and I suppose it remained in the midst of the camp from that day forward. There was no use for it after Israel entered Canaan; but, as long as they were in the wilderness, it was probably exhibited in the centre of the camp, hard by the tabernacle door, upon a lofty standard. Aloft, and open to the gaze of all, hung this image of a dead snake, the perpetual cure for serpent-venom. Had it been made of other materials, it might have been broken, or have decayed; but a serpent of brass would last as long as fiery serpents pestered the desert camp. As long as there was a man bitten, there was the serpent of brass to heal him. What a comfort is this, that Jesus is still able to save to the uttermost all that come unto God by Him, seeing He ever liveth to make intercession for them! The dying thief beheld the brightness of that serpent of brass as he saw Jesus hanging at his side, and it saved him; and so may you and I look and live, for He is "Jesus Christ, the same yesterday, and to-day, and for ever."

> " Faint my head, and sick my heart,
> Wounded, bruis'd, in every part,
> Satan's fiery sting I feel
> Poison'd with the pride of hell:
> But if at the point to die,
> Upward I direct mine eye,
> Jesus lifted up I see,
> Live by Him who died for me.

I hope I do not overlay my subject by these figures. I wish not to do so, but to make it very plain to you. All you that are really guilty, all you who are bitten by the serpent, the sure remedy for you is to look to Jesus Christ, who took our sin upon Himself, and died in the sinner's stead, "being made sin for us, that we might be made the righteousness of God in Him." Your only remedy lies in Christ, and nowhere else. Look unto Him, and be ye saved.

III. This brings us, in the third place, to consider THE APPLICATION OF THE REMEDY, or the link between the serpent-bitten man and the brass serpent which was to heal him. What was the link? It was of the most simple kind imaginable. The brazen serpent might have been, if God had so ordered it, carried into the tent where the sick man was, but it was not so. It might have been applied to him by rubbing : he might have been expected to repeat a certain form of prayer, or to have a priest present to perform a ceremony, but there was nothing of the kind ; he had only to look. It was well that the cure was so simple, for the danger was so frequent. Bites of the serpent came in many ways; a man might be gathering sticks, or merely walking along, and be bitten. Even now, in the desert, serpents are a danger. Mr. Sibree says that, on one occasion, he saw what he thought to be a round stone, beautifully marked. He put forth his hand to take it up, when to his horror he discovered that it was a coiled-up living serpent. All the day long, when fiery serpents were sent among them, the Israelites must have been in danger. In their beds and at their meals, in their houses and when they went abroad, they were in danger. These serpents are called by Isaiah "flying serpents," not because they do fly, but because they contract themselves and then suddenly spring up, so as to reach to a considerable height, and a man might be well buskined and yet not be beyond the reach of one of these malignant reptiles. What was a man to do when he was bitten? Nothing but stand outside his tent door, and look to the place where gleamed afar the brightness of the serpent of brass, and the moment he looked he was healed. He had nothing to do but to look: no priest was wanted, no holy water, no hocus-pocus, no mass-book, nothing but a look. A Romish bishop said to one of the early Reformers, when he preached salvation by simple faith, "O Mr. Doctor, open that gap to the people, and we are undone!" And so indeed they are, for the business and trade of priestcraft are ended for ever if men may simply trust Jesus and live. Yet it is even so. Believe in Him, ye sinners, for this is the spiritual meaning of looking, and at once your sin is forgiven, and what perhaps is more, its deadly power ceases to operate within your spirit. There is life in a look at Jesus; is not this simple enough?

But please to notice how *very personal* it was. A man could not be cured by anything anybody else could do for him. If he had been bitten by the serpent, and had refused to look to the serpent of brass, and had gone to his bed, no physician could help him. A pious mother might kneel down and pray for him, but it would be of no use. Sisters might come in and plead, ministers might be called in to pray that the man might live; but he must die despite their prayers if he did not look. There was only one hope for his life—*he must look to that serpent of brass.* It is just so with you. Some of you have written to me begging me to pray for you: so I have, but it avails nothing unless you yourselves believe in Jesus Christ. There is not beneath the copes of heaven, nor in heaven, any hope for any one

of you unless you will believe in Jesus Christ. Whoever
you may be, however much bitten of the serpent, and however near to die, if you will look to the Saviour, you shall
live; but if you will not do this, you must be damned, as
surely as you live. At the last great day I must bear
witness against you that I have told you this straight out
and plainly. " He that believeth and is baptized shall be
saved ; but he that believeth not shall be damned." There is
no help for it ; you may do what you will, join what Church
you please, take the Lord's Supper, be baptized, go through
severe penances, or give all your goods to feed the poor,
but you are a lost man unless you look to Jesus, for this is
the one remedy ; and even Jesus Christ Himself cannot, will
not, save you unless you look to Him. There is nothing in
His death to save you, there is nothing in His life to save
you, unless you will trust Him. It has come to this, *you
must look*, and look for yourself, if you would be saved.

And then, again, it is *very instructive*. This looking,
what did it mean ? It meant this—self-help must be
abandoned, and God must be trusted. The wounded man
would say, " I must not sit here and look at my wound, for
that will not save me. See there where the serpent struck
me ; the blood is oozing forth, black with the venom ! How
it burns and swells! My very heart is failing. But all
these reflections will not ease me. I must look away from
this to the uplifted serpent of brass." It is idle to look
anywhere except to God's one ordained remedy. The
Israelites must have understood as much as this, that God
requires us to trust Him, and to use His means of salvation.
We must do as He bids us, and trust in Him to work our
cure ; and if we will not do this, we shall die eternally.

This way of curing was intended that they might magnify

the love of God, and attribute their healing entirely to divine grace. The brazen serpent was not merely a picture, as I have shown you, of God's putting away sin by spending His wrath upon His Son, but it was a display of divine love. And this I know because Jesus Himself said, " As Moses lifted up the serpent in the wilderness, even so must the Son of man be lifted up. . . . For God so loved the world, that He gave His only-begotten Son "—plainly saying that the death of Christ upon the cross was an exhibition of God's love to men ; and whosoever looks to that grandest display of God's love to man, namely, His giving His only-begotten Son to become a curse for us, shall surely live. Now, when a man was healed by looking at the serpent, he could not say that he healed himself; for he only looked, and there is no virtue in a look. A believer never claims merit or honour on account of his faith. Faith is a self-denying grace, and never dares to boast. Where is the great credit of simply believing the truth, and humbly trusting Christ to save you? Faith glorifies God, and so our Lord has chosen it as the means of our salvation. If a priest had come and touched the bitten man, he might have ascribed some honour to the priest; but when there was no priest in the case, when there was nothing except looking to that brazen serpent, the man was driven to the conclusion that God's love and power had healed him. I am not saved by anything that I have done, but by what the Lord has done. To that conclusion God will have us all come ; we must all confess that, if saved, it is by His free, rich, sovereign, undeserved grace displayed in the person of His dear Son.

IV. Allow me one moment upon the fourth head, which is, THE CURE EFFECTED. We are told in the text that " if a

serpent had bitten any man, *when* he beheld the serpent of
brass, he lived;" that is to say, *he was healed at once.* He
had not to wait five minutes, nor five seconds. Dear
hearer, did you ever hear this before? If you have not, it
may startle you; but it is true. If you have lived in the
blackest sin that is possible up to this very moment, yet if
you will now believe in Jesus Christ, you shall be saved
before the clock ticks another time. It is done like a flash
of lightning; pardon is not a work of time. Sanctification
needs a lifetime, but justification needs no more than a
moment. Thou believest, thou livest. Thou dost trust to
Christ, thy sins are gone, thou art a saved man the instant
thou believest. "Oh!" saith one, "that is a wonder." It
is a wonder, and will remain a wonder to all eternity. Our
Lord's miracles, when He was on earth, were mostly instan-
taneous. He touched the fevered ones, and they were able
to get up and minister to Him. No doctor can cure a fever
in that fashion, for there is a resultant weakness left after
the heat of the fever is abated. Jesus works perfect cures;
and whosoever believeth in Him, though he hath only
believed one minute, is justified from all his sins. Oh, the
matchless grace of God!

This remedy healed again and again. Very possibly,
after a man had been healed, he might go back to his work,
and be attacked by a second serpent, for there were broods
of them about. What had he to do? Why, to look again;
and if he was wounded a thousand times, he must look a
thousand times. You, dear child of God, if you have sin
on your conscience, look to Jesus. The healthiest way of
living where serpents swarm is never to take your eye off
the brazen serpent at all. Ah, ye vipers, ye may bite if ye
will; as long as my eye is upon the brazen serpent I defy

your fangs and poison-bags, for I have a continual remedy at work within me! Temptation is overcome by the blood of Jesus. "This is the victory that overcometh the world, even our faith."

This cure was of universal efficacy to all who used it. There was not one case in all the camp of a man that looked to the serpent of brass and yet died, and there never will be a case of a man that looks to Jesus who remains under condemnation. The believer *must* be saved. Some of the people had to look from a long distance. The pole could not be equally near to everybody; but so long as they could see the serpent, it healed those that were afar off as well as those who were nigh. Nor did it matter if their eyes were feeble. All eyes were not alike keen; and some may have had a squint, or a dimness of vision, or only one eye, but if they did but look they lived. Perhaps the man could hardly make out the shape of the serpent as he looked. "Ah!" he said to himself, "I cannot discern the coils of the brazen snake, but I can see the shining of the brass;" and he lived. Oh, poor soul, if thou canst not see the whole of Christ, nor all His beauties, nor all the riches of His grace, yet if thou canst but see Him who was made sin for us, thou shalt live. If thou sayest, "Lord, I believe; help Thou mine unbelief," thy faith will save thee; a little faith will give thee a great Christ, and thou shalt find eternal life in Him.

Thus I have tried to describe the cure. Oh, that the Lord would work that cure in every sinner here at this moment! I do pray that He may.

It is a pleasant thought that if they looked to that brazen serpent by any kind of light they lived. Many beheld it in the glare of noon, and saw its shining coils, and lived; but

I should not wonder that some were bitten at night, and by the moonlight they drew near, and looked up and lived. Perhaps it was a dark and stormy night, and not a star was visible. The tempest crashed overhead, and from the murky cloud out flashed the lightning, cleaving the rocks asunder. By the glare of that sudden flame the dying man made out the brazen serpent, and though he saw but for a moment, yet he lived. So, sinner, if your heart is wrapped in tempest, and if from out of the cloud there comes but one single flash of lightning, look to Jesus Christ by it, and you shall live.

V. I close with this last matter of consideration : here is A LESSON FOR THOSE WHO LOVE THEIR LORD. What ought we to do? We should imitate Moses, whose business it was to set the brazen serpent upon a pole. It is your business and mine to lift up the gospel of Christ Jesus, so that all may see it. All Moses had to do was to hang up the brazen serpent in the sight of all. He did not say, " Aaron, bring your censer, and bring with you a score of priests, and make a perfumed cloud." Nor did he say, " I myself will go forth in my robes as lawgiver, and stand there." No, he had nothing to do that was pompous or ceremonial ; he had but to exhibit the brass serpent, and leave it naked and open to the gaze of all. He did not say, " Aaron, bring hither a cloth of gold, wrap up the serpent in blue and scarlet and fine linen." Such an act would have been clean contrary to his orders. He was to keep the serpent unveiled. Its power lay in itself, and not in its surroundings. The Lord did not tell him to paint the pole, or to deck it with the colours of the rainbow. Oh, no ; any pole would do ! The dying ones did not want to see the pole ; they only needed to behold the serpent. I dare say he would make a neat pole, for God's work should be done decently; but still the serpent was the sole thing to look at. This is what we have to do with our Lord. We must preach *Him*, teach *Him*, and make *Him* visible to all. We must not conceal Him by our attempts at eloquence and learning. We must have done with the polished lancewood pole of fine speech, and those bits of scarlet and blue, in the form of grand sentences and poetic periods. Everything must be done that Christ may be seen, and nothing must be allowed which hides Him. Moses may go away and go to bed when the serpent is once uplifted. All that is wanted is that the brazen serpent should be within view both by day and night. The preacher may hide himself, so that nobody may know who he is, or where he is; for if he has set forth Christ, he is best out of the way.

Now, you teachers, teach your children Jesus. Show them Christ crucified. Keep Christ before them. You young men that try to preach, do not attempt to do it grandly. The true grandeur of preaching is for Christ to be grandly displayed in it. No other grandeur is wanted. Keep self in the background, but set forth Jesus Christ among the people, evidently crucified among them; none but Jesus, none but Jesus. Let him be the sum and substance of all your teaching.

Some of you have looked to the brazen serpent, I know, and you have been healed; but what have you done with the brazen serpent since? You have not come forward to confess your faith, and join the Church. You have not spoken to any one about his soul. You have put the brazen serpent into a chest, and hidden it away. Is this right? Bring it out, and set it on a pole. Publish Christ and His salvation. He was never meant to be treated as a curiosity in a museum; He is intended to be exhibited in the highways, that those who are sin-bitten may look at Him. "But I have no proper pole," says one. The best sort of pole to exhibit Christ upon is a high one, so that He may be seen the further. Exalt Jesus. Speak well of His name. I do not know any other virtue that there can be in the pole but its height. The more you can speak in your Lord's praise, the higher you can lift Him up, the better; but for all other styles of speech there is nothing to be said. Do lift Christ up. "Oh!" says one, "but I have not a long standard." Then lift Him up on such as you have, for there are short people about who will be able to see by your means. I think I told you once of a picture which I saw of the brazen serpent. I want the Sunday-school teachers to listen to this. The artist represented all sorts of people clustering round the pole; and as they looked, the horrible snakes dropped off their arms, and they lived. There was such a crowd around the pole that a mother could not get near it. She carried a little babe, which a serpent had bitten. You could see the blue marks of the venom. As she could get no nearer, the mother held her child aloft, and turned its little head that it might gaze with its infant eye upon the brazen serpent, and live. Do this with your little children, you Sunday-school teachers. Even while they are yet little, pray that they may look to Jesus Christ and live; for there is no bound set to their age. Old men, snake-bitten, came hobbling on their crutches. "Eighty years old am I," saith one, "but I have looked to the brazen serpent, and I am healed." Little boys were brought out by their mothers, though as yet they could hardly speak plainly, and they cried in child-language,

"I look at the great snake, and it bless me." All ranks,
and characters, and dispositions, and both sexes, looked and
lived. Who will look to Jesus at this good hour? O dear
souls, will you have life or no? Will you despise Christ,
and perish? If so, your blood be on your own skirts. I
have told you God's way of salvation; lay hold on it.
Look to Jesus at once. May His Spirit gently lead you
so to do! Amen.

HEALING BY THE STRIPES
OF JESUS.

HEALING BY THE STRIPES
OF JESUS.

Preached at the Metropolitan Tabernacle, May 9, 1880; being the Two Thousandth published Sermon.

"With His stripes we are healed."—ISA. liii. 5.

BEING one evening in Exeter Hall, I heard our late beloved brother, Mr. Mackay, of Hull, make a speech, in which he told us of a person who was under very deep concern of soul, and felt that he could never rest till he found salvation. So, taking the Bible into his hand, he said to himself, "Eternal life is to be found somewhere in this Word of God; and if it be here, I will find it, for I will read the Book right through, praying to God over every page of it, if perchance it may contain some saving message for me." He told us that the earnest seeker read on through Genesis, Exodus, Leviticus, and so on; and though Christ is there very evidently, he could not find Him in the types and symbols. Neither did the holy histories yield him comfort, nor the Book of Job. He passed through the Psalms, but did not find his Saviour there; and the same was the case with the other books till he reached Isaiah. In this prophet he read on till near the end, and then, in the fifty-third chapter, these words arrested his delighted attention,

"*With His stripes we are healed.*"   "Now I have found it,"
says he.   "Here is the healing that I need for my sin-sick
soul, and I see how it comes to me through the sufferings
of the Lord Jesus Christ.   Blessed be His name, I am
healed!"   It was well that the seeker was wise enough to
search the Sacred Volume; it was better still that, in that
Volume, there should be such a life-giving word, and that the
Holy Spirit should reveal it to the seeker's heart.   I said
to myself, "That text will suit me well, and peradventure
a voice from God may speak through it yet again to some
other awakened sinner."   May He, who by these words
spoke to the chamberlain of the Ethiopian queen, who also
was impressed with them while in the act of searching the
Scripture, speak also to many who shall hear or read this
sermon!   Let us pray that it may be so.   God is very
gracious, and He will hear our prayers.

The object of my discourse is very simple: I would come
to the text, and I would come *at* you.   May the Holy
Spirit give me power to do both to the glory of God!

I. In endeavouring to come to the full meaning of the
text, I would remark, first, that GOD, IN INFINITE MERCY,
HERE TREATS SIN AS A DISEASE.   "With His stripes"—
that is, the stripes of the Lord Jesus—"we are healed."
Through the sufferings of our Lord, sin is pardoned, and we
are delivered from the power of evil: this is regarded as
the healing of a deadly malady.   The Lord in this present
life treats sin as a disease.   If He were to treat it at once as
sin, and summon us to His bar to answer for it, we should
at once sink beyond the reach of hope, for we could not
answer His accusations, nor defend ourselves from His
justice.   In great mercy He looks upon us with pity, and for
the while treats our ill manners as if they were diseases to

be cured rather than rebellions to be punished. It is most gracious on His part to do so; for while sin is a disease, it is a great deal more. If our iniquities were the result of an unavoidable sickness, we might claim pity rather than censure; but we sin wilfully, we choose evil, we transgress in heart, and therefore we bear a moral responsibility which makes sin an infinite evil. Our sin is our crime rather than our calamity: however, God looks at it in another way for a season. That He may be able to deal with us on hopeful grounds, He looks at the sickness of sin, and not as yet at the wickedness of sin. Nor is this without reason, for men who indulge in gross vices are often charitably judged by their fellows to be not only wholly wicked, but partly mad. Propensities to evil are usually associated with a greater or less degree of mental disease; perhaps, also, of physical disease. At any rate, sin is a spiritual malady of the worst kind.

Sin is a disease, for *it is not essential to manhood*, nor an integral part of human nature as God created it. Man was never more fully and truly man than he was before he fell; and He who is specially called "the Son of man" knew no sin, neither was guile found in His mouth; yet was He perfectly man. Sin is abnormal; a ·sort of cancerous growth, which ought not to be within the soul. Sin is disturbing to manhood; sin unmans a man. Sin is sadly destructive to man; it takes the crown from his head, the light from his mind, and the joy from his heart. We may name many grievous diseases which are the destroyers of our race, but the greatest of these is sin: sin, indeed, is the fatal egg from which all other sicknesses have been hatched. It is the fountain and source of all mortal maladies.

It is a disease, because *it puts the whole system of the man out of order* It places the lower faculties in the higher place, for it makes the body master over the soul. The man should ride the horse; but in the sinner the horse rides the man. The mind should keep the animal instincts and propensities in check; but in many men the animal crushes the mental and the spiritual. For instance, how many live as if eating and drinking were the chief objects of existence: they live to eat, instead of eating to live! The faculties are thrown out of gear by sin, so that they act fitfully and irregularly; you cannot depend upon any one of them keeping its place. The equilibrium of the life-forces is grievously disturbed. Even as a sickness of body is called a disorder, so is sin the disorder of the soul. Human nature is out of joint, and out of health, and man is no longer man: he is dead through sin, even as he was warned of old, "In the day that thou eatest thereof thou shalt surely die." Man is marred, bruised, sick, paralyzed, polluted, rotten with disease, just in proportion as sin has shown its true character in him.

Sin, like disease, operates to weaken man. The moral energy is broken down so as scarcely to exist in some men. The conscience labours under a fatal consumption, and is gradually ruined by a decline; the understanding has been lamed by evil, and the will is rendered feeble for good, though forcible for evil. The principle of integrity, the resolve of virtue, in which a man's true strength really lies, is sapped and undermined by wrong-doing. Sin is like a secret flow of blood, which robs the vital parts of their essential nourishment. How near to death in some men is even the power to discern between good and evil! The apostle tells us that, when we were yet without strength, in

due time Christ died for the ungodly; and this being without strength is the direct result of the sickness of sin, which
has weakened our whole manhood.

*Sin is a disease which in some cases causes extreme pain
and anguish, but in other instances deadens sensibility.*   It
frequently happens that, the more sinful a man is, the less
he is conscious of it.   It was remarked of a certain
notorious criminal that many thought him innocent because,
when he was charged with murder, he did not betray the
least emotion.   In that wretched self-possession there was,
to my mind, presumptive proof of his great familiarity with
crime: if an innocent person is charged with a great
offence, the mere charge horrifies him.   It is only by
weighing all the circumstances, and distinguishing between
sin and shame, that he recovers himself.   He who can do
the deed of shame does not blush when he is charged with
it.   The deeper a man goes in sin, the less does he allow
that it is sin.   Like a man who takes opium, he acquires
the power to take larger and larger doses, till that which
would kill a hundred other men has but slight effect upon
him.   A man who readily lies is scarcely conscious of the
moral degradation involved in being a liar, though he may
think it shameful to be called so.   It is one of the worst
points of this disease of sin that it stupefies the understanding, and causes a paralysis of the conscience.

By-and-by sin is sure to cause pain, like other diseases
which flesh is heir to; and when its awakening comes, what
a start it gives!   Conscience one day will awake, and fill
the guilty soul with alarm and distress, if not in this world,
yet certainly in the next.   Then will it be seen what an
awful thing it is to offend against the law of the Lord.

Sin is a disease which pollutes a man.   Certain diseases

render a man horribly impure. God is the best Judge of
purity, for He is thrice-holy, and He cannot endure sin.
The Lord puts sin from Him with abhorrence, and prepares
a place where the finally unclean shall be shut up by themselves. He will not dwell with them here, neither can they
dwell with Him in heaven. As men *must* put lepers apart
by themselves, so justice must put out of the heavenly
world everything which defileth. O my hearer, shall the
Lord be compelled to put you out of His presence because
you persist in wickedness?

And this disease, which is so polluting, is, at the same
time, *most injurious* to us, from the fact that it prevents the
higher enjoyment and employment of life. Men exist in
sin, but they do not truly live : as the Scripture saith, such
an one is dead while he liveth. While we continue in sin,
we cannot serve God on earth, nor hope to enjoy Him for
ever above. We are incapable of communion with perfect
spirits, and with God Himself; and the loss of this communion is the greatest of all evils. Sin deprives us of
spiritual sight, hearing, feeling, and taste, and thus deprives
us of those joys which turn existence into life. It brings
upon us true death, so that we exist in ruins, deprived of all
which can be called life.

This disease is fatal. Is it not written, "The soul that
sinneth, it shall die"? "Sin, when it is finished, bringeth
forth death." There is no hope of eternal life for any man
unless sin be put away. This disease never exhausts itself
so as to be its own destroyer. Evil men wax worse and
worse. In another world, as well as in this present state,
character will, no doubt, go on to develop and ripen, and
so the sinner will become more and more corrupt as the
result of his spiritual death. O my friends, if you refuse

Christ, sin will be the death of your peace, your joy, your prospects, your hopes, and thus the death of all that is worth having! In the case of other diseases, nature may conquer the malady, and you may be restored; but in this case, apart from divine interposition, nothing lies before you but eternal death.

God, therefore, treats sin as a disease, because it *is* a disease; and I want you to feel that it is so, for then you will thank the Lord for thus dealing with you. Many of us have felt that sin is a disease, and we have been healed of it. Oh, that others could see what an exceedingly evil thing it is to sin against the Lord! It is a contagious, defiling, incurable, mortal sickness.

Perhaps somebody says, "Why do you raise these points? They fill us with unpleasant thoughts." I do it for the reason given by the engineer who built the great Menai Tubular Bridge. When it was being erected, some brother engineers said to him, "You raise all manner of difficulties." "Yes," he said, "I raise them that I may solve them." So do we at this time dilate upon the sad state of man by nature, that we may the better set forth the glorious remedy of which our text so sweetly speaks.

II. God treats sin as a disease, and HE HERE DECLARES THE REMEDY WHICH HE HAS PROVIDED. "With His stripes we are healed."

I ask you very solemnly to accompany me in your meditations for a few minutes, while I bring before you *the stripes of the Lord Jesus.* The Lord resolved to restore us, and therefore he sent His only-begotten Son, "Very God of very God," that He might descend into this world to take upon Himself our nature, to secure our redemption. He lived as a man among men; and in due

time, after thirty years or more of service, the time came
when He should do us the greatest service of all, namely,
stand in our stead, and bear the chastisement of our peace.
He went to Gethsemane, and there, at the first taste of our
bitter cup, He sweat great drops of blood. He went to
Pilate's hall, and Herod's judgment-seat, and there drank
draughts of pain and scorn in our room and place. Last
of all, they took Him to the cross, and nailed Him there
to die—to die in our stead, "the Just for the unjust, to
bring us to God."

The word "stripes" is used to set forth *our Saviour's
sufferings*, both of body and of soul. The whole of
Christ was made a sacrifice for us; His whole manhood
suffered. As to His *body*, it shared with His mind in a
grief that never can be described. In the beginning of
His passion, when He emphatically suffered instead of us,
He was in an agony, and from His bodily frame a bloody
sweat distilled so copiously as to fall to the ground. It is
very rarely that a man sweats blood. There have been one
or two instances of it, and they have been followed by
almost immediate death ; but our Saviour lived—lived after
an agony which, to any one else, would have proved fatal.
Ere He could cleanse His face from this dreadful crimson,
they hurried Him to the high priest's hall. In the dead of
night they bound Him, and led Him away. Anon they
took Him to Pilate and to Herod. These scourged Him,
and their soldiers spat in His face, and buffeted Him, and
put on His head a crown of thorns. Scourging is one of
the most awful tortures that can be inflicted by malice. It
is to the eternal disgrace of Englishmen that they should
have permitted the "cat" to be used upon the soldier;
but to the Roman, cruelty was so natural that he made

his common punishments worse than brutal.   The Roman scourge is said to have been made of the sinews of oxen, twisted into knots, and into these knots were inserted slivers of bone, and hucklebones of sheep; so that every time the scourge fell upon the bare back, "the plowers made deep furrows."   Our Saviour was called upon to endure the fierce pain of the Roman scourge, and this not as the *finis* of His punishment, but as a preliminary to crucifixion. To this they added buffeting, and plucking of the hair: they spared Him no form of pain.   In all His faintness, through bleeding and fasting, they made Him carry His cross until another was forced, by the forethought of their cruelty, to bear it, lest their Victim should die on the road. They stripped Him, and threw Him down, and nailed Him to the wood.   They pierced His hands and His feet.   They lifted up the tree, with Him upon it, and then dashed it down into its place in the ground, so that all His limbs were dislocated, according to the lament of the twenty-second psalm, "I am poured out like water, and all My bones are out of joint."   He hung in the burning sun till the fever dissolved His strength, and He said, "My heart is like wax; it is melted in the midst of My bowels.   My strength is dried up like a potsherd; and My tongue cleaveth to My jaws; and Thou hast brought Me into the dust of death."   There He hung, a spectacle to God and men.   The weight of His body was first sustained by His feet, till the nails tore through the tender nerves; and then the painful load began to drag upon His hands, and rend those sensitive parts of His frame.   How small a wound in the hand has brought on lockjaw!   How awful must have been the torment caused by that dragging iron tearing through the delicate parts of the hands and feet!   Now

were all manner of bodily pains centred in His tortured
frame. All the while His enemies stood around, pointing
at Him in scorn, thrusting out their tongues in mockery,
jesting at His prayers, and gloating over His sufferings.
He cried, "I thirst," and then they gave Him vinegar
mingled with gall. After a while He said, "It is finished."
He had endured the utmost of appointed grief, and had
made full vindication to Divine justice; then, and not till
then, He gave up the ghost. Holy men of old have
enlarged most lovingly upon the bodily sufferings of our
Lord, and I have no hesitation in doing the same, trusting
that trembling sinners may see salvation in these painful
"stripes" of the Redeemer.

To describe the outward sufferings of our Lord is not
easy: I acknowledge that I have failed. But His *soul-
sufferings*, which were the soul of His sufferings, who can
even conceive, much less express, what they were? At
the very first I told you that He sweat great drops of blood.
That was His heart driving out its life-floods to the surface
through the terrible depression of spirit which was upon
Him. He said, "My soul is exceeding sorrowful, even
unto death." The betrayal by Judas, and the desertion of
the twelve, grieved our Lord; but the weight of our sin
was the real pressure on His heart. Our guilt was the
olive-press which forced from Him the moisture of His
life. No language can ever tell His agony in prospect of
His passion; how little, then, can we conceive the passion
itself? When nailed to the cross, He endured what no
martyr ever suffered; for martyrs, when they have died,
have been so sustained of God that they have rejoiced
amid their pain; but our Redeemer was forsaken of His
Father, until He cried, "My God, My God, why hast Thou

forsaken Me?" That was the bitterest cry of all, the utmost depth of His unfathomable grief. Yet was it needful that He should be deserted, because God must turn His back on sin, and consequently upon Him who was made sin for us. The soul of the great Substitute suffered a horror of misery, instead of that horror of hell into which sinners would have been plunged had He not taken their sin upon Himself, and been made a curse for them. It is written, "Cursed is every one that hangeth on a tree;" but who knows what that curse means?

The remedy for your sins and mine is found in the substitutionary sufferings of the Lord Jesus, and in these only. These "stripes" of the Lord Jesus Christ were on our behalf. Do you enquire, "Is there anything for us to do, to remove the guilt of sin?" I answer: There is nothing whatever for you to do. By the stripes of Jesus we are healed. All those stripes He has endured, and left not one of them for us to bear.

"But must we not believe on Him?" Ay, certainly! If I say of a certain ointment that it heals, I do not deny that you need a bandage with which to apply it to the wound. Faith is the linen which binds the plaster of Christ's reconciliation to the sore of our sin. The linen does not heal; that is the work of the ointment. So faith does not heal; that is the work of the atonement of Christ.

Does an enquirer reply, "But surely I must do something, or suffer something"? I answer: You must put nothing with Jesus Christ, or you greatly dishonour Him. In order to your salvation, you must rely upon the wounds of Jesus Christ, and nothing else; for the text does not say, "His stripes help to heal us," but, "With His stripes we are healed."

"But we must repent," cries another. Assuredly we must, and shall, for repentance is the first sign of healing; but the stripes of Jesus heal us, and not our repentance. These stripes, when applied to the heart, work repentance in us : we hate sin because it made Jesus suffer.

When you intelligently trust in Jesus as having suffered for you, then you discover the fact that God will never punish you for the same offence for which Jesus died. His justice will not permit Him to see the debt paid, first, by the Surety, and then again by the debtor. Justice cannot twice demand a recompense : if my bleeding Surety has borne my guilt, then I cannot bear it. Accepting Christ Jesus as suffering for me, I have accepted a complete discharge from judicial liability. I have been condemned in Christ, and there is, therefore, now no condemnation to me any more. This is the groundwork of the security of the sinner who believes in Jesus : he lives because Jesus died in his room and place and stead ; and he is acceptable before God because Jesus is accepted. The person for whom Jesus is an accepted Substitute must go free ; none can touch him ; he is clear. O my hearer, wilt thou have Jesus Christ to be thy Substitute? If so, thou art free. "He that believeth on Him is not condemned." Thus "with His stripes we are healed."

III. I have tried to put before you the disease and the remedy ; I now desire to notice the fact that THIS REMEDY IS IMMEDIATELY EFFECTIVE WHEREVER IT IS APPLIED. The stripes of Jesus do heal men ; they have healed many of us. It does not look as if it could effect so great a cure, but the fact is undeniable. I often hear people say, "If you preach up this faith in Jesus Christ as saving men, they

will be careless about holy living." I am as good a witness
on that point as anybody, for I live every day in the midst
of men who are trusting to the stripes of Jesus for their
salvation, and I have seen no ill effect following from such
a trust; but I have seen the very reverse. I bear testimony
that I have seen the very worst of men become the very
best of men by believing in the Lord Jesus Christ. These
stripes heal in a surprising manner the moral diseases of
those who seemed past remedy.

The character is healed. I have seen the drunkard
become sober, the harlot become chaste, the passionate
man become gentle, the covetous man become liberal, and
the liar become truthful, simply by trusting in the sufferings
of Jesus. If it did not make good men of them, it would
not really do anything for them, for you must judge men
by their fruits, after all ; and if the fruits are not changed,
the tree is not changed. Character is everything : if the
character be not set right, the man is not saved. But we
say it without fear of contradiction, that the atoning
sacrifice, applied to the heart, heals the disease of sin. If
you doubt it, try it. He that believes in Jesus is sanctified
as well as justified ; by faith he becomes henceforth an
altogether changed man.

The conscience is healed of its smart. Sin crushed the
man's soul; he was spiritless and joyless, but the moment
he believed in Jesus he leaped into light. Often you can
see a change in the very look of the man's face ; the cloud
flies from the countenance when guilt goes from the conscience. Scores of times, when I have been talking with
those bowed down with sin's burden, they have looked as
though they were qualifying for an asylum through inward
grief; but they have caught the thought, " Christ stood for

me ; and if I trust in Him, I have the sign that He did so, and I am clear," and their faces have been lit up as with a glimpse of heaven.

Gratitude for such great mercy causes a change of thought towards God, and so *it heals the judgment*, and by this means the affections are turned in the right way, and *the heart is healed*. Sin is no longer loved, but God is loved, and holiness is desired. *The whole man is healed*, and the whole life changed. Many of you know how light of heart faith in Jesus makes you, how the troubles of life lose their weight, and the fear of death ceases to cause bondage. You rejoice in the Lord, for the blessed remedy of the stripes of Jesus is applied to your soul by faith in Him.

The fact that " with His stripes we are healed " is a matter in evidence. I shall take liberty to bear my own witness. If it were necessary, I could call thousands of persons, my daily acquaintances, who can say that with the stripes of Jesus they are healed; but I must not therefore withhold my personal testimony. If I had suffered from a dreadful disease, and a physician had given me a remedy which had healed me, I should not be ashamed to tell you all about it ; but I would quote my own case as an argument with you to try my physician. Years ago, when I was a youth, the burden of my sin was exceedingly heavy upon me. I had fallen into no gross vices, and should not have been regarded by any one as being specially a transgressor ; but I regarded myself as such, and I had good reason for so doing. My conscience was sensitive because it was enlightened ; and I judged that, having had a godly father and a praying mother, and having been trained in the ways of piety, I had sinned against much light, and consequently

there was a greater degree of guilt in my sin than in that
of others who were my youthful associates, but had not
enjoyed my advantages. I could not enjoy the sports of
youth because I felt that I had done violence to my
conscience. I would seek my chamber, and there sit
alone, read my Bible, and pray for forgiveness; but peace
did not come to me. Books such as Baxter's *Call to the
Unconverted*, and Doddridge's *Rise and Progress*, I read
over and over again. Early in the morning I would
awake, and read the most earnest religious books I could
find, desiring to be eased of my burden of sin. I was not
always thus dull, but at times my misery of soul was very
great. The words of the weeping prophet and of Job were
such as suited my mournful case. I would have chosen
death rather than life. I tried to do as well as I could, and
to behave myself aright; but in my own judgment I grew
worse and worse. I felt more and more despondent. I
attended every place of worship within my reach, but I
heard nothing which gave me lasting comfort till one day
I heard a simple preacher of the gospel speak from the
text, "Look unto Me, and be ye saved, all the ends of
the earth." When he told me that all I had to do was to
"look" to Jesus—to Jesus the crucified One—I could
scarcely believe it. He went on, and said, "Look, look,
look!" He added, "There is a young man, under the
left-hand gallery there, who is very miserable : he will have
no peace until he looks to Jesus;" and then he cried,
"Look! Look! Young man, look!" I did look; and
in that moment relief came to me, and I felt such overflowing joy that I could have stood up, and cried, "Hal-
lelujah! Glory be to God, I am delivered from the burden
of my sin!" Many days have passed since then; but my

faith has held me up, and compelled me to tell out the story of free grace and dying love. I can truly say—

"E'er since by faith I saw the stream
Thy flowing wounds supply,
Redeeming love has been my theme,
And shall be till I die."

I hope to sit up in my bed in my last hours, and tell of the stripes that healed me. I hope some young men, yea, and old men before me, will at once try this remedy; it is good for all characters and all ages. "With His stripes we are healed." Thousands upon thousands of us have tried and proved this remedy. We speak what we do know, and testify what we have seen. God grant that men may receive our witness through the power of the Holy Spirit!

I want a few minutes' talk with those who have not tried this marvellous heal-all. Let us come to close quarters. Friend, you are by nature in need of soul-healing as much as any of us, and one reason why you do not care about the remedy is, because you do not believe that you are sick. I saw a pedlar one day, as I was walking out; he was selling walking-sticks. He followed me, and offered me one of the sticks. I showed him mine—a far better one than any he had to sell—and he withdrew at once. He could see that I was not likely to be a purchaser. I have often thought of that when I have been preaching: I show men the righteousness of the Lord Jesus, but they show me their own, and all hope of dealing with them is gone. Unless I can prove that their righteousness is worthless, they will not seek the righteousness which is of God by faith. Oh, that the Lord would show you your disease, and then you would desire the remedy!

It may be that you do not care to hear of the Lord Jesus Christ. Ah, my dear friends! you will have to hear of Him one of these days, either for your salvation or your condemnation. The Lord has the key of your heart, and I trust He will give you a better mind; and whenever this shall happen, your memory will recall my simple discourse, and you will say, "I do remember. Yes, I heard the preacher declare that there is healing in the wounds of Jesus."

I pray you do not put off seeking the Lord; that would be great presumption on your part, and a sad provocation to Him. But, should you have put it off, I pray you do not let the devil tell you it is too late. It is never too late while life lasts. I have read in books that very few people are converted after they are forty years of age. My solemn conviction is that there is but little truth in such a statement. I have seen as many people converted at one age as at another in proportion to the number of people who are living at that age. Any first Sunday in the month you may see the right hand of fellowship given to from thirty to eighty people who have been brought in during the month; and if you take stock of them, there will be found to be a selection representing every age, from childhood up to old age. The precious blood of Jesus has power to heal long-rooted sin. It makes old hearts new. If you were a thousand years old, I would exhort you to believe in Jesus, and I should be sure that His stripes would heal you. Your hair is nearly gone, old friend, and furrows appear on your brow; but come along! You are rotting away with sin, but this medicine meets desperate cases! Poor, old, tottering pensioner, put your trust in Jesus, for with His stripes the old and the dying are healed!

Now, my dear hearers, you are at this moment either

healed or not. You are either healed by grace, or you are
still in your natural sickness. Will you be so kind to yourselves as to enquire which it is? Many say, "We know
what we are;" but certain more thoughtful ones reply,
"We don't quite know." Friend, you ought to know, and
you should know. Suppose I asked a man, "Are you a
bankrupt or not?" and he said, "I really have no time to
look at my books, and therefore I am not sure." I should
suspect that he could not pay twenty shillings in the
pound; should not you? Whenever a man is afraid to
look at his books, I suspect that he has something to be
afraid of. So, whenever a person says, "I don't know my
condition, and I don't care to think much about it," you
may pretty safely conclude that things are wrong with him.
You ought to know whether you are saved or not.

"I hope I am saved," says one; "but I do not know
the date of my conversion." That does not matter at all.
It is a pleasant thing for a person to know his birthday;
but when persons are not sure of the exact date of their
birth, they do not, therefore, infer that they are not alive.
If a person does not know *when* he was converted, that is
no proof that he is not converted. The point is, do you
trust Jesus Christ? Has that trust made a new man of
you? Has your confidence in Christ made you feel that
you have been forgiven? Has that made you love God
for having forgiven you, and has that love become the
mainspring of your being, so that out of love to God you
delight to obey Him? Then you are a healed man. If
you do not believe in Jesus, be sure that you are still un-
healed, and I pray you look at my text until you are led
by grace to say, "I am healed, for I have trusted in the
stripes of Jesus."

Suppose, for a moment, you are not healed, let me ask the question, "*Why are you not?*" You know the gospel : why are you not healed by Christ? "I don't know," says one. But, my dear friend, I beseech you do not rest until you do know.

"I can't get at it," says somebody. The other day a young girl was putting a button on her father's coat. She was sitting with her back to the window, and she said, "Father, I can't see ; I am in my own light." He said, "Ah, my daughter, that is where you have been all your life !" This is the position of some of you spiritually. You are in your own light: you think too much of yourselves. There is plenty of light in the Sun of Righteousness, but you get in the dark by putting self in the way of that Sun. Oh, that your self might be put away ! I read a touching story the other day as to how one found peace. A young man had been for some time under a sense of sin, longing to find mercy ; but he could not reach it. He was a telegraph clerk, and being in the office one morning he had to receive and transmit a telegram. To his great surprise, he spelt out these words : "Behold the Lamb of God, which taketh away the sin of the world." A gentleman, out for a holiday, was telegraphing a message in answer to a letter from a friend who was in trouble of soul. It was meant for another, but he that transmitted it received eternal life, as the words came flashing into his soul.

Oh, dear friends, get out of your own light, and at once "Behold the Lamb of God, which taketh away the sin of the world"! I cannot telegraph the words to you, but I would put them before you so plainly and distinctly that every one in trouble of soul may know that they are meant for him. There lies your hope—not in yourself, but in the

Lamb of God. Behold Him; and as you behold Him your sin shall be put away, and by His stripes you shall be healed.

If, dear friend, you are healed, this is my last word to you; then *get out of diseased company.* Come away from the companions who have infected you with sin. Remember what the Lord says upon this matter: "Come out from among them, and be ye separate, saith the Lord, and touch not the unclean thing; and I will receive you, and will be a Father unto you, and ye shall be My sons and daughters, saith the Lord Almighty."

Next, if you are healed, praise the Healer, and acknowledge what He has done for you. There were ten lepers healed, but only one returned to praise the healing hand. Do not be among the ungrateful nine. If you have found Christ, confess His name. Confess it in His own appointed way. "He that believeth and is baptized shall be saved." When you have thus confessed Him, speak out for Him. Tell what Jesus has done for your soul, and dedicate yourself to the holy purpose of spreading abroad the message by which you have been healed.

I met this week with something that pleased me, about how one man, being healed, may be the means of blessing to another. Many years ago I preached a sermon in Exeter Hall, which was printed, and entitled, "Salvation to the Uttermost." A friend, who lives not very far from this place, was in the city of Para, in Brazil. Here he heard of an Englishman in prison, who had in a state of drunkenness committed a murder, for which he was confined for life. Our friend went to see him, and found him deeply penitent, but quietly restful, and happy in the Lord. He had felt the terrible wound of blood-guiltiness in his soul, but it had been healed, and he felt the bliss of pardon.   Here is the story of the poor man's conversion as I have it :—" A young man, who had just completed his contract with the gas-works, was returning to England, but before doing so he called to see me, and brought with him a parcel of books. When I opened it, I found that they were novels ; but, being able to read, I was thankful for anything.   After I had read several of the books, I found a sermon (No. 84), preached by C. H. Spurgeon, in Exeter Hall, on June 8th, 1856, from the words, 'Wherefore He is able also to save them to the uttermost,' etc. (Heb. vii. 25).   In his discourse, Mr. Spurgeon referred to Palmer, who was then lying under sentence of death in Stafford Gaol, and in order to bring home this text to his hearers, he said that if Palmer had committed many other murders, if he repents and seeks God's pardoning love in Christ, even he will be forgiven ; I then felt that if Palmer could be forgiven, so might I.   I sought, and, blessed be God, I found.   I am pardoned, I am free ; I am a sinner saved by grace.   Though a murderer, I have not yet sinned ' beyond the uttermost,' blessed be His holy name ! "   It made me very happy to think that a poor condemned murderer could thus be con-verted.   Surely there is hope for every hearer and reader of this sermon, however guilty he may be !

If you know Christ, tell others about Him.   You do not know what good there is in making Jesus known, even though all you can do is to give a tract, or repeat a verse. Dr. Valpy, the author of a great many class-books, wrote the following simple lines as his confession of faith :—

"In peace let me resign my breath,
    And Thy salvation see ;
My sins deserve eternal death,
    But Jesus died for me."

Valpy is dead and gone ; but he gave those lines to dear old Dr. Marsh, the Rector of Beckenham, who put them over his study mantel-shelf.   The Earl of Roden came in and read them. " Will you give me a copy of those lines ? " said the good earl.   " I shall be glad," said Dr. Marsh, and he copied them.   Lord Roden took them home, and put them over *his* mantel-shelf.   General Taylor, a Waterloo hero, came into the room, and noticed them.   He read them over and over again, while staying with Earl Roden, till his lordship remarked, "I say, friend Taylor, I should think you know those lines by heart."   He answered, " I do know them by heart ; indeed, my very heart has grasped their meaning."   He was brought to Christ by that humble rhyme.   General Taylor handed those lines to an officer in the army, who was going out to the Crimean war.   He came home to die ; and when Dr. Marsh went to see him, the poor soul in his weakness said, " Good sir, do you know this verse which General Taylor gave to me ?   It brought me to my Saviour, and I die in peace."   To Dr. Marsh's surprise, he repeated the lines :—

> " In peace let me resign my breath,
>   And Thy salvation see ;
> My sins deserve eternal death,
>   But Jesus died for me."

Only think of the good which four simple lines may do. Be encouraged all of you who know the healing power of the wounds of Jesus.   Spread this truth by all means. Never mind how simple the language.   Tell it out : tell it out everywhere, and in every way, even if you cannot do it in any other way than by copying a verse out of a hymn-book.   Tell it out that by the stripes of Jesus we are healed. May God bless you, dear friends !   Pray for me that this sermon of mine, which is numbered TWO THOUSAND, may be a very fruitful one.

OUR MANIFESTO.

OUR MANIFESTO.

Preached at an Assembly of Ministers of the Gospel, April 25, 1890.

" But I certify you, brethren, that the gospel which was preached of me is not after man."—GAL. i. 11.

To me it is a pitiful sight to see Paul defending himself as an apostle ; and doing this, not against the gainsaying world, but against cold-hearted members of the Church. They said that he was not truly an apostle, for he had not seen the Lord ; and they uttered a great many other things derogatory to him. To maintain his claim to the apostleship, he was driven to commence his Epistles with "Paul, an apostle of Jesus Christ," though his work was a self-evident proof of his call. If, after God has blessed us to the conversion of many, some of these should raise a question as to our call to the ministry, we may count it a fiery trial ; but we shall not conclude that a strange thing has happened to us. There is much more room to question our call to the ministry than to cast a doubt upon Paul's apostleship. This indignity, if it be put upon us, we can cheerfully bear for our Master's sake. We need not wonder, dear brethren, if our ministry should be the subject of attack, because this has been the lot of those who have gone before us ; and we should lack one great seal of our acceptance with God if we did not receive the unconscious homage of enmity which is always paid to the faithful by the ungodly world. When the devil is not troubled *by* us, he does not trouble *us*. If his kingdom is not shaken, he will not care about us or our work, but will let us enjoy inglorious ease. Be comforted by the experience of the apostle of the Gentiles : he is peculiarly our apostle, and we may regard his experience as a type of what we may expect while we labour among the Gentiles of our own day.

The treatment which has been given to eminent men while they have lived has been prophetic of the treatment of their reputations after death. This evil world is unchangeable in antagonism to true principles, whether their advocates be dead or living. They said more than eighteen hundred years ago, "Paul, what of him ?" They say so still. It is not unusual to hear dubious persons profess to differ from the apostle, and they even dare to say, "There I do not agree with Paul." I remember the first time that I heard this expression I looked at the individual with astonishment. I was amazed that such a pigmy as he should say this of the great apostle. Altogether apart from Paul's inspiration, it seemed like a cheese-mite differing from a cherub, or a handful of chaff discussing the verdict of the fire. The individual was so utterly beneath observation that I could not but marvel that his conceit should have been so outspokenly shameless. Notwithstanding this objection, even when supported by learned critics, we still agree with the inspired servant of God. It is our firm conviction that to differ from Paul's Epistles is to differ from the Holy Ghost, and to differ from the Lord Jesus Christ, whose mind Paul has fully expressed. It is remarkable that Paul's writings should be so assailed; but this warns us that when we have gone to our reward, our names will not be free from aspersion, nor our teaching from opposition. The noblest of the departed are still slandered. Be not careful as to human judgment of yourself in death or in life; for what does it matter? Your real character no man can injure but yourself; and if you are enabled to keep your garments clean, all else is not worth a thought.

To come more closely to our text: we do not claim to be able to use Paul's words exactly in the full sense which he could throw into them; but there is a sense in which, I trust, we can each one say, "I certify you, brethren, that the gospel which was preached of me is not after man." We may not only say this, but we ought to be able to say it with thorough truthfulness. The form of expression goes as far as Paul was wont to go towards an oath when he says, "I certify you, brethren." He means, I assure you, most certainly—I would have you to be certain of it—"that the gospel which was preached of me is not after man." On this point he would have all the brethren certified past all doubt.

From the context we are sure that he meant, first of all, that *his gospel was not received by him from men.* His reception of it in his own mind was not after men. And next, he meant, that *the gospel itself was not invented by men.* If I can hammer out these two statements, we will then *draw practical conclusions therefrom.*

I. First, TO US THE GOSPEL IS NOT AFTER MEN AS TO THE MODE BY WHICH WE HAVE RECEIVED IT. In a certain sense we received it from men as to the outward part of the reception, for we were called by the grace of

God through parental influence, or through a Sabbath-school teacher, or by the ministry of the Word, or by the reading of a godly book, or by some other agency. But in Paul's case none of these things were used. He was distinctly called by the Lord Jesus Christ Himself speaking to him from heaven, and revealing Himself in His own light. It was necessary that Paul should not be indebted to Peter, or James, or John, even in the way in which many of us are indebted to instrumentality; so that he might truly say, "I neither received it of man, neither was I taught it, but by the revelation of Jesus Christ." Yet we also can say this in another sense. We also have received the gospel in a way beyond the power of man to convey it to us : men brought it to our ear, but the Lord Himself applied it to our heart. The best of the saints could not have brought it home to our hearts, so as to regenerate, convert, and sanctify us by it. There was a distinct act of God the Holy Ghost by which the instrumentality was made effectual, and the truth was rendered operative upon our souls.

So I note that *not one among us has received the gospel by birthright.* We may be the children of holy parents, but we are not therefore the children of God. To us it is clear that "that which is born of the flesh is flesh," and nothing more. Only "that which is born of the Spirit is spirit." Yet we hear of persons whose children do not need con-version. They are spoken of as being free from natural corruption, and born children of God, having a grace within which only needs to be developed. I am sorry to say that my father did not find me such a child. He found out early in my life that I was born in sin, and shapen in iniquity, and that folly was bound up in my heart. Friends and teachers soon perceived in me a natural depravity; and assuredly I have found it in myself: the sad discovery needed no very minute research, for the effect of the evil stared me in the face in my character. This tradition as to our being born with a holy nature is gaining foothold in the professing Church, though contrary to Scripture, and even to the confessions of faith which are still avowedly maintained. Certain preachers hardly dare formulate it as a doctrine; but it is with them a kind of chaotic belief that there may be productions of the flesh which are very superior, and will serve well enough without the new birth of the Spirit. This tacit belief will lead up to birthright membership; and that is fatal to any Christian community, wherever it comes to be the rule. Without conversion, in certain fellowships, the young people drift into the Church as a matter of course, and the Church becomes only a part of the world, with the Christian name affixed to it. May we never in our Churches sink into that condition! That religion which is a mere family appendage is of little worth. The true seed are " born, not of blood, nor of the will of the flesh, nor of the will of man, but of God." We have not received our faith by tradition from our parents; and yet some of us, if true faith could be so received, would certainly have thus received it, for if we are not Hebrews of the Hebrews, yet according to our family-tree we are Puritans of the Puritans, descended through many generations of believers. Of this we make small account before God, though we are not ashamed of it before men. We have no father in our spiritual life but the Lord Himself, and we have not received that life, or the gospel, by any carnal parentage, but of the Lord alone.

Brethren, we have not received the gospel, nor do we now receive it, *because of the teaching of any man, or set of men.* Do you receive anything because Calvin taught it? If so, you had need look to your foundations. Do you believe a doctrine because John Wesley preached it? If so, you have reason to mind what you are at. God's way, by which we are to receive the truth, is to receive it by the Holy Ghost. It is helpful to me to know what such and such a minister believed. The judgment of a holy, godly, clear-sighted, gifted divine is not to be despised; it deserves to have due weight with us. He is as likely to be right as we are; and we should differ from a grace-taught man with some hesitancy. But it is a very different thing to say, "I believe it on this good man's authority." In our raw state as young Christians, it may not be injurious to receive truth from pastors and parents, and so on; but if we are to become *men* in Christ Jesus, and teachers of others, we must quit the childish habit of dependence on others, and search for ourselves. We may now leave the egg, and get rid of the pieces of shell as quickly as may be. It is our duty to search the Scriptures to see whether these things be so; and more, it is our wisdom to cry for grace to appropriate each truth, and let it dwell in our inmost nature. It is time that we should be able to say, "This truth is now as personally my own as if I had never heard it from lip of man. I receive it because it has been written on my own heart by the Lord himself. Its coming to me is not after men."

There is an opinion current in certain circles that you must not receive anything unless it is taught you of men: the word "men" being swallowed up and hidden away, but being there, after all, under the term "*the Church*." The

Church is set up as the great authority. If she has
sanctioned it, you dare not question it; if she decrees, it
is yours to obey. But this is to receive a gospel "after
man" with a vengeance. And the process involved is a
strange one. You must trace a dogma as coming through
a continuous visible Church, and this will lead you through
the *Cloaca Maxima* of old Rome. Though truth be
manifestly clear and pure, and prove itself to be the water
of life to you, yet you must not accept it; but you must
betake yourself to the mudded stream which can be traced
through the foul channel of a continuous Church, which
for ages has apostatized. My dear brethren, a doctrine's
being believed by what may in courtesy be called "the
Church" is no voucher for it: the most of us would almost
regard it as being a question to be raised whether teaching
can be true which has been vouched for by those great
worldly corporations which have usurped the name of
Churches of Christ. Several sects claim apostolical succession, and if any possess it, the Baptists are the most
likely, since they practise the ordinances as they were
delivered; but we do not even care to trace our pedigree
through the long line of martyrs, and of men abhorred by
ecclesiastics. If we could do this without a break, the
result would be of no value in our eyes; for the rag of
"apostolical succession" is not worth warehouse room.
Those who contend for the fiction may monopolize it
if they will. We do not receive the revelation of God
because it has been received by a succession of fathers,
monks, abbots, and bishops. We are right glad when we
perceive that certain of them saw the truth of God, and
taught it; but that fact does not make it truth to us. We
would each one say, "I certify you, brethren, that the

gospel which was preached of me is not after man." We
never think of quoting the community of men called "the
Church" as the ultimate authority with conscience. "We
have not so learned Christ."

Furthermore, I hope I shall speak for all of you here
when I say that *we have received the truth personally by the
revelation of it to our own souls by the Spirit of the Lord.*
Albeit that in so large a company as this I fear there may
be a Judas, and the "Lord, is it I?" may well be passed
round with holy self-suspicion; yet we can all say, unless
fearfully deceived, that we have received the truth which
we preach by the inward teaching of the Holy Spirit. Let
us turn to our diaries, though the dates are now far away
in the long-ago. We remember when the light broke in,
and revealed our lost estate, and thus began the groundwork of our teaching. Ah, friends! the darker doctrines
which make up the foil of the priceless jewels of the gospel,
do you not remember when you received them with power?
That I was guilty, I believed, for I was so taught; but
then and there I *knew* in my soul that it was so. Oh, how
I knew it! Guilty before God, "condemned already," and
lying under the present curse of a broken Law, I was sore
dismayed. I had heard the Law of God preached, and
I had trembled as I heard it; but now I felt an inward
conviction of personal guilt of the most piercing character.
I saw myself a sinner; and what a sight is that! Fearful-
ness took hold upon me, and shame and dread. Then
I saw how true was the doctrine of the sinfulness of sin;
and what a punishment it must involve. That doctrine I
no longer received of men.

The gracious doctrine of peace through the precious
blood of Jesus, we also know by inward personal teaching.

We used to hear and sing of the great Sacrifice, and of the love of Him who bore our sins in His own body on the tree; but now we stood at the cross-foot: for ourselves we beheld that dear face, and gazed into the eyes so full of pity, and saw the hands and feet that were fastened to the wood for our sakes. Oh, when we saw the Lord Jesus, as our Surety, smarting for our offence, then we received the truth of redemption and atonement in a way that was "not after man"!

Yes, those godly men who have gone to heaven did preach the gospel to us fully and earnestly, and they laboured to make known Christ to us; but to reveal the Son of God in us was beyond their power. They could as easily have created a world as have made these truths vital to us. We say, therefore, each one from his inmost soul, " I certify you, brethren, that the gospel which was preached of me is not after man;" so far as the way by which we have come to know and feel it within our own souls.

Since our first days we have experienced a gradual opening up of the gospel to our understanding, but in all that process, our real progress has been of God, and not of men. Brethren, you read commentators—that is to say, if your own comments are worth hearing; you read the books of godly men—that is to say, if you yourselves ever say anything worth reading; yet your spiritual learning, if it be true and real, is of the Lord's imparting. Do we learn anything, in the most emphatic sense of learning, unless we are taught of the Lord? Is it not essential that God the Spirit should lay home the truth which has been spoken to you even by the ablest instructor? You have continued to be students ever since you left College; but your Tutor has been the Holy Spirit. By no other method can our spirits

learn the truth of God but by the teaching of the Spirit
of God. We can receive the shell and the outer form of
theology, but the real Word of the Lord itself comes by the
Holy Spirit, who leads us into all truth.

How sweetly the Spirit has taught us *in meditation !*
Have you not often been surprised and overcome with
delight as Holy Scripture has opened up, as if the gates of
the golden city had been set back for you to enter? I am
sure that you did not then gather your knowledge from
men, because it was all fresh to you as you sat alone with
no book before you but the Bible, and yourself receptive,
scarcely thinking out matters, but drinking them in as the
Lord brought them to you. A few minutes' silent openness
of soul before the Lord has brought us in more treasure of
truth than hours of learned research. The truth is something
like those stalactite caverns and grottoes of which we have
heard, which you must enter and see for yourself if you
would really know their wonders. If you should venture
there without light or guide, you would run great risks ; but
with blazing flambeaux, and an instructed leader, your
entrance is full of interest. See ! your guide has taken you
through a narrow winding passage, where you have to creep
or go on bended knees ! At last he has brought you out
into a magnificent hall ; and when the torches are held
aloft, the far-off roof sparkles and flashes back the light as
from countless jewels of every hue ! You now behold
nature's architecture ; and cathedrals are henceforth toys
to you. As you stand in that vast pillared and jewelled
palace, you feel how much you owe to your guide, and to
his flaming torch. Thus the Holy Spirit leads us into all
truth, and sheds light on the eternal and the mysterious.
This He does in certain cases very personally. Then He

fills us with complete forgetfulness of all our immediate surroundings, and we commune only with the truth. I can well understand how philosophers, while working out an absorbing problem, have seemed lost, and oblivious of all the world besides. Have you never felt a holy absorption in the truth while the Spirit has filled you with its glorious vision? It has been so with many of the saints while taught of God. They are not likely to give up to popular clamour what they have thus received.

How often has the Lord taught His servants His own truth *in the school of tribulation!* We speak well of meditation : it is as silver; but tribulation is as much fine gold. Tribulation not only worketh patience ; but patience brings experience, and in experience there is a deep and intimate knowledge of the things of God which cometh by no other means. Do you know what it is to be in such pain that you could not bear one turn more of the screw, and have you then in faintness fallen back upon your pillow, and felt that even then you could not be more happy unless you were caught up to the third heaven? Then has it been verified to some of us that we can do all things through Christ that strengtheneth us. While lying in passive peace, it may be you have seen a Scripture come forth like a star between the cloud-rifts of a tempest, and it has shone with such lustre as only the Lord God could have given to it. Depression of spirit and torture of body have been forgotten, while the bright promise has made your soul full of light. There is a place in the far-back desert which you can never forget. There grows a bush. A very unpromising object is a bush : but it is sacred to you ; for there the Lord revealed Himself to you, and the bush burned with fire, but was not consumed. You will never unlearn the lesson of the burning bush. Do we ever know any truth till the Holy Spirit burns it into us, and engraves it on our soul as with an iron pen, and with the point of a diamond? There are ways of learning for which we are very grateful; but the surest way of learning divine truth is by having the Word "engrafted" so as to take living hold upon the soul. Then we do not believe it only; we give our life to it : it lives in us, and at the same time we live upon it. Such truth throbs in every pulse; for it has quickened the heart. We do not question it; we cannot, for it lives in us, and colours our being. The devil insinuates questions; but we are not accountable for what he pleases to do, and we care the less, because he now whispers into a deaf ear. When once the soul itself has received the truth, and it has come to permeate the entire being, we are not accessible to those doubts which aforetimes pierced us like poisoned arrows.

I may add, concerning many of the truths of God, and the whole gospel system, that we have learned the truth thereof *in the field of sacrifice and service with our Lord*, so that to us it is "not after man." If you do not believe in human depravity, accept a pastorate in this wicked London, and if you are true to your commission, you will doubt no more ! If you do not believe in the necessity of the Holy Spirit to regenerate, take a charge over a cultured and polished congregation, that will hear all your rhetoric, and will remain as worldly and as frivolous as it was before. If you do not believe in the power of the atoning blood, never go and see believers die, for you will find that they trust in nothing else. A dying Christ is the last resort of the believer.

> " When every earthly prop gives way,
> He then is all my strength and stay."

If you do not believe in the election of grace, live where multitudes of men come under your notice, and persons most unlikely are called out from among them in surprising ways, and it will grow upon you. Here comes one who says, "I have neither father, mother, brother, sister, nor friend who ever enters a place of worship." "How came you to believe?" "I heard a word in the street, sir, quite by accident, that brought me to tremble before God." Here is the election of grace. Here comes another, dark in mind, troubled in soul, and she is a member of a family all of them members of your Church, all happy and rejoicing in the Lord; and yet this poor creature cannot lay hold upon Christ by faith. To your great joy, you set before her Christ in all His fulness of grace, and she becomes the brightest of the whole circle; for they never knew the darkness as she did, and they can never rejoice in the light as she delights in it. To find a greatly-loving saint you must find one who has had much forgiven. The woman that was a sinner is the only one that will wash Christ's feet. There is raw material in a publican which you seldom find in a Pharisee. A Pharisee may polish up into an ordinary Christian; but somehow there is a charming touch about the pardoned sinner which is lacking in the other. There is an election of grace, and you cannot help noticing, as you go about, how certain believers enter into the inner circle, while others linger in the outer courts. The Lord is sovereign in His gifts, and doeth as He wills; and we are called to bow before His sceptre within the Church as well as at its portal. The longer I live, the more sure I am that salvation is all of grace, and that the Lord gives that grace according to His own will and purpose.

Once more, some of us have received the gospel because

of *the wonderful unction that has gone with it at times to our souls.* I hope that none of us will ever fall into the snare of following the guidance of impressions made upon us by texts which happen to come prominently before our minds. You have judgments, and you must not lay them aside to be guided by accidental impressions. But for all that, and at the back of all that, there is not a man here that has led an eventful, useful life, but must confess that certain of those acts of his life, upon which his whole history has hinged, are connected with influences upon his mind which were produced, as he believes, by supernatural agency. A passage of Holy Writ, which we had read a hundred times before, took us captive, and became the master of every thought. We steered by it as men trust the pole-star, and we found that our voyage was made easy thereby. Certain texts are, to our memory, sweet as wafers made with honey; for we know what they once did for us, and the recollection is refreshing. We have been revived from a fainting-fit, nerved for a desperate effort, or fired for a sacrifice, by a Scripture which became no longer a word in a book, but the very voice of God to our soul—even that voice of the Lord, which is full of majesty. Have you not noticed how a turn of a word in a text has made it seem all the more fitted for you? It looked a very small point; but it was essential to its effect, just as a small notch in a key may be the exact form which makes it fit the lock. How much may hang on what seems, to the unspiritual, to be nothing more than a slight verbal distinction, or an unimportant turn of expression! A thought of primary importance may turn upon the singular or plural of a word. If it be the Greek word itself, the importance cannot be overestimated; but in an English word, in the translation, there may be well-nigh equal force, according as the word is true to the original. The many, who can only read our marvellous English Bible, come to prize its words because the Lord has blessed them to their souls. A simple Welsh friend believed that our Lord must have been a Welshman, "because," said he, "He always speaks *to me* in Welsh." To me it has often seemed as if the Well-beloved of my soul had been born in my native village, had gone to my school, and had passed through all my personal experiences; for He knows me better than I know myself. Although I know He was of Bethlehem and Judæa, yet He seems like one of London, or of Surrey. Nay, more; I see in Him more than manhood could have made Him; I discern in Him a nature more than that of man; for He enters the inmost recesses of my soul, He reads me like an open page, He comforts me as one brought up with me, He dives into my deepest griefs, and attends me in my highest joys. I have secrets in my heart which only He knows. Would God His secret were with me as mine is with Him up to the measure of my capacity! It is because of that wonderful power which the Lord Jesus has over us through His sacred Word that we receive that Word from Him, and receive it as "not of man."

What is unction, my brethren? I fear that no one can help me by a definition. Who can define it? But yet we know where it is, and we certainly feel where it is not. When that unction perfumes the Word, it is its own interpreter, it is its own apologist, it is its own confirmation and proof, to the regenerate mind. Then the Word of God deals with us as no word of man ever did or could. We have not received it, therefore, of men. Constantly receiving the divine Word as we do, it comes to us with an energy ever fresh and forcible. It comes to us especially with a sanctifying power, which is the very best proof of its coming from the thrice-holy God. Philosophers' words may teach us what holiness is, but God's Word makes us holy. We hear our brethren exhort us to aspire to high degrees of grace, but God's Word lifts us up to them. The Word is not merely an instrument of good, but the Holy Spirit makes it an active energy within the soul to purge the heart from sin, so that it can be said, "Ye are clean through the Word which I have spoken unto you." When thus cleansed, you know that the Word is true. You are sure of it, and you no longer need even the most powerful book of "evidences." You have the witness in yourself, the evidence of things not seen, the seal of eternal verity.

I have taken all this time upon how we receive the gospel, and therefore I must perforce be brief upon a further point.

II. TO US THE TRUTH ITSELF IS NOT AFTER MEN. I desire to assert this plainly. If any man thinks that the gospel is only one of many religions, let him candidly compare the Scriptures of God with other pretended revelations. Have you ever done so? I have made it a College exercise with our brethren. I have said, "We will read a chapter of the Koran." This is the Mahometan's holy book. A man must have a strange mind who should mistake that rubbish for the utterances of inspiration. If he is at all familiar with the Old and New Testaments, when he hears an extract from the Koran, he feels that he has met with a foreign author : the God who gave us the Pentateuch could have had no hand in many portions of the Koran. One of the most modern pretenders to inspiration is the Book of Mormon. I could not blame you should you laugh

outright while I read aloud a page from that farrago.
Perhaps you know the Protevangelion, and other apocryphal
New Testament books. It would be an insult to the
judgment of the least in the kingdom of heaven to suppose
that he could mistake the language of these forgeries for
the language of the Holy Ghost. I have had several pretended revelations submitted to me by their several authors,
for we have more of the prophetic clan about than most
people know of; but no one of them has ever left on my
mind the slightest suspicion of his sharing the inspiration
of John or Paul. There is no mistaking the inspired
Books if you have any spiritual discernment. Once let the
divine light dawn in the soul, and you perceive a colouring
and a fashion in the product of inspiration which are not
possible to mere men. Would one who doubts this write
us a fifth Gospel? Would any one among our poets
attempt to write a new Psalm, which could be mistaken for
a Psalm of David? I do not see *why* he could not, but
I am sure he cannot. You can give us new psalmody,
for it is an instinct of the Christian life to sing the praises
of God; but you cannot match the glory of divinely-
inspired song. Therefore we receive the Scripture, and
consequently the gospel, as "not after man."

You say, perhaps, "You are comparing books, and
forgetting that your theme is the gospel." But this is only
in appearance. I do not care to waste your time by asking
you to compare the gospels of men. There is not another
gospel that I know of that is worth the comparison for
a single minute. "Oh, but," they say, "there is a gospel
that is much wider than yours." Yes, I know that it is
much wider than mine; but to what does it lead? They
say that what is nicknamed Calvinism has a very narrow

door. There is a word in Scripture about a strait gate and
a narrow way; and therefore I am not alarmed by the
accusation. But then there are rich pastures when you
once enter within, and this renders it worth while to enter
in by the strait gate. Certain other systems have very
wide doors; but they lead you into small privileges, and
those of a precarious tenure. I hear certain invitations
which might run as follows : "Come, ye disconsolate; but
if you come, you will be disconsolate still, for there will be
no *eternal* life made sure to you, and you must preserve
your own souls, or perish after all." But I shall not enter
into any comparisons, for they are odious in this case.

The gospel, *our gospel, is beyond the strain and reach of
human thought.* When men have exercised themselves to
the very highest in original conceptions, they have never
yet thought out the true gospel. If it is such a commonplace thing as the critics would have us believe, why did it
not arise in the minds of the Egyptians or Chinese? Great
minds often run in the same groove; why did not other
great minds run in the same grooves as those of Moses, or
Isaiah, or Paul? I think it is a fair thing to say that, if
it is such a commonplace form of teaching, it might have
arisen among the Persians or Hindoos; or, surely, we might
have found something like it among the great teachers of
Greece. Did any of these think out the doctrine of free
and sovereign grace? Did they guess at the Incarnation
and Sacrifice of the Son of God? No, even with the aid
of our inspired Book, no Mahometan, to my knowledge,
has taught a system of grace in which God is glorified as to
His justice, His love, and His sovereignty. That sect has
grasped a certain sort of predestination which it has defaced
into blind fate ; but even with that to help them, and the

unity of the Godhead as a powerful light to aid them, they
have never thought out a plan of salvation so just to God
and so pacifying to the troubled conscience as the method
of redemption by the substitution of our Lord Jesus.

I will give you another proof, which, to my mind, is
conclusive that our gospel is not after men ; and it is this—
that *it is immutable, and nothing that man produces can be
so called.* If man makes a gospel—and he is very fond of
doing it, like children making toys—what does he do ? He
is very pleased with it for a few moments, and then he
pulls it to pieces, and makes it up in another way; and
this continually. The religions of " modern thought " are
as changeable as the mists on the mountains. See how
often science has altered its very basis ! Science is
notorious for being most scientific in destruction of all the
science that has gone before it. I have sometimes indulged
myself, in leisure moments, in reading ancient natural
history; and nothing can be more comic. Yet this is by
no means an abstruse science. In twenty years' time, some
of us may probably find great amusement in the serious
scientific teaching of the present hour, even as we do now
in the systems of the last century. It may happen that, in
a little time, the doctrine of evolution will be the standing
jest of schoolboys. The like is true of the modern divinity
which bows its knee in blind idolatry of so-called science.
Now we say, and do so with all our heart, that the gospel
which we preached forty years ago we will still preach in
forty years' time if we are alive. And, what is more, that
the gospel which was taught of our Lord and His apostles
is the only gospel now on the face of the earth. Ecclesiastics have altered the gospel, and if it had not been of
God it would have been stifled by falsehood long ago ; but

because the Lord has made it, it abideth for ever. Everything human is before long moon-struck, so that it shifts
with every phase of the lunar orb; but the Word of the
Lord is not after men, for it is the same yesterday, to-day,
and for ever.

It cannot be after men, again, because *it is so opposed to
human pride.* Other systems flatter men, but this speaks
the truth. Hear the dreamers of to-day cry up the dignity
of human nature! How sublime is man! But point me
to a single syllable in which the Word of God sets itself to
the extolling of man. On the contrary, it lays him in the
very dust, and reveals his condemnation. Where is boasting then? It is excluded: the door is shut in its face.
The self-glorification of human nature is foreign to Scripture, which has for its grand object the glory of God. God
is everything in the gospel which I preach, and I believe
that He is all in all in your ministry also. There is a
gospel in which the work and the glory are divided between
God and man, and salvation is not altogether of grace;
but in our gospel "salvation is of the Lord." Man never
could nor would have invented and devised a gospel which
would lay him low, and secure to the Lord God all the
honour and the praise. This seems to me to be clear
beyond all question; and hence our gospel is not after
men.

Again, it is not after men, because *it does not give sin
any quarter.* I have heard that an Englishman has pro-
fessed himself a Mahometan because he is charmed by the
polygamy which the Arabian prophet allows his followers.
No doubt the prospect of four wives would win converts
who would not be attracted by spiritual considerations. If
you preach a gospel which makes allowances for human

nature, and treats sin as if it were a mistake rather than a crime, you will find willing hearers. If you can provide absolution at small cost, and can ease conscience by a little self-denial, it will not be wonderful if your religion becomes fashionable. But our gospel declares that the wages of sin is death, and that we can only have eternal life as the gift of God; and that this gift always brings with it sorrow for sin, a hatred towards it, and an avoidance of it. Our gospel tells a man that he must be born again, and that without the new birth he will be lost eternally, while with it he will obtain everlasting salvation. Our gospel offers no excuse or cloak for sin, but condemns it utterly. It presents no pardon except through the great Atonement, and it will give that man no security who tries to harbour any sin in his bosom. Christ died for sin; and we must die to sin, or die eternally. If we preach the gospel faithfully, we must preach the Law. You cannot fully preach salvation by Christ without setting Sinai at the back of the picture, and Calvary in the front. Men must be made to feel the evil of sin before they will prize the great Sacrifice which is the head and front of our gospel. This is not to the taste of this or any other age; and therefore I am sure man did not invent it.

We know that the gospel of our Lord Jesus Christ is not of men, because *our gospel is so suitable for the poor and the illiterate.* The poor, according to the usual fashion of men, are overlooked. Parliament has enclosed all the commons, so that a poor man cannot keep a goose; I doubt not that, if it were likely to be effectual, we should soon hear of a Bill for distributing the freeholds of the stars among certain skylords. It is evident that a fine property in the celestial regions is, at the present time, unregistered

in any of our courts. Well, they may sooner enclose and
assign the sun, moon, and stars than the gospel of our
Lord Jesus. This is the poor man's common. "The poor
have the gospel preached to them." Yet there are not a
few nowadays who despise a gospel which the common
people can hear and understand; and we may be sure that
a plain gospel never came from them, for their taste does
not lie in that direction. They want something abstruse,
or, as they say, "thoughtful." Do we not hear this sort of
remark, "We are an intellectual people, and need a cultured ministry. Those evangelistic preachers are all very
well for popular assemblies, but we have always been select,
and require that preaching which is abreast of the times"?
Yes, yes, and their man will be one who will not preach
the gospel unless it be in a clouded manner; for if he does
declare the gospel of Jesus, the poor will be sure to intrude
themselves, and shock my lords and ladies. Brethren, our
gospel does not know anything about high and low, rich
and poor, black and white, cultured and uncultured. If it
makes any difference, it prefers the poor and the down-
trodden. The great Founder of it says, "I thank Thee,
O Father, Lord of heaven and earth, because Thou hast
hid these things from the wise and prudent, and hast
revealed them unto babes." We praise God that He has
chosen the base things, and things that are despised. I
hear it boasted of a man's ministry, although it gradually
diminishes the congregation, that it is doing a great work
among "thoughtful young men." I confess that I am not
a believer in the existence of these thoughtful young men :
those who mistake themselves for such I have generally
found to be rather conceited than thoughtful. Young men
are all very well, and so are young women, and old women

also; but I am sent to preach the gospel to every creature, and I cannot limit myself to thoughtful young men. I certify to you that the gospel which I have preached is not after men, for it knows nothing of selection and exclusiveness, but it values the soul of a sweep or a dustman at the same price as that of the Lord Mayor, or of her Majesty.

Lastly, we are sure that the gospel we have preached is not after men, because *men do not take to it*. It is opposed even to this day. If anything is hated bitterly, it is the out-and-out gospel of the grace of God, especially if that hateful word "sovereignty" is mentioned with it. Dare to say, "He will have mercy on whom He will have mercy, and He will have compassion on whom He will have compassion," and furious critics will revile you without stint. The modern religionist not only hates the doctrine of sovereign grace, but he raves and rages at the mention of it. He would sooner hear you blaspheme than preach election by the Father, atonement by the Son, or regeneration by the Spirit. If you want to see a man worked up till the Satanic is clearly uppermost, let some of the new divines hear you preach a free-grace sermon. A gospel which is after men will be welcomed by men; but it needs a divine operation upon the heart and mind to make a man willing to receive into his inmost soul this distasteful gospel of the grace of God.

My dear brethren, do not try to make it tasteful to carnal minds. Hide not the offence of the cross, lest you make it of none effect. The angles and corners of the gospel are its strength: to pare them off is to deprive it of power. Toning down is not the increase of strength, but the death of it. Why, even among the sects, you must have noticed that their distinguishing points are the horns

of their power; and when these are practically omitted, the
sect is effete! Learn, then, that if you take Christ out of
Christianity, Christianity is dead. If you remove grace out
of the gospel, the gospel is gone. If the people do not
like the doctrine of grace, give them all the more of it.
Whenever its enemies rail at a certain kind of gun, a wise
military power will provide more of such artillery. A great
general, going in before his king, stumbled over his own
sword. "I see," said the king, "your sword is in the
way." The warrior answered, "Your majesty's enemies
have often felt it to be so." That our gospel offends the
King's enemies, is no cause for regret to us.

Dear friends, if it be so that we have not received the
gospel from man, but from God, *let us continue to receive
truth by the divinely-appointed channel of faith.* Are you
sure that you ever will to the full *understand* the truth of
God? With most of us the understanding is like a narrow
postern gate to the city of Mansoul, and the great things of
God cannot be so cut down as to be brought in by that
entrance. The door is not wide enough. But our city has
a great gate called faith, through which even the infinite
and eternal may be admitted. Give over the hopeless
effort of dragging into the mind by efforts of reason that
which can so readily come into you by the Holy Ghost
through faith. We that speak against rationalism are
ourselves apt to reason too much; and there is nothing so
unreasonable as to hope to receive the things of God by
reasoning them out. Let us believe them upon the divine
testimony; and when they try us, and even when they
seem to grate upon the sensibilities of humanity, let us
receive them none the less for that. We are not to be

judges of what God's truth ought to be ; we are to accept it as the Lord reveals it.

Next, *let us, each one, expect opposition if he receives the truth from the Lord,* and especially opposition from one person who is both near and dear to him—namely, himself. There is a certain " old man " who is yet alive, and he is no lover of the truth ; but, on the contrary, he is a partisan of falsehood. I heard a gracious policeman say that, when he stood in Trafalgar Square, and fellows of the baser sort kicked him and the other police, he felt a bone of the old man stirring within him. Ah, we have felt that bone too often ! The carnal nature opposes the truth, for it is not reconciled to God, neither indeed can be. Let us pray the Lord to conquer our pride, that the truth may dominate us, despite our evil hearts. As to the outside world opposing, we are not at all alarmed by that fact, for it is exactly what we were taught to expect. We are now unmoved by opposition. The captain of a ship minds not if a little spray breaks over him.

Remember that, if you did not receive the truth except through the power of the Spirit of God, you cannot expect others to do so. They will not believe your report unless the arm of the Lord be revealed to them. But then, if faith be the Holy Ghost's work, we need not fear that men can destroy it. Those who attempt to change our belief may well be a little dubious as to their success in the task they have undertaken. If faith be a divine work within our souls, we may defy all sophistries, flatteries, temptations, and threats. We shall be divinely obstinate: those who would pervert us will have to give us up. Possibly they will call us bigots, or hard-shells, or even idiots; but this also signifies little if our names are written in heaven.

Let us also conclude from our subject that *if these things come to us from God, we can safely rest our all upon them.* If they came to us from men, they would probably fail us at a crisis. Did you ever trust men, and not rue the day ere the sun was down? Did you ever rely on an arm of flesh without discovering that the best of men are but men at the best? But if these things come from God, they are eternal and all-sufficient. We can both live and die upon the everlasting gospel. Let us deal more and more with God, and with Him only. If we have obtained light from Him, there is more of blessing to be had. Let us go to that same Teacher, that we may learn more of the deep things of God. Let us bravely believe in the success of the gospel which we have received. We believe *in* it : let us believe *for* it. We will not despair though the whole visible Church should apostatize. When invaders had surrounded Rome, and all the country lay at their mercy, a piece of land was to be sold, and a Roman citizen bought it at a fair price. The enemy was there, but the patriot felt quite sure that he would be dislodged. The enemy might destroy the Roman State. Let him try it ! Be you of the same mind concerning the gospel that you preach. The God of Jacob is our Refuge, and none can stand against His eternal power and Godhead. The everlasting gospel is our banner, and with Jehovah to maintain it, our standard never shall be lowered. In the power of the Holy Ghost truth is invincible. Come on, ye hosts of hell, and armies of the aliens ! Let craft and criticism, priestcraft and rationalism, do their best, or their worst ! The Word of the Lord endureth for ever, even that Word which by the gospel is preached unto men !

A MEMORABLE MILESTONE.

A MEMORABLE MILESTONE.

Sermon preached in the Metropolitan Tabernacle on Thursday evening, March 25, 1886; the twenty-fifth anniversary of Mr. Spurgeon's first sermon in the Tabernacle.

"I have preached righteousness in the great congregation: lo, I have not refrained my lips, O Lord, Thou knowest. I have not hid Thy righteousness within my heart; I have declared Thy faithfulness and Thy salvation: I have not concealed Thy lovingkindness and Thy truth from the great congregation. Withhold not Thou Thy tender mercies from me, O Lord: let Thy lovingkindness and Thy truth continually preserve me."—Ps. xl. 9-11.

SOMETIMES, dear friends, we should take a review of life. There are occasions when men feel bound to do so, and the retrospect may be full of profit to themselves. I find that many look back in hours of trouble. A dark cloud brings them to a pause. They might have continued to run on with very little thought, but sorrow calls them to a halt. They are driven to God in prayer, and at such times it is not unusual for them, if God has been gracious to them in the past, to recollect all that goodness, and to mention it while they are pleading at the mercy-seat. They say, "He hath dealt well with His servant. The Lord hath helped me hitherto." They look back, and see the Ebenezers which they have raised in past years, and they cry, "Hath God forgotten to be gracious?"

> "Can He have taught me to trust in His name,
> And thus far have brought me to put me to shame?"

Thus they drive their griefs away, and the remembrance of past mercies helps them to snatch firebrands from the altars of the bygone years, wherewith to kindle the sacrifice of the present moment.

Men are also accustomed to review their lives when they are brought near to the verge of the grave. It is helpful, when we fear that life is about to end, to begin to add it up, to see what the sum total reaches. "Set thine house in order; for thou shalt die, and not live." And a part of the setting of the house in order is to remember the past, and look at what we have done, and what God has done; and set the one against the other, that we may repent of the sin, and may hope because of the mercy. Now, albeit that we may not ourselves be brought so near to death's door as that, yet during the past month or so we have, as a people, been continually going to the sepulchre. I think that there were seven notable brethren and sisters who fell asleep last week, so constantly have death's arrows been flying amongst us; and therefore, as we are come to the margin of the river, and must ourselves shortly put off this tabernacle, let us look back a little, and remember all the way whereby the Lord our God has led us.

I think, however, that without going to those occasions either of great sorrow or of apprehended departure, men are quite right in estimating time, and taking note of some periods as peculiarly noteworthy. Twenty-five years—a quarter of a century—have passed over our heads since I preached my first sermon in this house. It was opened with songs of joy; but many who were with us then are in glory now, and many of you were not even born then. To those who were at the opening of the Tabernacle, it must seem almost an old building now. I hear people talk of " the dear old Tabernacle," and well they may, for a quarter of a century is no mean period in the history of a building or a church. There has been a great deal done in those twenty-five years, and we have, both personally and as a Church, enjoyed abounding mercy. I did not think it right to let to-night pass over without offering devout thanksgiving to the Lord for all His lovingkindness to us, and endeavouring to say a word that should make us feel more fully our indebtedness to God, and our determination to be more than ever consecrated to His service.

This text, though it belongs first of all, in the divinest and fullest sense, to our gracious Master, belongs also to David, and through David to those whom God has called to bear testimony to the gospel of His grace. We can say, and we do say, humbly but most earnestly—and I know that there are many brethren here who can say, each one of his own ministry, and many brothers and sisters here who can say, too, after their measure, altering the words here and there somewhat—" I have preached righteousness in the great congregation : lo, I have not refrained my lips, O Lord, Thou knowest. I have not hid Thy righteousness within my heart ; I have declared Thy faithfulness and Thy salvation : I have not concealed Thy lovingkindness and Thy truth from the great congregation."

I. Coming, then, to our text, here is, first, A CONTINUAL TESTIMONY. Let us think of it.

Many of you have borne testimony for God in your homes, as well as in your lives; some of you have borne that testimony in your classes in the Sunday-school ; some in the street ; some in cottage meetings ; some in larger assemblies. We, especially, who are called to the public ministry of the Word, have borne this testimony in "the great congregation." But all of us who are the Lord's servants have borne our testimony according to our opportunities and abilities.

It has been imperfect, but it has been sincere. In looking back upon our testimony for God, we could almost wish to obliterate it because of its imperfections; but we can truthfully say that it has been sincerely borne up to the measure of capacity given. It has been borne without a doubt, without any mental reservation, with intensity of spirit—borne because it could not be helped. I have preached the gospel to you, my brethren and sisters, because I have believed it. If what I have preached to you be not true, I am a lost man. For me there is no joy in life and no hope in death except in that gospel which I have continually preached here. It is not to me a theory. I would scarcely stop at saying that it is a belief. It has become matter of absolute fact to me. It is interwoven with my consciousness. It is part of my being. Every day makes it dearer to me; my joys bind me to it, my griefs drive me to it. All that is behind me, all that is before me, all that is above me, all that is beneath me, everything compels me to say that my testimony has been borne from my heart, and mind, and soul, and strength; and I am grateful to God that I can say this, putting it as the text puts it, " O Lord, Thou knowest," if others do not, that it is so.

I feel grateful to God that I can say this because of *the subjects of the testimony.* The first subject of the psalmist's testimony had been God's "righteousness." That is the main point to be noted in all testimony for God, —God's positive righteousness in Himself; God's way of righteousness by which He justifies the ungodly; God's method of spreading righteousness in the world by the power and energy of His Holy Spirit. I, for one, believe in a God who punishes sin. I have never flattered you with the idea that sin is a trifle, and that in some future age it may expiate itself. Nay, the righteousness of God has seemed to me to be a dark background upon which to draw the bright lines of His everlasting love in Christ Jesus. In the expiation of Christ, the righteousness of God is vindicated to the full. He is "just, and the Justifier of Him that believeth in Jesus." I ask for no pardon to be given to me unrighteously. My conscience could not be satisfied with a forgiveness that came to me unjustly. The glory of God would be dishonoured thereby. There would be a blot upon the heavenly statute-book if sin were pardoned without atonement. But we have preached the righteousness of God; and we feel that, in doing so, we lay a sure foundation, upon which to build the comfort and hope of the believer in Christ Jesus.

In addition to the righteousness of God, the psalmist had preached His "faithfulness." The Lord keeps all His promises. He is the Faithful Promiser, and what He promises He performs. There is no lie in Him, nor change, nor shadow of a turning. "Hath He said, and shall He not do it?" Which of His promises ever failed? Has He drawn back even in the least degree from His covenant, or altered the word which has gone forth out of His lips? Our testimony has not been borne to a fickle God, and a feeble salvation, which saves for a time, and after all does not really save, but suffers saints to fall away, and perish everlastingly. Nay, we have given unfaltering utterance to that declaration of our Lord, "I give unto My sheep eternal life; and they shall never perish, neither shall any pluck them out of My hand." We believe in everlasting love, in an everlasting covenant, ordered in all things and sure ; and therefore righteousness and faithfulness have been the two foundations of our ministry, upon which we have tried to build a gospel worth our preaching and worth your having.

Then the psalmist says that he had borne testimony to two things in conjunction with each other : " Thy lovingkindness and Thy truth." Oh, brothers and sisters, what a theme is here ! " Thy lovingkindness." God's generous mercy, His overflowing love, His kinned-ness, His kindness to His chosen, whom He has made to be a people near unto Himself, to whom He manifests His very soul. That word "loving," added to the word " kindness," makes it a gem doubly precious. Where is there among words any other equal to this,—"lovingkindness"? I have exulted to preach to you the lovingkindness of the Lord. I needed not to be driven to this happy task. I have almost needed sometimes to be stopped when I have passed the hour, and my theme has carried me away. Oh, the lovingkindness of the Lord to those that put their trust under the shadow of His wings! That is a subject on which one might preach for ever, and yet not exhaust it.

And then His "truth"—God's truth; the truth of His Word; the truth of His Son ; the truth of the great doctrines which are given to us in the gospel. I have not preached to you any sort of speculation. I have never sought to invent new forms of truth. It shall be seen one day whose thoughts shall stand, God's thoughts or man's; and it shall be seen which is the true ministry, that which takes up God's Word, and echoes it, or that which boils it down until the very life is extracted from it. I have no sympathy with the preaching which degrades God's truth into a hobby-horse for its own thought, and only looks upon Scripture as a kind of pulpit from which it may thunder out its own opinions. Nay, if I have gone beyond what that Book has taught, may God blot out everything that I have said! I beseech you, never believe me if I go an atom beyond what is plainly taught there. I am content to live and to die as the mere repeater of Scriptural teaching : as a person who has thought out nothing, and invented nothing ; as one who never thought that to be any part of his calling ; but who concluded that he was to take the message from the lips of God to the best of his ability, and simply to be a mouth for God to the people, mourning much that anything of his own should come between, but never thinking that he was somehow to refine that message to adapt it to the brilliance of this wonderful century, and then to hand it out as being so much his own that he might take some share of the glory of it. Nay, nay ; we have aimed at nothing of the kind. "I have declared *Thy* faithfulness and *Thy* salvation : I have not concealed *Thy* lovingkindness and *Thy* truth from the great congregation." Nothing have we preached as our own. If there has been anything of our own, we do bitterly take back those words, and eat them, and repent that ever we should have been guilty of such sin and folly. The things which we have learned of God our Father, and of His Son Jesus Christ, by His Holy Spirit, we have sought to speak unto you.

Now, dear friends, let me say, next, that this text describes *a work which has been done under great difficulties.* It does seem a very easy thing simply to have a message and to tell it. Yes, it appears so ; but it is not so easy as it

looks at first sight. I do not suppose that you always find
your servants deliver your messages accurately. Did you
ever sit round a table, and tell one person a story, and
ask him to tell it to his neighbour? Let each one whisper it;
and by the time it gets to the end of the table you will not
know the story at all; it will have been altered so much.
There is a tendency in the minds of all of us to alter what
we tell, and it is a struggle to keep to the exact truth.
Besides, this is an age which likes pretty things, and something fresh and new; and it is not easy always to swim up-
stream, and to go against the tendency of the times, and the
spirit of the age. We have no particular desire to be thought
fools any more than anybody else; and we know where all
the wisdom is; at least, we ought to know, for we hear
often enough about it. Ask the brethren of the "modern
thought" school if they have not all the wisdom that is to
be had nowadays. If they do not say that they have, many
of them act as if they thought they had. No, friends, it
is not so easy, after all, just to keep to the plain truth.
There is a brother who has struck out something wonderfully fresh. We read his book; shall we not at least go
with him a little way? You shall find, brethren, that if you
determine to hold fast the faith once for all delivered to
the saints, you will have a battle to fight, in which you will
be beaten unless you rely upon God for strength. If you
are willing to let truth go, well, it is a small matter of
neglect, and it is soon done; and then you will be greeted
with, "Hail fellow! Well met." But if you mean to
declare God's truth, you will need His help in the struggle.

But, although this testimony is borne under difficulties,
it is attended with unutterable pleasure. Oh, the delight of
preaching the gospel! I often say to young men who

apply for admission to the College, "Don't you become a minister if you can help it." And I say to everybody,— Do not become a minister if you can help it; but if you cannot help it, if a divine destiny drives you on, thank God that it is so! You are a happier man, if you are able to preach the gospel, than if you had been elected to a throne. There is no business like it under heaven. I have heard some say that our professional study of the Word of God may be a hindrance to our growth in the divine life. I know what they mean, and there is some truth in their words; but to me, the preaching of the gospel has been a continual means of grace, and I can say with the Apostle Paul, "Unto me, who am less than the least of all saints, is this *grace* given, that I should preach among the Gentiles the unsearchable riches of Christ." It really is a grace to be permitted to preach the gospel, and it brings grace with it. Brethren in the ministry, have you not read the Bible much more because you have had to preach the blessed truths revealed in it? Have you not been driven to your knees much more because you have had to deal with anxious souls, and to lead the people of God? I am sure that it is so; and I thank God for having a calling which does not take me away from the mercy-seat, but drives me to it. I am grateful that I have a message which I am glad to tell, glad to tell anywhere, a message which never needs to be concealed, but which brings joy to us in telling it, and salvation to our hearers in listening to it. Blessed be God that we have such a story to tell!

I could say much more about this first point, but I must not, for our time is so short. This must suffice upon the continual testimony.

II. Now, secondly, the text mentions A REMARKABLE

AUDIENCE. The psalmist says, twice over, "I have preached righteousness in *the great congregation ;*" and yet again, "I have not concealed Thy lovingkindness and Thy truth from *the great congregation.*"

It is *astonishing to the preacher* that there should be a great congregation to hear the gospel. I do not know how you think of it, but if anybody had been set here to speak so many times a week, the same person, for twenty-five years, and he had been speaking upon politics, I wonder whether he would have had a crowded congregation at the end of the time. My friend Mr. Varley speaks right mightily ; but if he had been preaching upon total abstinence for twenty-five years, I am sure that some would have totally abstained from coming to hear him. If I had had to preach here upon—well, what topic shall I say ?—the object that the Liberation Society has in view, I am afraid that I should have liberated many of you from attendance long before this. All other subjects are exhaustible ; but give us that Book, and give us the Holy Ghost, and we may preach on for ever. We shall never get to the end of it. I have heard of two infidels, one of whom said to his fellow, "If you had to go to jail for twelve months, and you could only have one book, what book would you choose?" He was very surprised when his companion said, "Oh, I should take the Bible !" The first one said, "But you do not believe in it ; I wonder that you should choose it." "Oh ! but," rejoined his friend, "it is no end of a book." And so it is. It is "no end of a book." Jerome used to say, "I adore the infinity of Holy Scripture ;" and well he might. Now, you should look at my Bible at home, marked with all the texts I have preached from. There are thirty-one completed volumes of my sermons ; thirty-two is going on. Well, I have all those texts marked from which I have preached. Of course, in addition to the thirty-two volumes in the regular weekly series, there are many more volumes printed. I sometimes make the outline of a sermon, and then, when I turn to my Bible, I find that I have preached from that text, and the sermon has been published, and I say, " That will not do for a Sunday morning." I do not want to have the same subject again oftener than I can help; but the same text may be taken, and a new sermon readily enough made from it, for there is a springing well in Holy Scripture, never exhausted. The great congregation wants continually to come to hear repetitions of the same thing. Young man, just beginning to preach, do not be afraid to stick to your texts. That is the best way to get variety in your discourses. Saturate your sermons with Bibline, the essence of Bible truth, and you will always have something new to say.

But the great congregation, when I think of it, *how encouraging it is!* It is always good fishing where there are plenty of fish. We are bound to go and angle for a single soul, wherever there is one to be found. Some do great service for the Master who take the fish one by one ; but oh, what a delight it is to have the great seine-net of the gospel, and throw it into such a lake as this, God being with you ! How encouraging it is !

But then, dear friends, when we think of this great con-gregation, *what solemn thoughts come over one's mind !* I come down to this platform sometimes, and get another look at this great congregation, and I am staggered. Time after time I have felt as if I could run away sooner than face this tremendous throng again, and speak to them once more. O sirs, to think of all these being dying men and dying women, and to think that this gospel that I preach is needed by them all, and may be refused by many with awful consequences, and may be accepted by some (it will be, thank God) with consequences of unutterable joy! To think that we shall have to give an account of how we have preached, and how you have heard! To think that we shall all meet again at the judgment-seat, to give an account of every Sunday and every Thursday service! If Xerxes could not restrain a tear at the thought of his myriads of men passing away, who can look at congregations like this without being moved with compassion? Yes, yes; it is not easy to preach to a great congregation so as to be able to say at the last, " I am pure from the blood of all men, for I have not shunned to declare unto you all the counsel of God."

The sight of this great congregation gathered to-night *suggests many memories.* I recollect some dear ones that used to sit here, and there, and there, and there. I can almost see them now; some dear grey heads, that used to be our glory, that are now with God; some young and ardent spirits, that were taken away before they reached their prime. You sit where sat some who loved your Master well, and served Him faithfully. Worthily occupy their places, beloved friends.

But excuse me if I say no more upon this topic. My brain seems in a whirl, as dissolving views pass before my memory in quick succession. If you want to see life and death, stand here. I feel like the captain of a vessel on the bridge. I am looking down on you who are the passengers and crew; but yet, from another point of view, I seem to be looking at real waves that sweep by, and more come, and others follow; ever a succession of changes, nothing abiding. How long shall we abide? How soon shall we, too, also go? Well, it is something to have preached Christ to this great congregation. It is something to believe that those who have not received Him are without excuse. It is much better to believe that many have received Him, and that we shall meet them in the glory-land, rejoicing in that glorious sacrifice by which they have been cleansed from sin, in that dear Saviour by whose life and death they have been quickened, and made heirs of eternal glory.

III. I have only a very few minutes left, in which to expatiate upon the last point, and that is, THE SUGGESTED PRAYER. May I just give you an outline of what I would have said if we could have spared more time? The prayer of the psalmist is,—" Withhold not Thou Thy tender mercies from me, O Lord : let Thy lovingkindness and Thy truth "—the things which he had preached—" continually preserve me."

This prayer is *suitable for the preacher*, and he prays it now. Taking David's words, and making them my own, I pray to the Lord at this moment,—" Withhold not Thou Thy tender mercies from *me*, O Lord : let Thy loving-kindness and Thy truth continually preserve *me*."

The prayer is also *suitable for every Christian here*. Let me read it, and let every Christian pray it now : " Withhold not Thou Thy tender mercies from *me*, O Lord : let Thy lovingkindness and Thy truth continually preserve *me*."

With a little alteration, *this prayer may suit you who are not yet saved*, but who desire to be : " Withhold not Thou Thy tender mercies from *me*, O Lord." Are you praying it? Is not this a good night in which to pray that prayer? The signs are all propitious. There is " the

sound of a going in the tops of the mulberry-trees." There
are tokens for good abroad. There is dew about to-night.
Now, therefore, pray this prayer if thou hast never prayed
before ; and God help thee to claim the answer by appro-
priating faith !

It seems to me that this prayer was suggested to the
psalmist by at least three things.

First, *it was suggested by the great congregation.* David
seems to say, "O Lord, there are so many, but withhold
not Thy tender mercies from me."

> " Lord, I hear of showers of blessing
> Thou art scattering, full and free ;
> Showers, the thirsty land refreshing ;
> Let some droppings fall on me,
>   Even me."

Next, *the subject suggested it.* " Thy truth, Thy lovingkindness, O Lord ; let these preserve me. I hear of Thy
goodness ; I cannot bear to miss it. I hear of Thy truth ;
I would not be a stranger to it. Lord, bless even me ! "

Then there was another cause why David specially put
up such a prayer as that—*the future suggested it.* The
psalmist expected to suffer great trials and serious afflictions,
and therefore he prayed, " Let Thy lovingkindness and Thy
truth continually preserve me."

Now, as a congregation, we have completed twenty-five
years in this building ; but we must not reckon that we
have got to the end of our struggles, or even to the end of
our sins. O brothers and sisters, this is only a part of the
way to heaven. I think that I told you, once before, that
some friends, when they raise an Ebenezer, sit down on
the top of it, and say, " Here we are going to stop." I
remember that that night I put a sharp iron spike on the

top of "the stone of help," that nobody might sit upon it; and I do the same again. Let none of us sit down at the end of this twenty-fifth year, and say, "We have come so far, and here we are going to stay." Long nights of darkness lie beyond, there are giants to be fought, mountains to be climbed, rivers to be crossed. Who dreams of ease, while he is here in the enemy's country? Out with your sword, man! You have not done with the battle. Awake, thou that sleepest! Thou hast not come yet to the place of resting. This is the place for watching, and praying, and wrestling, and struggling. Therefore do we pray, "Withhold not Thou Thy tender mercies from me." We are getting older; we are getting weaker; we are, perhaps, getting sillier. Who knows that all our years will bring us good news? They may bring us evil if we trust to our past experience. We want God now as much with us as ever we did. Therefore let us cry to Him, "From this night do Thou bless us more and more."

The poor psalmist was in great trouble when he prayed this prayer. He says, "Innumerable evils have compassed me about." Therefore he says, "Withhold not Thou Thy tender mercies from me."

He adds, "Mine iniquities have taken hold upon me." If there is one here whose conscience is accusing him, and who is guilty before his God, let him pray this prayer because of his iniquities.

He goes on to say, "I am not able to look up." If that is your case, if you cannot look up, pray the Lord to look down, and cry to Him never to take His mercy from you.

David further says, concerning his iniquities, "They are more than the hairs of my head : therefore my heart faileth

me." Well, when our heart does fail us, let us recollect the
mercy which has helped us so long, and let us cast ourselves
again upon that mercy for all that lies before us.

I am not going to venture upon any prophecy. I
attended, on Wednesday, the funeral of our beloved brother
Dr. Stanford. You may attend mine before this year is
over; or I may attend yours. If you could draw up the
curtain that hides the future, you would not wish to do it,
would you? But be just so that, if you live, you are
prepared to live; and if you die, you are prepared to die.
I think that the best thing you can do is to do the next
thing that comes to you, and to do it thoroughly well. I
was here last Monday. I had no rest from spiritual work
from three in the afternoon till half-past nine at night; and
about the middle of it I felt, "Well, I do not know how I
shall get through this long, long afternoon of seeing enquirers
and candidates for Church-fellowship." And I said to a
brother, "How am I to do it all?" However, there was a.
cup of tea in front of me, and I said, "I think I will drink
that tea; that is the next thing to be done." Oftentimes
that will be your best course, just do the next thing you can
do when you are saying to yourself, "How shall I do if I
live to be old?" When you go home to-night, eat your
supper, and go to bed to the glory of God; and when you
get up in the morning, do not think about what you are
going to do at night. Do what comes to you when you
begin the day's work, and keep right straight on. If you
can see a step at a time, that is about as far as you need
to see. Do not begin prying into the future; but just go
straight on from day to day, depending on God for the
mercy and grace and strength of the day. That is the
way to live, and I am persuaded that is the way to die.

Mr. Wesley said, "If I knew that I was to die to-night, and I had an engagement to attend such a class-meeting, I should go to it. I have promised to call and see old Betty So-and-so on the way back. I should call in to see her. I have then to go home, and have family prayer. I would do that. Then I should take my boots off, and I should go to bed, just as I am going to do if I am not going to die." Oh, do not let death be a sort of addition to the programme, which was not calculated upon; but so live that whenever it comes—if it come while we are sitting here to-night—you are ready for it. Then yours will be a happy life, a joyful life, a useful life. Secularism teaches us that we ought to look to this world. Christianity teaches us that the best way to prepare for this world is to be fully prepared for the next. Why, it elevates and glorifies the secularism, which else would trail in the mire, if our con-versation, our citizenship, is in heaven, even while we are on the earth. God bless you, beloved! Let us praise His name for all the mercies of the past quarter of a century, and trust His grace for all the future.

THE HOLY SPIRIT GLORIFY-
ING CHRIST.

THE HOLY SPIRIT GLORI-
FYING CHRIST.

Preached at the Metropolitan Tabernacle on Lord's-day evening,
April 12, 1891.

"He shall glorify Me : for He shall receive of Mine, and shall shew it unto you."—JOHN xvi. 14.

THE needs of spiritual men are very great, but they cannot be greater than the power of the divine Trinity is able to meet. We have one God,—Father, Son, and Holy Ghost,—one in three and three in one; and that blessed Trinity in unity gives Himself to sinners that they may be saved. In the first place, every good thing that a sinner wants is in the Father. The prodigal son was wise when he said, "I will arise, and go to my father." Every good and perfect gift comes from God the Father, the first Person in the blessed Trinity, because every good gift and every perfect gift can only be found in Him. But the needy soul says, "How shall I get to the Father? He is infinitely above me. How shall I reach up to Him?" In order that you might obtain the blessings of grace, God was in Christ Jesus, the second ever-blessed Person of the sacred Trinity. Let me read you part of the verse that follows my text: "All things that the Father hath are

Mine." So, you see, everything is in the Father first; and the Father puts all things into Christ. "It pleased the Father that in Him should all fulness dwell." Now you can get to Christ because He is man as well as God. He is "God over all, blessed for ever;" but He came into this world, was born of the Virgin Mary, lived a life of poverty, "suffered under Pontius Pilate, was crucified, dead, and buried." He is the conduit-pipe, conveying to us all blessings from the Father. In the Gospel of John we read, "Of His fulness have all we received, and grace for grace." Thus you see the Father, with every good thing in Himself, putting all fulness into the Mediator, the Man Christ Jesus who is also the Son of God.

Now I hear a poor soul say, "But I cannot even get to Christ; I am blind and lame. If I could get to Him, He would open my eyes; but I am so lame that I cannot run or even walk to Him. If I could get to Him, He would give me strength; but I lie as one dead. I cannot see Christ, or tell where to find Him." Here comes in the work of the Holy Spirit, the third Person of the blessed unity. It is His office to take of the things of Christ, and show them unto saints and sinners, too. We cannot see them, but we shall see them fast enough when He shows them to us. Our sin puts a veil between us and Christ. The Holy Spirit comes and takes the veil away from our heart, and then we see Christ. It is the Holy Spirit's office to come between us and Christ, to lead us to Christ, even as the Son of God comes between us and the Father, to lead us to the Father; so that we have the whole Trinity uniting to save a sinner, the triune God bowing down out of heaven for the salvation of rebellious men. Every time we dismiss you from this house of prayer, we pronounce upon you the

blessing of the sacred Trinity: "May the grace of our
Lord Jesus Christ, and the love of God, and the communion
of the Holy Ghost be with you!" And you want all that to
make a sinner into a saint, and to keep a saint from going
back to be a sinner again. The whole blessed Godhead,
Father, Son, and Holy Spirit, must work upon every soul
that is ever to be saved.

See how divinely they work together—how the Father
glorifies the Son, how the Holy Spirit glorifies Jesus, how
both the Holy Spirit and the Lord Jesus glorify the Father!
These three are one, sweetly uniting in the salvation of the
chosen seed.

To-night our work is to speak of the Holy Spirit. Oh,
what a blessed Person He is; not merely a sacred influence, but a divine Person, "very God of very God."
He is the Spirit of holiness to be reverenced, to be
spoken of with delight, yet with trembling; for remember,
there is a sin against the Holy Ghost. A word spoken
against the Son of man may be forgiven, but blasphemy
against the Holy Ghost (whatever that may be, I know not,)
is put down as a sin beyond the line of divine forgiveness.
Therefore reverence, honour, and worship God the Holy
Spirit, in whom lies the only hope that any of us can ever
have of seeing Jesus, and so of seeing God the Father.

First, to-night, I shall try to speak of *what the Holy
Spirit does:* "He shall receive of Mine, and shall shew it
unto you;" secondly, I shall seek to set forth *what the
Holy Spirit aims at:* "He shall glorify Me: for He shall
receive of Mine, and shall shew it unto you;" and, thirdly,
I shall explain how *in both these things He acts as the Comforter,* for we read, in the seventh verse, that our Saviour
says, "If I go not away, the Comforter will not come unto

you;" and it is of the Comforter that He says, "He shall glorify Me: for He shall receive of Mine, and shall shew it unto you." Much of our time has already gone, therefore I will be studiedly brief. But I want to talk personally to every one of my hearers to-night. You have come through the wet to hear the gospel. Now do hear it; and God grant that you may hear it with your inner as well as with your outer ears!

I. First, we are to consider, WHAT THE HOLY SPIRIT DOES. Jesus says, "He shall receive of Mine, and shall shew it unto you."

The Holy Ghost, then, *deals with the things of Christ.* How I wish that all Christ's ministers would imitate the Holy Spirit in this respect! When you are dealing with the things of Christ, you are on Holy Ghost ground; you are following the track of the Holy Spirit. Does the Holy Ghost deal with science? What is science? Another name for the ignorance of men. Does the Holy Ghost deal with politics? What are politics? Another name for every man getting as much as he can out of the nation. Does the Holy Ghost deal with these things? Nay, my brethren, " He shall receive of Mine." Oh, my brother, the Holy Ghost will leave you if you go gadding about after these insignificant trifles! He will leave you, if you are for magnifying yourself, and your wisdom, and your plans; for the Holy Spirit is taken up with the things of Christ. " He shall receive of Mine, and shall shew it unto you." I like what Mr. Wesley said to his preachers. "Leave other things alone," said he; "you are called to win souls." So I believe it is with all true preachers. We may let other things alone. The Holy Ghost, who is our Teacher, will own and bless us if we keep to His line of things. O preacher of the gospel, what canst thou receive like the things of Christ? And what canst thou talk of so precious to the souls of men as the things of Christ? Therefore, follow thou the Holy Ghost in dealing with the things of Christ.

Next, the Holy Spirit *deals with feeble men.* "He shall receive of Mine, and shall shew it unto you." "Unto you." He is not above dealing with simple minds. He comes to those who have no training, no education, and He takes the things of Christ, and shows them to such minds. The greatest mind of man that was ever created was a poor puny thing compared with the infinite mind of God. We may boast about the great capacity of the human intellect; but what a narrow and contracted thing it is at its utmost width! and for the Holy Spirit to come and teach the little mind of man, is a great condescension. But we see the condescension of the Holy Ghost even more when we read, "Not many wise men after the flesh, not many mighty, not many noble, are called;" and when we hear the Saviour say, "I thank thee, O Father, Lord of heaven and earth, because Thou hast hid these things from the wise and prudent, and hast revealed them unto babes." The Holy Ghost takes of the things of Christ, and shows them to those who are babes compared with the wise men of this world. The Lord Jesus might have selected princes to be His apostles; He might have gathered together twelve of the greatest kings of the earth, or at least twelve senators from Rome; but He did not so. He took fishermen, and men belonging to that class, to be the pioneers of His kingdom; and God the Holy Ghost takes of the things of Christ, high and sublime as they are, and shows them unto men like these apostles were, men ready to follow where

the Lord led them, and to learn what the Lord was willing
to teach them.

If you think of the condescension of the Holy Spirit in
taking of the things of Christ, and showing them unto us,
you will not talk any more about coming down to the level
of children when you talk to them. I remember a young
man who was a great fool, but did not know it, and therefore was all the greater fool; once, speaking to children,
he said, "My dear children, it takes a great deal to
bring a great mind down to your capacities." You cannot
show me a word of Christ of that kind. Where does the
Holy Ghost ever talk about its being a great come-down
for Him to teach children, or to teach us? Nay, nay;
but He glorifies Christ by taking of His things, and showing
them unto us, even such poor ignorant scholars as we are.

If I understand what is meant here, I think that it
means, first, that the Holy Ghost *helps us to understand
the words of Christ.* If we will study the teaching of the
Saviour, it must be with the Holy Spirit as the light to
guide us; He will show us what Christ meant by the words
He uttered. We shall not lose ourselves in the Saviour's
verbiage; but we shall get at the inner meaning of Christ's
mind, and be instructed therein; for the Lord Jesus says,
"He shall receive of Mine, and shall shew it unto you." A
sermon of Christ, even a single word of Christ, set in the
light of the Holy Spirit, shines like a diamond; nay, like a
fixed star, with light that is never dim. Happy men and
happy women who read the words of Christ in the light
shed upon them by the Holy Ghost! But I do not think
that this is all that the text means.

It means this: "Not only shall He reveal My words,
but My *things;*" for Christ says, "All things that the

Father hath are Mine: therefore said I, that He shall take of Mine, and shall shew it unto you."

Now, while I talk very briefly upon this important theme, try to follow me, and may the Holy Spirit help us all to learn what Christ means.

The Holy Ghost takes the *nature* of Christ, and shows it unto us. It is easy to say, "I believe Him to be God and man;" but the point is, to apprehend that He is God, and therefore able to save, and even to work impossibilities; and to believe that He is man, and therefore feels for you, sympathizes with you, and is a brother born to help you in your adversities. May the Holy Ghost make you see the God-Man to-night! May He show you the humanity and the Deity of Christ, as they are most blessedly united in His adorable person; and you will be greatly comforted thereby.

The Holy Ghost shows to us the *offices* of Christ. He is Prophet, Priest, King. Especially to you, sinner, Christ is a Saviour. Now, if you know that He takes up the work of saving sinners, and that it is His business to save men, why then, dear friend, surely you will have confidence in Him, and not be afraid to come to Him! If I wanted my shoes mended, I should not take my hat off when I went into a cobbler's shop, and say, "Please excuse me. May I beg you to be so good as to mend my shoes?" No, it is his trade; it is his business. He is glad to see me. "What do you want, sir?" says he; and he is glad of work. And when Christ puts over His door, "Saviour," I, wanting to be saved, go to Him, for I believe that He knows His calling, and that He can carry it out, and that He will be glad to see me, and that I shall not be more glad to be saved than He will be to save me. I want you to catch that idea. If the Holy Spirit will show you that, it will bring you very near to joy and peace to-night.

May the Holy Ghost also show you Christ's *engagements*. He has come into the world engaged to save sinners. He pledged Himself to the Father to bring many sons unto glory, and He must do it. He has bound Himself to His Father, as the Surety of the covenant, that He will bring sinners into reconciliation with God. May the Holy Ghost show that fact to you; and right gladly you will leap into the Saviour's arms !

It is very sweet when the Holy Spirit also shows us the *love* of Christ—how intensely He loves men, how He loved them of old, for His delights were with the sons of men —not because He had redeemed them ; but He redeemed them because He loved them, and delighted in them. Christ has had an eternal love to His people.

> " His heart is made of tenderness,
>   His bowels melt with love."

It is His heaven to bring men to heaven. It is His glory to bring sons to glory. He is never so happy as when He is receiving sinners. But if the Holy Ghost will show you the depth and the height, the length and the breadth, of the love of Christ to sinners, it will go a long way towards bringing all who are in this house to-night to accept the Saviour.

But when the Holy Ghost shows you the *mercy* of Christ —how willingly He forgives ; how He passes by iniquity, transgression, and sin ; how He casts your sins into the sea, throws them behind God's back, puts them away for ever ;— ah ! when you see this, then will your hearts be won to Him.

Specially I would desire the Holy Ghost to show you the *blood* of Christ. A Spirit-taught view of the blood of

Christ is the most wonderful sight that ever a weeping eye beheld. There is your sin, your wicked, horrible, damnable sin; but Christ comes into the world, and takes the sin, and suffers in your room and place and stead; and the blood of such a one as He, perfect man and infinite God—such blood as was poured out on Calvary's tree—must take away sin. Oh, for a sight of it! If any of you are now despairing, and the Holy Ghost will take of the blood of Christ, and show it unto you, despair will have no place in you any longer. It must be gone, for "the blood of Jesus Christ His Son cleanseth us from all sin," and he that believeth in Him is forgiven all his iniquities.

And if the Holy Ghost will also take of the *prayers* of Christ, and show them unto you, what a sight you will have! Christ on earth, praying till He gets into a bloody sweat; Christ in heaven, praying with all His glorious vestments on, accepted by the Father, glorified at the Father's right hand, and making intercession for transgressors, praying for you, praying for all who come to God by Him, and able, therefore, to save them to the uttermost;—this is the sight you will have. A knowledge of the intercession of Christ for guilty men is enough to make despair flee away once for all. I can only tell you these things; but if the Holy Ghost will take of them, and show them unto you, oh, beloved, you will have joy and peace to-night through believing!

One thing I must add, however, and then I will leave this point, upon which we could dilate for six months, I think; that is, that *whatever the Holy Ghost shows you, you may have.* Do you see that? He takes of the things of Christ, and shows them to us; but why? Not as a boy at school

does to one of his companions when he is teasing him.
I remember often seeing it done.   He pulls out of his
pocket a beautiful apple, and shows it to his schoolmate.
"There," says he, "do you see that apple?   Is he going to
say, "Now I am going to give you a piece of it"?   No,
not he.   He only shows him the apple just to tantalize him.
Now, it would be blasphemy to imagine that the Holy
Ghost would show you the things of Christ, and then say,
"You cannot have them."   No, whatever He shows you,
you may have.   Whatever you see in Christ, you may have.
Whatever the Holy Ghost makes you to see in the person
and work of the Lord Jesus, you may have it.   And He
shows it to you on purpose that you may have it, for He is
no Tantalus to mock us with the sight of a blessing beyond
our reach; He waits to bless us.   Lay that thought up in
your heart; it may help you some day, if not now.   You
remember what God said to Jacob, "The land whereon
thou liest, to thee will I give it."   If you find any promise
in this Book, and you dare to lie down upon it, it is
yours.   If you can just lie down and rest on it, it is
yours; for it was not put there for you to rest on it
without its being fulfilled to you.   Only stretch thyself
on any covenant blessing, and it is yours for ever.   God
help us so to do!

II.   But now, secondly, and very briefly, let us consider,
WHAT THE HOLY SPIRIT AIMS AT.   Well, He aims at this,
Jesus says, "He shall glorify Me."   When He shows us
the things of Christ, His object is to glorify Christ.   The
Holy Spirit's object is to make Christ appear to be great
and glorious to you and to me.   The Lord Jesus Christ is
infinitely glorious; and even the Holy Ghost cannot make
Him glorious except to our apprehension; but His desire

is that we may see and know more of Christ, that we may honour Him more, and glorify Him more.

Well, how does the Holy Spirit go about this work? In this simple way, by *showing us the things of Christ.* Is not this a blessedly simple fact, that when even the Holy Ghost intends to glorify Christ, all that He does is to show us Christ? Well, but does He not put fine words together, and weave a spell of eloquence? No; He simply shows us Christ. Now, if you wanted to praise Jesus Christ to-night, what would you have to do? Why, you would only have to speak of Him as He is—holy, blessed, glorious! You would show Him, as it were, in order to praise Him, for there is no glorifying Christ except by making Him to be seen. Then He has the glory that rightly belongs to Him. No words are wanted, no descriptions are needed. "He shall glorify Me: for He shall receive of Mine, and shall shew it unto you."

And is it not strange that Christ should be glorified by His *being shown to you?* *To you,* my dear friend! Perhaps you are saying, "I am a nobody." Yes, but Christ is glorified by being shown to you. "Oh, but I am very poor, very illiterate, and besides, very wicked!" Yes, but Christ is glorified by being shown to you. Now, a great king or a great queen would not be rendered much more illustrious by being shown to a little Sunday-school girl, or exhibited to a crossing-sweeper boy. At least, they would not think so; but Christ does not act as an earthly monarch might. He reckons it to be His glory for the poorest pair of eyes that ever wept to look by faith upon Him. He reckons it to be His greatest honour for the poorest man, the poorest woman, or the poorest child that ever lived, to see Him in the light in which the Holy Ghost sets Him. Is not this a blessed truth? I put it very simply and briefly. The Holy Ghost, you see, glorifies Christ by showing Him to sinners. Therefore, if you want to glorify Christ, do the same. Do not go and write a ponderous tome, and put fine words together. Tell sinners, in simple language, what Christ is. "I cannot praise Him," says one. You do not want to praise Him. Say what He is. If a man says to me, "Show me the sun," do I say, "Well, you must wait till I strike a match and light a candle, and then I will show you the sun"? That would be ridiculous, would it not? And for our candles to be held up to show Christ, is absurd. Tell what He is. Tell what He is to you. Tell what He did for you. Tell what He did for sinners. That is all. "He shall glorify Me: for He shall receive of Mine, and shall shew it unto you."

I will not say more on this point, except that if any one of us is to glorify Christ, we must talk much of Him. We must tell what the Holy Spirit has told to us; and we must pray the Holy Spirit to bless to the minds of men the truth we speak, by enabling them to see Christ as the Spirit reveals Him.

III. But now, thirdly, in both of these things,—showing unto us the things of Christ, and glorifying Christ,—THE HOLY SPIRIT IS A COMFORTER. Gracious Spirit, be a Comforter now to some poor struggling ones in the Tabernacle, by showing them the things of Christ, and by glorifying Him in their salvation!

First, in showing to men the things of Christ the Holy Spirit is a Comforter. *There is no comfort like a sight of Christ.* Sinner, your only comfort must lie in your Saviour, in His precious blood, and in His resurrection from the

dead.   Look that way, man !   If you look inside, you will
never find any comfort there.   Look where the Holy Ghost
looks.   "He shall receive of Mine, and shall shew it unto
you."   When a thing is shown to you, it is meant for you
to look at it.   If you want real comfort, I will tell you
where to look, namely, to the person and work of the Lord
Jesus Christ.   "Oh !"   say you, "but I am a wretched
person."   I know you are.   You are a great deal worse
than you think you are.   "Oh, but I think myself the worst
that ever lived."   Yes, you are worse than that !   You do
not know half your depravity.   You are worse than you
ever dreamed that you were.   But that is not where to look
for comfort.   "I am brutish," says one; "I am proud; I
am self-righteous; I am envious; I have everything in me
that is bad, sir, and if I have a little bit that is good
sometimes, it is gone before I can see it.   I am just
lost, ruined, and undone."   That is quite true; but I
never told you to look there.   Your comfort lies in this,
"He shall receive of Mine,"—that is of Christ's—"and
shall shew it unto you."   Your hope of transformation,
of gaining a new character altogether, of eternal life, lies
in Christ, who quickeneth the dead, and maketh all things
new.   Look away from self, and look to Christ, for He alone
can save you.

 A sight of Christ is the destruction of despair.   "Oh, but
the devil tells me that I shall be cast into hell !   There is
no hope for me."   What matters it what the devil tells
you?   He was a liar from the beginning.   Let him say
what he likes; but if you will look away to Christ, there will
be an end of the devil's power over you.   If the Holy Ghost
shows you what Christ came to do on the cross, and what
he is doing on His throne in heaven, there will be an end

to these troublous thoughts from Satan, and you will be comforted.

Dear child of God, are you *in sorrow* to-night? May the Holy Ghost take of the things of Christ, and show them unto you! There is an end to sorrow when you see Jesus, for sorrow itself is so sweetly sanctified by the companionship of Christ which it brings to you, that you will be glad to drink of His cup and to be baptized with His baptism.

Are you *in want* to-night, without even a place where to lay your head? So, too, was He. " The Son of man hath not where to lay His head." Go to Him with your trouble. He will help you to bear your poverty. He will help you to get out of it, for He is able to help you in temporal trials as well as in spiritual ones. Therefore go you to Christ. All power is given unto Him in heaven and in earth. Nothing is too hard for the Lord. Go your way to Him, and a sight of Him will give you comfort.

Are you *persecuted ?* Well, a sight of the thorn-crowned brow will take the thorn out of persecution. Are you very, very low? I think that you have all heard the story I am about to tell you, but some of you have, perhaps, forgotten it. Many years ago, when this great congregation first met in the Surrey Music Hall, and the terrible accident occurred, when many persons were either killed or wounded in the panic, I did my best to hold the people together till I heard that some were dead, and then I broke down like a man stunned, and for a fortnight or so I had little reason left. I felt so broken in heart that I thought that I should never be able to face a congregation again ; and I went down to a friend's house, a few miles away, to be very quiet and still. I was walking round his garden, and I well remember the spot, and even the time, when this passage came to me, " Him hath God exalted with His right hand to be a Prince and a Saviour ; " and this thought came into my mind at once, "You are only a soldier in the great King's army, and you may die in a ditch; but it does not matter what becomes of you as long as your King is exalted. *He*—HE is glorious. God hath highly exalted Him." You have heard of the old French soldiers when they lay a-dying. If the emperor came by, when they were ready to expire, they would just raise themselves up and give one more cheer for their beloved leader. " *Vive l'Empereur !* " would be their dying words. And so I just thought, " *He* is exalted. What matters it about me ? " and in a moment my reason was perfectly restored. I was as clear as possible. I went into the house, had family prayer, and came back to preach to my congregation on the following Sabbath, restored only by having looked to Jesus, and having seen that He was glorious. If He is to the front, what does it matter what happens to us? Rank on rank we will die in the battle if He wins the victory. Only let the Man on the White Horse win ; let the King who died for us, and washed us in His precious blood, be glorified, and it is enough for us.

Thus, you see, when the Holy Ghost takes of the things of Christ, and shows them unto us, He acts as a Comforter in His very best and most effectual way.

But now, lastly, *when Christ is glorified in the heart, He acts as a Comforter, too.* I believe, brethren, that we should not have half the trouble that we have if we thought more of Christ. The fact is, that we think so much of ourselves that we get troubled. But some one says, " But I have so many troubles." Why should you not have a great many troubles? Who are you that you should not have troubles? "Oh, but I have had loss after loss which you do not know of!" Very likely, dear friend. I do not know of your losses, but is it any wonder that you should have then? "Oh!" says one, "I seem kicked about like a football." Why should you not be? What are you? "Oh!" said one poor penitent to me the other night, "for me to come to Christ, sir, after my past life, seems so mean." I said, "Yes, so it is; but, then, you *are* mean. It was a mean business of the prodigal son to come home, and eat his father's bread and the fatted calf after he had spent his substance in riotous living." It was a mean thing, was it not? But, then, the father did not think it mean. He clasped him to his bosom, and welcomed him home. Come along, you mean sinners, you that have served the devil, and now want to run away from him! Steal away from Satan at once, for my Lord is ready to receive you. You have no idea how willing He is to welcome you. He is so ready to forgive, that you have not yet guessed how much sin He can forgive. "All manner of sin and blasphemy shall be forgiven unto men." Up to your necks in filth, in your very hearts saturated with the foulest iniquity; yet, if you come to Christ, He will wash you whiter than snow. "Come now, and let us reason together, saith the Lord: though your sins be as scarlet, they shall be as white as snow; though they be red like crimson, they shall be as wool." Come along, and try my Lord. Have exalted ideas of Christ. Oh, if a man will but have great thoughts of Christ, he shall then find his troubles lessening, and his sins disappearing! You have been putting Christ on a wrong scale altogether, I see. Perhaps even you people of God have not thought of Christ as you ought to do. I have heard of

a certain commander who had led his troops into a rather
difficult position. He knew what he was at, but the
soldiers did not all know; and there would be a battle on
the morrow. So he thought that he would go round from
tent to tent, and hear what the soldiers said. He listened,
and there was one of them saying to his fellows, " See what
a mess we are in now ! Do you see, we have only so many
cavalry, and so many infantry, and we have only a small
quantity of artillery. And on the other side there are so
many thousands against us, so strong, so mighty, that we
shall be cut to pieces in the morning." And the general
drew aside the canvas, and there they saw him standing,
and he said, " How many do you count *me* for ? " He had
won every battle that he had ever been engaged in. He
was the conqueror of conquerers. " How many do you
count me for ? " O souls, you have never counted Christ
for what He is ! You have put down your sins, but you
have never counted what kind of a Christ He is who has
come to save you. Rather do like Luther, who says that
when the devil came to him, he brought him a long sheet
containing a list of his sins, or of a great number of them,
and Luther said to him, " Is that all ? " " No," said the
devil. " Well, go and fetch some more, then." Away went
Satan to bring him another long list, as long as your
arm. Said Luther, " Is that all ? " "Oh, no ! " said the
devil, " I have more yet." " Well, go and bring them all,"
said Luther. " Fetch them all out, the whole list of them."
Then it was a very long black list. I think that I have
heard that it would have gone round the world twice. I
know that mine would. Well, what did Luther say when
he saw them all? He said, " Write at the bottom of them,
' The blood of Jesus Christ His Son cleanseth us from all

sin !'." It does not matter how long the list is when you write those blessed words at the end of it. The sins are all gone then. Did you ever take up from your table a bill for a very large sum? You felt a kind of flush coming over your face. You looked down the list. It was a rather long list of items, perhaps, from a lawyer or a builder. But when you looked at it, you saw that there was a penny stamp at the bottom, and that the account was receipted. "Oh !" you said, "I do not care how long it is ; for it is all paid." So, though your sins are very many, if you have a receipt at the bottom,—if you have trusted Jesus,—your sins are all gone, drowned in the Red Sea of your Saviour's blood, and Christ is glorified in your salvation. May God the Holy Ghost bring every unsaved one here to-night to repentance and faith in our Lord Jesus Christ! The Lord bless every one of you, for His name's sake ! Amen.

BIBLIOGRAPHY.

[Except where otherwise stated, the following works are all published by Messrs. Passmore and Alabaster, Paternoster Buildings, London.

An asterisk (*) denotes that the work is out of print.]

The New Park Street Pulpit. 1855–61. Sermons, etc.

* *" Come, ye Children."* A Sermon on Psalm xxxiv. 11. Addressed to Sunday-school Teachers. 1856.

* *Six Sermons, with other Articles from " The Baptist Messenger."* 1856.

* *Sermons delivered in Exeter Hall, Strand.* Selected from "The New Park Street Pulpit." 1856.

* *The Pulpit Library.* Sermons, etc. 2 vols. 1856–58.

* *The New Park Street Library.* Edited by C. H. Spurgeon. 1856.

Spurgeon's Penny Illustrated Almanack. Edited by C. H. Spurgeon. 1856–92.

* *Our National Sins.* A Sermon on Micah vi. 9. 1857.

The Saint and his Saviour; or, The Progress of the Soul in the Knowledge of Jesus. Hodder and Stoughton. 1857. New Editions, 1867, 1880, and 1889.

Fast-day Services, held in the Crystal Palace, Sydenham, October 7, 1857 ; consisting of prayers, hymns, exposition, and sermon. ("The New Park Street Pulpit.") 1857.

De Propaganda Fide. A Lecture before the Young Men's Christian Association. (See Young Men's Christian Association Lectures.) James Nisbet and Co. 1859.

Morning by Morning ; or, Daily Readings for the Family or the Closet. 1860. Fifteenth Thousand, 1878. One Hundred and Fifteenth Thousand, 1891.

* *The Great Social Evil.* A Sermon on John viii. 10, 11. 1860.

° *The Gorilla, and the Land he inhabits.* A Lecture. 1861.

* *Illustrious Lord Mayors.* A Lecture. 1861.

Metropolitan Tabernacle Pulpit. Sermons. 1862–92.

Counterfeits. A Lecture. (See Young Men's Christian Association Lectures.) James Nisbet and Co. 1862.

Gleanings among the Sheaves. 1864.

Spurgeon's Gems : being brilliant passages selected from Mr. Spurgeon's discourses. 1865.

The Sword and the Trowel. Edited by C. H. Spurgeon. 1865–92.

The Pleasant Catechism concerning Christ : with Pleasant Stories, Illustrations, and Hymns, etc. Preface by C. H. Spurgeon. 1865.

Rev. C. H. Spurgeon's Anecdotes and Stories. Collected and arranged by O. Creyton. Houlston and Sons. 1866.

Two Letters from Mr. Spurgeon. One to the Evangelical Alliance, signifying his withdrawal from that Association ; another to the Christian public, proving that his accusations are neither novel nor singular, etc. 1866.

Our Own Hymn-Book. A Collection of Psalms and Hymns for Public Worship. Compiled by C. H. Spurgeon. 1866.

Preface to Bunyan's *Water of Life.* 1868.

John Ploughman's Talk ; or, Plain Advice for Plain People. 1868. Three Hundred and Eightieth Thousand, 1892.

The Treasury of David : containing an Original Exposition of the Book of Psalms. 7 vols. 1870–85.

Feathers for Arrows ; or, Illustrations for Preachers and Teachers. 1870. Thirty-second Thousand, 1891.

Evening by Evening; or, Readings at Eventide for the Family or the Closet. 1870. Eighty-fifth Thousand, 1891.

The Interpreter; or, Scripture for Family Worship. Arranged and annotated by C. H. Spurgeon. With Hymns. 1873.

* *My Run to Naples and Pompeii.* A Lecture, etc. 1873.

Types and Emblems: being a collection of sermons at the Metropolitan Tabernacle, etc. 1873.

The Interpreter Hymn-Book. To be used in connection with *The Interpreter Family Bible.* 1874.

Our Own Penny Hymn-Book: being Hymns selected from *Our Own Hymn-Book.* 1874.

Flashes of Thought: being One Thousand Extracts from the works of C. H. Spurgeon, alphabetically arranged. 1874.

Lectures to my Students. First Series, 1875. Thirty-fourth Thousand. Second Series, 1876. Nineteenth Thousand.

Trumpet-Calls to Christian Energy. A collection of sermons preached at the Metropolitan Tabernacle on Sunday and Thursday evenings. 1875.

Introduction to V. J. Charlesworth's *Life and Anecdotes of Rowland Hill.* Hodder and Stoughton. 1876.

Commenting and Commentaries. Two Lectures, with a catalogue of Biblical commentaries, and remarks thereon. 1876. Thirteenth Thousand.

The Metropolitan Tabernacle, its History and Work. Illustrated. 1876.

A Man in Christ. An Address delivered to Members of the Stock Exchange, December 4, 1876.

Christ's Glorious Achievements, set forth in seven sermons. ("Spurgeon's Shilling Series.") 1877.

The Claims of God. An Address to Men of Business, etc. 1877.

Faith in Christ. An Address to Men of Business, etc. 1877.

First Things First. An Address delivered at the Mansion House to the members of the Banks' Prayer Union. 1877.

Seven Wonders of Grace. (" Spurgeon's Shilling Series.") 1877.

The Mourner's Comforter : being seven discourses upon Isaiah lxi. 1–3. ("Spurgeon's Shilling Series.") 1878.

The Spare Half-Hour. (" Spurgeon's Shilling Series.") Papers reprinted from *The Sword and the Trowel.* 1878.

The Bible and the Newspaper. ("Spurgeon's Shilling Series.") 1878.

Speeches at Home and Abroad. Edited by G. H. Pike. 1878.

Eccentric Preachers. ("Spurgeon's Shilling Series.") 1879.

The Spurgeon Birthday Book and Autographic Register. Compiled from the works of C. H. Spurgeon. 1879.

Memorial Volume, containing sermons and addresses delivered in the Metropolitan Tabernacle to commemorate the twenty-fifth year of Mr. Spurgeon's pastorate. 1879.

John Ploughman's Pictures ; or, More of his Plain Talk for Plain People. 1880. One Hundred and Thirtieth Thousand, 1891.

" *Be of Good Cheer :* " the Saviour's comforting exhortation enlarged upon. (" Spurgeon's Shilling Series.") 1881.

Farm Sermons. 1882.

Illustrations and Meditations ; or, Flowers from a Puritan's Garden. Distilled and dispensed by C. H. Spurgeon. 1883.

The Present Truth. A collection of sermons preached at the Metropolitan Tabernacle on Sunday and Thursday evenings. 1883.

The Despised Friend. Extracted from *The Saint and his Saviour.* Hodder and Stoughton. 1883.

Welcome to Jesus. Floral Tracts. Four Packets. Drummond's Tract Depôt, Stirling. 1883.

Preface to T. Spurgeon's *Gospel of the Grace of God.* 1884.

The Clue of the Maze. 1884.

My Sermon Notes. 2 vols. Vol. I., 1884; Vol. II., 1885.

Mr. Spurgeon's Jubilee. Report of the proceedings at the Metropolitan Tabernacle, June 18th and 19th, 1884.

The Spurgeon Album, containing a sketch of Mr. Spurgeon's life and his numerous institutions, with photographic views, and portraits of Mr. and Mrs. Spurgeon. 1884.

Storm Signals : being a collection of sermons preached on Sunday and Thursday evenings. 1885.

All of Grace. An earnest word with those who are seeking salvation by Jesus Christ. 1886. Fortieth Thousand, 1891.

Gospel Temperance. An Address. National Temperance Publication Depôt. 1886.

According to Promise; or, The Method of the Lord's Dealing with His Chosen People. 1887. Thirtieth Thousand, 1891.

The Golden Alphabet : being a Commentary upon the 119th Psalm. By C. H. Spurgeon, etc. 1887.

Indices to C. H. Spurgeon's Sermons. 1855-91 inclusive.

The Cheque-Book of the Bank of Faith : being precious promises, arranged for daily use, with comments. 1888.

Around the Wicket Gate; or, A Friendly Talk with Seekers concerning Faith in the Lord Jesus Christ. 1889.

The Salt-Cellars : being a Collection of Proverbs, together with Homely Notes thereon. 2 vols. 1889. Thirtieth Thousand, 1891.

Sermons in Candles. Illustrations which may be found in common candles. 1890.

Twelve Sermons Series. (Christmas Sermons. New Year's Sermons. Sermons on the Death and Passion of Christ. Sermons on the Resurrection. Striking Sermons. Soul-winning Sermons. Sermons on various subjects.) 1890.

The Greatest Fight in the World. 1891.

Memories of Stambourne, with Personal Remarks, Recollections, and Reflections. 1891.

Messages to the Multitude: being representative sermons chosen by Mr. Spurgeon for this volume in the series known as "Preachers of the Age." Sampson Low & Co. 1892.

Also, numerous tracts for adults, and booklets for general distribution, covering the entire period of his ministry.

Mr. Spurgeon's posthumous work, a *Commentary on the Gospel according to Matthew,* will be issued at an early date.

From the Usher's Desk to the Tabernacle Pulpit. The Authorized (popular) Life of C. H. Spurgeon. Illustrated. By R. Shindler. The proof-sheets of this work were revised at Mentone during Mr. Spurgeon's last illness. 1892.

It is perhaps a matter of public interest to state in this connection that a large number of unprinted Sermons by Mr. Spurgeon are in possession of his representatives : and it is understood that these will appear week by week, at all events for several years to come, in the series known as the *Metropolitan Tabernacle Pulpit.*

LONDON : PRINTED BY WILLIAM CLOWES AND SONS, LIMITED,
STAMFORD STREET AND CHARING CROSS.

Preachers of the Age.

Uniform Crown 8vo Volumes, with Photogravure Portraits.
Cloth extra, 3s. 6d. *each.*

VOLUMES ALREADY PUBLISHED.

I. By His Grace THE ARCHBISHOP OF CANTERBURY.
LIVING THEOLOGY.
"Full of wise counsels and generous sympathies."—*Times.*

II. By the Rev. ALEXANDER MACLAREN, D.D.
THE CONQUERING CHRIST. (*Second Edition.*)
"Doctrinal yet practical, full of literary feeling and suppressed spiritual passion, evangelical without being narrow, moral without ceasing to be evangelical; sermons no man could hear without profit, and every man may read with advantage. Nonconformity still knows how to rear and appreciate preachers."—*The Speaker.*

III. By the LORD BISHOP OF DERRY.
VERBUM CRUCIS.
"The eloquent Dr. Alexander has done a rare thing for him—he has published a volume of sermons. . . . The man of culture, thought, trained observation, and holy life reveals himself in every line."—*Glasgow Herald.*

IV. By the Rev. HUGH PRICE HUGHES, M.A.
ETHICAL CHRISTIANITY.

V. By the LORD BISHOP OF WAKEFIELD.
THE KNOWLEDGE OF GOD.
"He has the rare power of making deep things plain, and the sermons often assume the form of a talk to his hearers."—*Scotsman.*

VI. By the Rev. H. R. REYNOLDS, D.D.
LIGHT AND PEACE.

VII. By the Rev. Canon KNOX LITTLE.
THE JOURNEY OF LIFE.

VIII. By the Rev. C. H. SPURGEON.
MESSAGES TO THE MULTITUDE.

LONDON : SAMPSON LOW, MARSTON & COMPANY, LIMITED,
St. Dunstan's House, FETTER LANE, FLEET STREET, E.C.

𝔓𝔯𝔢𝔞𝔠𝔥𝔢𝔯𝔰 𝔬𝔣 𝔱𝔥𝔢 𝔄𝔤𝔢

(Continued).

Uniform Crown 8vo Volumes, with Photogravure Portraits.
Cloth extra, **3s. 6d.** *each.*

VOLUMES IN PREPARATION.

IX. By the LORD BISHOP OF RIPON.

SERMONS.

X. By the Rev. A. M. FAIRBAIRN, D.D., Principal of Mansfield College, Oxford.

FAITH AND DUTY.

XI. By the Rev. HANDLEY C. G. MOULE, M.A., Principal of Ridley Hall, Cambridge.

CHRIST IS ALL.

XII. By the Rev. J. OSWALD DYKES, D.D., Principal of the English Presbyterian College, London.

PLAIN WORDS ON GREAT THEMES.

Other volumes in preparation, which will be duly announced.

Mr. SPURGEON, in the February number of *The Sword and the Trowel*, thus speaks of the " Preachers of the Age " Series :—

" The idea of issuing a set of volumes of sermons as specimens of the discourses of the period, is a very good one. Messrs. Sampson Low & Co. are carrying out the plan in capital style, giving for three and sixpence a strongly-bound crown octavo volume, adorned with a first-class portrait, and containing about a dozen sermons. The first three names which appear upon the list of ' Preachers of the Age' are those of the Archbishop of Canterbury, Dr. Maclaren, and the Bishop of Derry and Raphoe. These three volumes are before us, together with first sheets of sermons by C. H. Spurgeon. Messrs. Hughes, Knox Little, Reynolds, Fairbairn, Dykes, etc., will follow in quick succession ; but C. H. S. cannot promise that his set will be ready for some little time, for he is ordered to ' hasten slowly.' "

LONDON: SAMPSON LOW, MARSTON & COMPANY, LIMITED,
St. Dunstan's House, FETTER LANE, FLEET STREET, E.C.